Critical Perspectives on Global Governance

In this innovative study Jean Grugel and Nicola Piper aim to link theories of liberal global governance and rights-based development in a way that explores how rights can be made real.

The authors analyze the scope and effectiveness of rights-based governance in attaching a rights framework to emerging governance regimes and discourses as well as their utility for claiming rights in practice. In exploring how the architecture and instruments of global governance provide new spaces for political activism, as well as obstacles, the central argument highlights the importance of *claiming* rights. However, making claims first requires that issues such as poverty, workplace conditions or social exclusion are conceptualized, in a collective way, as rights *violations*. In order to be effective on the ground, rights must go beyond the purely legal domain, inherent in conceptions of liberal global governance as the 'rule of law' or 'good governance', and must inform state policies.

Moving away from the traditional focus on elites, states and global institutions, this book explores and analyzes how liberal global governance is really affecting ordinary people and how this can be both an opportunity and an obstacle to development, citizenship, voice and inclusion. To demonstrate this, case studies represent some of the most marginalized groups of people in Asia and Latin America: children and foreign workers. By taking a 'bottom-up' perspective, this study marks a shift from a vision of liberal global governance as a way to manage ordinary people, to one that posits global governance as a potential opportunity structure for political activism as well as a space of regulation.

This book will be of interest to students and researchers of politics, sociology, political geography, development studies and migration studies.

Jean Grugel is Professor of Politics at the University of Sheffield, UK.

Nicola Piper was Senior Research Fellow at the Asia Research Institute, National University of Singapore, during the research and drafting process of this book and has since taken up a Senior Lectureship in the Department of Geography at the University of Wales Swansea, UK.

RIPE SERIES IN GLOBAL POLITICAL ECONOMY

This series, published in association with the *Review of International Political Economy*, provides a forum for current debates in international political economy. The series aims to cover all the central topics in IPE and to present innovative analyses of emerging topics. The titles in the series seek to transcend a state-centred discourse and focus on three broad themes:

• the nature of the forces driving globalisation forward
• resistance to globalisation
• the transformation of the world order.

The series comprises two strands:

The *RIPE Series in Global Political Economy* aims to address the needs of students and teachers, and the titles will be published in hardback and paperback. Titles include

A Critical Rewriting of Global Political Economy
Integrating Reproductive, Productive and Virtual Economies
V. Spike Peterson

Contesting Globalization
Space and Place in the World Economy
André C. Drainville

Global Institutions and Development
Framing the World?
Edited by Morten Bøås and Desmond McNeill

Global Institutions, Marginalization, and Development
Craig N. Murphy

Critical Theories, International Relations and 'the Anti-Globalisation Movement'
The Politics of Global Resistance
Edited by Catherine Eschle and Bice Maiguashca

Globalization, Governmentality, and Global Politics
Regulation for the Rest of Us?
Ronnie D. Lipschutz, with James K. Rowe

Critical Perspectives on Global Governance
Rights and Regulation in Governing Regimes
Jean Grugel and Nicola Piper

Routledge/RIPE Studies in Global Political Economy is a forum for innovative new research intended for a high-level specialist readership, and the titles will be available in hardback only. Titles include:

1. Globalization and Governance*
Edited by Aseem Prakash and Jeffrey A. Hart

2. Nation-States and Money
The Past, Present and Future of National Currencies
Edited by Emily Gilbert and Eric Helleiner

3. The Global Political Economy of Intellectual Property Rights
The New Enclosures?
Christopher May

4. Integrating Central Europe
EU expansion and Poland, Hungary and the Czech Republic
Otto Holman

5. Capitalist Restructuring, Globalisation and the Third Way
Lessons from the Swedish Model
J. Magnus Ryner

6. Transnational Capitalism and the Struggle over European Integration
Bastiaan van Apeldoorn

7. World Financial Orders
An Historical International Political Economy
Paul Langley

8. The Changing Politics of Finance in Korea and Thailand
From Deregulation to Debacle
Xiaoke Zhang

9. Anti-Immigrantism in Western Democracies
Statecraft, Desire and the Politics of Exclusion
Roxanne Lynn Doty

10. The Political Economy of European Employment
European Integration and the Transnationalization of the (Un)Employment Question
Edited by Henk Overbeek

11. Rethinking Global Political Economy
Emerging Issues, Unfolding Odysseys
Edited by Mary Ann Tétreault, Robert A. Denemark, Kenneth P. Thomas and Kurt Burch

12. Rediscovering International Relations Theory
Matthew Davies and Michael Niemann

13. International Trade and Developing Countries*
Bargaining Coalitions in the GATT & WTO
Amrita Narlikar

14. The Southern Cone Model
The Political Economy of Regional Capitalist Development in Latin America
Nicola Phillips

15. The Idea of Global Civil Society
Politics and Ethics of a Globalizing Era
Edited by Randall D. Germain and Michael Kenny

16. Governing Financial Globalization
International Political Economy and Multi-Level Governance
Edited by Andrew Baker, David Hudson and Richard Woodward

*Also available in paperback

Critical Perspectives on Global Governance

Rights and regulation in governing regimes

Jean Grugel and Nicola Piper

Routledge
Taylor & Francis Group

LONDON AND NEW YORK

First published 2007
by Routledge
2 Park Square, Milton Park, Abingdon, Oxon OX14 4RN

Simultaneously published in the USA and Canada
by Routledge
270 Madison Avenue, New York, NY 10016

Routledge is an imprint of the Taylor & Francis Group, an informa business.

© 2007 Jean Grugel and Nicola Piper

Typeset in Times New Roman by
Taylor & Francis Books
Printed and bound in Great Britain by
Hobbs the Printers Ltd, Totton, Hampshire

British Library Cataloguing in Publication Data
A catalogue record for this book is available from the British Library

Library of Congress Cataloging in Publication Data
Grugel, Jean.
  Critical perspectives on global governance : rights and regulation in
governing regimes / Jean Grugel and Nicola Piper.
  p. cm. – (RIPE series in global political economy)
  Includes bibliographical references and index.
  1. Human rights–International cooperation. 2. Immigrants–Civil rights.
3. Emigration and immigration–International cooperation. 4. Children's
rights–International cooperation. 5. Regionalism (International
organization) I. Piper, Nicola. II. Title.
  JC571.G7852 2007
  325'.1–dc22
                                2007016782

ISBN 13: 978-0-415-36127-9 (hbk)
ISBN 13: 978-0-415-36128-6 (pbk)
ISBN 13: 978-0-203-93360-2 (ebk)

ISBN 10: 0-415-36127-3 (hbk)
ISBN 10: 0-415-36128-1 (pbk)
ISBN 10: 0-203-93360-5 (ebk)

Contents

Acknowledgements

A number of individuals and institutions have contributed to this volume to whom we owe a great deal of gratitude. Work on this project started when Nicola Piper was still Research Fellow with the Regulatory Institutions Network at the Australian National University where her deeper interests in issues of governance were nurtured. It continued when Jean was a Visiting Professor at the Barcelona Institute of International Studies (IBEI) in 2005–6. We would like to thank colleagues from both these institutions. We owe a special debt of gratitude to our mutual colleague and friend Assistant Professor Anders Uhlin (Lund University) for inviting us to Lund to participate in a workshop on 'Transnational Organization and Democratization of Global Governance', which gave us the opportunity to push on with the writing of the book.

We would also like to acknowledge the input of various colleagues who generously took the time to make constructive comments on our original book proposal. In particular, we are indebted to Professor Peter Drahos (Australian National University) and Tony Payne (University of Sheffield), both of whom made extremely helpful suggestions at the beginning of the project. Jean would like to thank Enrique Peruzzotti of the Universidad Di Tella, Buenos Aires, with whom she has carried out work on children's rights in Latin America, and Pia Riggirozzi of the University of Sheffield, who offered helpful advice and good company on research trips. She would also like to thank colleagues on the Non Governmental Public Action Programme, funded by the ERSC, which has served as an important source of inspiration for the research. We are both indebted to Henry Kippin, Danny Fitzpatrick and Adriana Montequin for research assistance at different stages of the project, and to Heidi Bagtazo, Editor for Politics and International Studies at Routledge, and her assistant Amelia McLaurin. Last but not least, we are deeply indebted to the numerous non-governmental organizations and individuals at various international organizations who shared their experiences with us in interviews and conversations, both electronic and verbal. Nicola would like specifically to single out the following individuals for their detailed insights in, and updates on, developments on the global and national policy levels: Ryszard Cholewinski, Patrick Taran, William Gois and Ellene Sana.

The concrete data and examples given in this book derive from many trips to the two regions under investigation here, Asia and Latin America, as well as Geneva, where the headquarters of many UN agencies are located. These trips would not have been possible had it not been for the various organizations that provided us with the necessary funding. Nicola would like to thank the Australian Research Council for awarding her grant no. DP0343303 (2001–4); the Asia Research Institute/National University of Singapore for an internal research grant to allow her to travel to Geneva (2005); and the Friedrich Ebert Foundation for a small grant to conduct further research in Malaysia (2005). Jean would like to acknowledge the research support of the ESRC for two awards – RES-000-22-0427 on New Regionalism and Transnational Collective Action in South America and RES-155-25-0012 on Civil Society and the Convention on the Rights of the Child in Argentina. The award for the Convention on the Rights of the Child in particular provided valuable research time and material for this book.

We would both like to thank our various friends and family who have helped the writing of the book in indirect, but hugely important, ways. In particular, Jean would like to thank Valerie Atkinson (for more than can ever be acknowledged here), Alicia Simione, Emma Ireland, Aletta Bonn, Sarah Alton, Hazel Smith and Jenny Pearce as well, of course, as Martin and the very lovely Anna. Nicola would like to thank Jennifer Wood, Joachim and Dorothea.

Jean Grugel, Sheffield
Nicola Piper, Singapore

List of Abbreviations

ADWU	Asian Domestic Workers' Union
AIDS	acquired immune deficiency syndrome
APEC	Asia-Pacific Economic Cooperation
APL	Alliance of Progressive Labour
APMRN	Asia Pacific Migration Research Network
ARI	Asia Research Institute
ASBO	anti-social behaviour order
ASEAN	Association of Southeast Asian Nations
BBC	British Broadcasting Corporation
BLA	bilateral agreement
CARAM Asia	Co-ordination of Action Research on AIDS and Mobility in Asia
CAT	Convention Against Torture and Other Cruel, Inhuman or Degrading Treatment or Punishment
CEDAW	Convention on the Elimination of All Forms of Discrimination Against Women
CERD	Convention on the Elimination of All Forms of Racial Discrimination
CESE	Comité économique et social européen
CFA	Centrale Franc Africain
CGG	Commission on Global Governance
CHIP	Childhood Poverty Research and Policy Centre, UK
COMMIT	Coordinated Mekong Ministerial Initiative Against Trafficking
CRC	UN Convention on the Rights of the Child
CRIN	Child Rights Information Network
CRM	UN International Convention on the Protection of the Rights of All Migrant Workers and their Families
CSACIDN	Comité de Seguimiento y Aplicacíon de la Convención sobre los Derechos del Niño, Argentina
CSO	civil society organization
DFES	Department for Education and Skills, UK

DFID	Department for International Development, UK
E Asia	East Asia
ECPAT	End Child Prostitution, Child Pornography and Trafficking of Children for Sexual Purposes
EESC	European Economic and Social Committee
ECOWAS	Economic Community of West African States
EPA	Economic Partnership Agreement
ERCOF	Economic Resource Center for Overseas Filipinos
EU	European Union
FDW	foreign domestic worker
FMLN	Frente Farabundo Martí para la Liberación Nacional, or Farabundo Martí National Liberation Front
FOM	Federal Office for Migration Switzerland
FUNABEM	Fundação Nacional do Bem-Estar do Menor
GATS	General Agreement on Trade in Services
GCCC	Gulf Cooperation Council Countries
GCIM	Global Commission on International Migration
GDP	gross domestic product
GNP	gross national product
GTZ	Gesellschaft fuer Technische Zusammenarbeit
HIV	human immunodeficiency virus
HKCTU	Hong Kong Confederation of Trade Unions
HRW	Human Rights Watch
HTA	Home-Town Association
ICCPR	International Covenant on Civil and Political Rights
ICESCR	International Covenant on Economic, Social and Cultural Rights
ICFTU	International Confederation of Free Trade Unions
ICFTU-APRO	International Confederation of Free Trade Unions-Asian Pacific Regional Organization
IFI	international financial institution
ILC	International Labour Congress
ILO	International Labour Organization
ILPA	Immigration Law Practitioners' Association
IMF	International Monetary Fund
IMWU	Indonesian Migrant Workers' Union
INGO	international non-governmental organization
IOM	International Organization for Migration
IPE	International Political Economy
IR	International Relations
IT	information technology
IUF	International Union of Food Workers
MFA	Migrant Forum in Asia
MoU	Memorandum of Understanding
MSAI	Migrants Savings and Alternative Investments

MTUC	Malaysian Trade Union Council
MWF	Migrant Workers' Forum
NAFTA	North American Free Trade Agreement
NGO	non-governmental organization
NICs	newly industrialized countries
NSPCC	National Society for the Prevention of Cruelty to Children, UK
NTUC	National Trade Union Council
OECD	Organization for Economic Co-Operation and Development
OFW	overseas Filipino worker
OHCHR	Office of the High Commissioner for Human Rights, UN
PDR	People's Democratic Republic
PR	permanent residency
PSI	Public Services International
RBA	rights-based approach
RCP	regional consultative processes
SAP	Structural Adjustment Programme
SE Asia	Southeast Asia
SE/E Asia	Southeast and East Asia
SMU	Social Movement Unionism
TUCP	Trade Union Congress of the Philippines
UK	United Kingdom
UN	United Nations
UNCTAD	United Nations Conference on Trade and Development
UNDP	United Nations Development Programme
UNFPA	United Nations Population Fund
UNHCR	United Nations High Commissioner for Refugees
UNICEF	United Nations Children's Fund
UNIFEM	United Nations Development Fund for Women
UNODC	United Nations Office on Drugs and Crime
UNRISD	United Nations Research Institute for Social Development
US/USA	United States of America
UNU	United Nations University
WIDER	World Institute for Development Economics Research
WTO	World Trade Organization

1   Global governance and rights

The relationship between global governance, rights-based regimes and ordinary people is the central concern of this book. The liberal defence of 'soft', norm-based global governance is that it produces a better and more ordered world in which rights can genuinely be made to matter. Does this claim hold up in practice? We explore this question by discussing what soft global governance means in two specific issue areas – namely, migrants and children. We examine how global rules have changed the global construction of migration and the relationship between states and children, the nature of the rules that are being developed to manage childhood and migration, and the extent to which these two work in practice to force states to make rights-based changes or allow non-governmental actors to advocate for rights.

Liberalism is a notoriously slippery concept and the liberal global shift in global politics that took place in the 1980s is fraught with contradiction and ambiguity. But however we understand it, individual rights certainly feature more prominently on the global agenda, at least discursively. The concept of rights has a purchase in contemporary global politics in a way that it did not before 1989. Nevertheless rights are being codified and claimed in the context of deepening global inequalities. Moreover, while rights charters are championed by the United Nations (UN) system, states are far more reluctant to endorse them and, consequently, try to limit their reach and effectiveness. In these circumstances, it is important to ask what rights mean, especially to vulnerable communities, what kind of rights are being codified and whether it is possible to make rights real through global legislation. Our task, in other words, is to examine the new global regimes or norms of rights from the perspective of whether they act as useful tools for tackling injustice and social, political and economic exclusion. Are the individual rights that normatively underpin contemporary global regimes being taken seriously by governments, and are they being made real? Does the new climate of rights-based global governance mean that rights can be more effectively claimed by or on behalf of ordinary people? Do international regimes that are organized around the principles of liberal rights serve to uphold them? To begin the enterprise, we need first to interrogate the movement towards global governance, explore what global governance has come to mean and discuss the relationship between rights and governance.

We argue in this chapter that it is important to take the globalization of rights seriously, even if rights are not being protected in practice. The global codification of rights limits the sovereignty of states in principle, by setting uniform and universal global standards. It creates a kind of constitution that can be used as a vehicle for making claims and legitimizes non-state action on behalf of vulnerable groups; it can also provide them with resources that open opportunities to exercise what Hertel (2006) has termed 'unexpected power' from below. Yet most analyses of liberal global governance fail to pay sufficient attention to the rights issue. We discuss why traditional approaches to global governance should be so blinkered in this respect. We go on to explore how rights can be brought into discussions of global governance. Although global governance is traditionally linked in a causal relationship with globalization and declining state authority, we see global rights regimes as being crucially dependent on states as well as global institutions and civil society organizations. Taking rights seriously means taking the state seriously. What we mean by this is that the significance of particular rights in particular settings depends on the capacity of states to implement certain reforms or, conversely, to block rights politics. It also depends on the efficacy of advocacy organizations. Even though non-state actors still have much less authority in global, domestic and local politics than states, there are nonetheless opportunities to put issues on global and national political agendas in new and sometimes effective ways.

Theorizing global governance

The concept of governance, and specifically global governance, began to capture the intellectual imagination in the 1990s. Global governance is now almost as ubiquitous as the related term 'globalization' and it is employed, in policy-making circles especially, with simplistic and perhaps even dangerous ease. For academics, governance debates have become central to almost all fields of social scientific enquiry. Even those who see the world as only 'partially globalized' nevertheless acknowledge the importance of the governance question (Keohane 2002). But what exactly do academics and policy-makers mean when they speak of 'global governance'?

Even a cursory glance at the debates reveals how little consistency there is in how the term is deployed. It is immediately striking how there is hardly any consensus as to whether global governance is a form of rule beyond or inclusive of states; very little understanding of the chain of delivery of global governance ordinances from the global level to states and communities; no common ground as regards the role of society-based actors in the provision/ contestation of global rules; and heated debate as to whether global governance is a way of reproducing or challenging global inequalities. Hoffmann and Ba (2005: 1–2) identify at least nine distinct academic usages of the term.

It is used to refer to: international regimes; international society; hegemonic stability; dynamics of globalization; the pursuit of IMF/World Bank/UN goals; global change; transformation in the global political economy; world government; and global civil society. These themes reflect different theoretical understandings of global processes and the global polity, although they all depend on the idea that new forms of order and norms are emerging.

The most common approach by far is a remarkably untheoretical, pro-Western one. It assumes that global governance constitutes quite straightforwardly an opportunity for the construction of a (pro-Western) system based on pluralism and liberal inclusion. This kind of thinking underpins the work of many influential global organizations and it shaped the thinking of the Commission on Global Governance (CGG). Set up with a membership of key politicians and global figures of authority with a brief to rethink the UN system in the 1990s after the Gulf War, the CGG was spurred on by a view that new ways to embed Western authority were needed. The CGG proclaimed global governance as a way to bridge global difference and manage the public/private mix in matters of policy-making. Global governance was conceptualized essentially as a modernization of the UN approach to order through multilateralism, accompanied by a role for selected civil society organizations. Global governance was defined as:

> the sum of the many ways individuals and institutions, public and private, manage their common affairs. It is a continuing process through which conflicting or diverse interests can be accommodated and cooperative action taken. It includes formal institutions and regimes empowered to enforce compliance, as well as informal arrangements that people and institutions either have agreed to or perceive to be in their interest ... governance ... must now be understood as also involving non-governmental organizations, citizens' movements, multinational corporations and the global market.
>
> (CGG 1995: 2–3)

This approach is also reflected in more academic work (Slaughter 2004). Some academic literature defines global governance essentially as sets of global bureaucratic networks, made up of generally well-intentioned individuals and held together by new technologies, which have the potential to deliver global public goods more efficiently and effectively than is presently the case. There is here, needless to say, an insufficient appreciation of the nature of states and the ways in which power is exercised and reproduced, globally and within nation states. For Slaughter, 'good' global governance is both (acceptably) elitist and consensual. It is:

> A brave new world [in which] government networks would not only produce convergence and informed divergence, improve compliance with international rules, and enhance international cooperation through

regulation by information. They would also regulate themselves in ways that would deliberately improve the governing performance of both actual and potential members; create forums for multilateral discussion and argument by all their members; and create opportunities to harness the positive rather than the negative powers of conflict.

(Slaughter 2004: 195)

In a bid to flee from descriptions such as these of unreal systems based on hopes rather than reality, others have suggested that global governance should be understood simply as shorthand for what used to be called international politics. Weiss (2000: 808), for example, defines global governance as a way:

to capture and describe the confusing and seemingly ever-accelerating transformation of the international system. States are central but their authority is eroding. Their creations, inter-governmental organizations, are no more in control than they ever were.

If we follow Weiss's lead, global governance becomes an arena of global policy-making, peopled with different actors, many of which are occupying spaces that were previously controlled by states, filled with politics, tensions, contestation and conflict. State-based actors fight to get heard and shape policy alongside international bureaucracies and the non-state sector. Resources matter, but power is increasingly diffuse. This approach certainly has a greater appreciation of the difficulties of institution-building and rule-making at the global level, the ambiguous nature of state power and the range of actors caught in global governance. But, at the same time, it does not capture or theorize the shift in global politics that is expressed by the concept of governance, and changes in the nature of policy delivery or the agenda of politics – the essence of the governance agenda, in short – go unremarked.

The need to develop more appropriate theoretical frameworks has most certainly been recognized. But different academic sub-disciplines have sought to build more rigorous approaches in different ways. We identify some of these approaches now. Whatever their many insights, however, they all pay insufficient attention to the key issue of rights within liberal governance.

Global governance in International Relations and International Political Economy

Nothing in the study of global politics emerges, like Aphrodite, fresh and instantly fully formed and concerns about the provision of order, the role of international organizations or the authority of international regimes, far from being wholly new issues, have always been at the heart of International Relations (IR). The realist–liberal divide, which is still so central to the discipline, is built on different approaches to order and, in particular, the nature of the state in providing and policing order. For realists, for whom a stout defence of sovereignty constitutes a moral position as well as an international reality, the idea that governance can originate in institutions and regimes independent of states is 'a contradiction in terms' (Gilpin 2002: 237). As a result, realist scholarship has sought to deny the governance *problematique*. Liberal internationalists, in contrast, have eagerly entered the fray.

Liberals have long argued that institutions and regimes above the state can and should play an independent role in the provision of global order and that the 'international' must be understood as the sum of different kinds of interactions: within markets, between citizens, communities and networks, as well as states. For liberals, not much has changed in the world; a state-centred world had long ceased to exist and globalization acts merely to confirm the fact that states must accommodate the authority of other actors. Liberal internationalists tend to see international institutions as a means to provide the basis for peace and democratic well-being, and have sometimes actively sought to shape them. The League of Nations was one such attempt after World War One and the institutions created after 1945, although they fell short of having a truly independent mandate, constituted a second try at creating institutions that try to regulate the behaviour of states. As McGrew (2002) shows, both the dynamics of transnational economic integration and the apparent diffusion of liberal democracy have renewed interest in the idea that international governance can provide for peace and democracy (see Russett and O'Neal 2001).

IR liberals have been charged with underplaying the scale and the impact of the vast range of changes, technological, political and cultural, which are covered by the umbrella term 'globalization'. The result has been the development of an intellectually diverse sub-field loosely known as global or globalization studies within IR and International Political Economy (IPE). Global governance is usually associated with economic globalization, declining sovereignty and the emerging authority of private actors in world politics. Politically, there are doubts as to whether states can, any longer, be said to speak for the community within its boundaries:

> Any discussion of global governance must start with an understanding of the changing fabric of international society. Woven into this are the complex processes known as globalization. Globalization refers to a historical process which transforms the spatial organization of social relations and transactions, generating transcontinental or inter-regional networks of interaction and the exercise of power.
>
> (McGrew and Held 2002: 1–2)

In sum, globalization appears as an immediate and direct challenge to the capacity and legitimacy of states, at the same time as it encourages the authority of private actors of various sorts, from banking to development non-governmental organizations (NGOs) and private military forces, to become involved in the provision of order. As a result, the first considered debates about governance that took into account the political changes wrought by globalization focused upon the challenges of order in a straightforwardly post-sovereign world. For McGrew and Held (2002), the diminished state was almost simply a 'fact', bringing in its wake a change to democracy; the pace and the scale of global inter-dependence and inter-connectedness generated urgent demands for new forms of global leadership and new global institutions.

This debate ultimately fed into new IPE studies, which, by a different intellectual route, had also arrived at globalization as the *deus ex machina* of change. Having emerged as a challenge to state-centric IR, most emblematically via Susan Strange's (1988) trenchant critique which suggested that authority had shifted definitively away from states to business and markets, new IPE gradually re-engaged with states via the study of governance. A new generation of IPE scholars has sought to sketch a more nuanced picture of the state under conditions of globalization. This is an important step forward, although, as Phillips (2005a: 96) notes, IPE still tends to treat states as essentially undifferentiated. Nevertheless, by positing a more holistic social science in which the domestic and international are integrated into a common analytical frame, along with a recognition of the inseparability of the political, social and economic domains (Underhill 2000), IPE is certainly more useful than traditional IR when it comes to discussing global governance because it is able to recognize the new realities of global power and is prepared to engage with the multiple dimensions of order and contestation. Additionally, because IPE takes a longer view of social change than either realism or liberalism have tended to, it has also been able to delineate rather more fully and imaginatively the various forms of global regulation that predated the Westphalian state system. It has, in other words, provided a historicized account of globalization and govern-ance. As IPE-informed studies now frequently note, Hedley Bull's (1977) striking metaphor of 'the new medievalism' recalls the various attempts at governing vast swathes of territories that pre-date the inter-state system – for example, the governance of medieval Europe through a mix of secu-lar and religious guidance and the pre-capitalist Roman, Greek or Inca empires.

This concern with global governance as changing forms of global archi-tecture is reflected in the work of Paul Cammack (2002) and Anthony Payne (2005a). Payne (2005a: 59) suggests that the study of global governance is a study of the new ways that power is constituted globally. There is certainly something appealing and clear in de-limiting global governance in this way, and it captures the possibility of approaching global governance through identifying distinct sets of issue areas within which power is exercised, rene-gotiated and institutionalized. In this formulation, global governance becomes sets of emergent regimes, norms and rules, as well as formally constituted agencies and institutions, which attempt to define and regulate global problems or conflicts. These institutions and rules are not of one piece. They do not make up as a single unifying structure, and there are confusions and contradictions within and between different governance regimes. Moreover, they are not necessarily fully legitimate or implemented systems – indeed the evidence points to contestation, fragility and difficulties of implementation. Some regimes have more reach and are policed more effectively than others. Power relations between states, international organizations, economic groups and civil society actors are constituted differently in different regimes. And, finally, the degree of flux and improvisation varies between different regimes. This messiness in global governance is recognized, and nicely captured, by Wilkinson and Hughes (2002: 2) who describe global governance in deceptively simple terms as 'the various patterns in which global, regional, national and local actors combine to govern particular areas'.

But new IPE approaches to global governance have some serious limitations too. In the first place, they have been bedevilled by the 'analytical economism' which is typical of IPE itself (Phillips 2005a) with the result that, with honourable exceptions (see Phillips 2005b; Wilkinson 2005), IPE has privileged studies of top-down economic and financial governance above all and, despite its apparent commitment to the notion of different regimes, it tends to offer quite sweeping generalizations about the whole of global governance based mainly on a detailed analysis of the architecture of economic governance. This has meant that IPE has failed to pay sufficient attention to the *politics* of global change and to the challenge of capturing the agency of ordinary people (Grugel 2005). Moreover, its focus on what happens in the 'core' of the global political economy or the developed world means that its analyses are often of limited value when it comes to trying to understand how governance shapes social and political action elsewhere.

International Law

Concerned with the role of law as a tool for global order, the study of international law provides an obvious route into discussions of global rule-making. The underlying normative premise of the field is that order, peace and progress can be achieved through 'good' international law. In contradiction to perceptions in IR, students of international law tend to assume that states will commit to the rules governing the global polity and that they have a propensity to comply with international directives (Chayes and Chayes 1998). More recently, however, doubts have been expressed about the extent to which states actually comply. Hathaway (2002), in particular, has provided considerable evidence to suggest that international law, by itself, does not induce compliance.

These debates are very suggestive in terms of understanding the politics of global governance. In so much as global governance is expressed through formal law-making, studies of compliance with international law represent an important point of departure. An understanding of the extent to which states enforce and implement new global rules is crucial. But most empirical studies of compliance with the new rules of governance are embryonic. Moreover, they have tended to focus on hard regimes of governance such as finance, where there are material incentives and direct and sustained pressure on states to carry out the new global directives. We simply do not know whether states behave similarly *vis-à-vis* projects of rights-based governance. Hathaway (2002) certainly suggests that it should not be assumed that states respond to global rights-based regimes in the same way as they do to security regimes or regimes of economic governance. She argues that state ratification of human rights legislation, far from being the dawn of a new age of global rights, may simply operate as a costless way for states to signal membership of the 'international community' since there are few mechanisms to enforce compliance. Neumayer (2005) has taken a more nuanced approach, which suggests that state compliance with rights-based regimes may depend on the extent to which there are strong civil society organizations able to push and police policy – that is, states can be made to comply with international law, but they do not have a natural propensity to do so.

Public Policy

An interest in global governance is not the exclusive preserve of scholars of IR or International Law. Indeed the very notion of governance is borrowed from Public Policy where it represents a way of thinking about the changes in policy delivery and state capacity and the shift towards the incorporation of society-based actors into domains that, in the past, were reserved for states. Governance is understood here as a search for order through the creation of norms and the generation of at least a superficial ideational harmony through networks in which the state 'does not occupy a privileged, sovereign position [but] can indirectly and imperfectly steer' (Rhodes 1996: 660). Public Policy, in fact, is the source of many of the standard metaphors of governance, including steering/rowing and disaggregated networks of rule. The shift to governance inside states transforms relationships between public and private bodies and, in the process, changes service delivery by bringing civil society actors in and creating some channels for influence by non-state actors over policy. This approach to global governance, then, would suggest the need to investigate the role of non-state actors and of resource exchanges in the making and the delivery of global policies.

Smith and Korzeniewicz (2005) transpose some of these concerns to the international arena; but they caution against assuming that increased interdependence between states and civil society necessarily strengthens the hand of non-governmental actors in the content of transnational policies:

> Rather than confronting the informational and transaction costs themselves, national leaders and international functionaries frequently find that cooperation ... can provide more effective and efficient 'private' solutions for implementing and monitoring the impact of politically sensitive subjects. In addition to the logics of delegation, self-regulation and monitoring, states and technocrats ... may also have specific strategic political motivations for promoting networks and certain modes of civil society participation. They frequently seek to neutralize or co-opt potentially anti-systemic movements to forestall lobbying efforts or public mobilizations.
>
> (Smith and Korzeniewicz 2005: 64)

Bringing non-state actors into policy networks, in other words, can serve to make state activities more legitimate and more efficient. It can strengthen, not weaken, the state, because states are usually able to delimit the activities of non-state actors and they are able to decide which actors they will work with. In this way, they create spaces of civil society inclusion and exclusion through the deployment of material and non-material incentives for inclusion. (Gaventa *et al.* 2002). This suggests that, by working with governments, non-state actors are taking the risk of enhancing the capacity of state actors to intervene and shape policies rather than creating spaces of autonomy for themselves. Moreover, it should be remembered that civil society actors are by no means the only non-state bodies trying to influence or participate in governing networks: 'Social movements are not moving to an empty space ... Transnational business already had privileged access to those governments' (O'Brien *et al.* 2000: 15). Business groups are at least equally empowered by governance – probably more so, given that liberalization of markets also strengthens their hand.

Public Policy approaches also remind us that civil society should not be conceptualized as a space of equals. The opportunity to engage with state actors over policy-making is not open to all civil society groups. Non-state actors are far more likely to be invited into governance networks if they can claim technical competence or expertise that state actors require or find attractive. Those organizations that are regarded as professional and proficient and/or produce forms of knowledge that governments need or cannot afford to ignore are more likely to gain access to policy-making circles. This is an important consideration, from a rights-based perspective. Which groups will be invited in? It is unlikely that civil society groups that advocate rejection of individualized rights, for example, will find themselves consulted; equally, it may be that groups that focus on social or economic rights, rather than political and civil rights, will also be seen as too critical to act as partners for states. By the same token, civil society groups without a base in city capitals can also often find themselves ignored by policy-makers because they are physically distant from the centres of decision-making.

Development Studies

Realism and liberalism tended to conceptualize the international system in terms of inter-state rivalry or the authority of states versus private interests, based on the experiences of advanced capitalist countries. Even IPE, which has tried to theorize the new politics of globalization, has mainly been concerned with developments within the North. But, for most of the world, these debates simply never made sense. Quite evidently, states in the developing world did not conform to realist and liberal models, even before globalization. They have always been shaped by external norms and conditionality. The 'global', in other words, could always be found deep within the state itself in the South, where it usually served to remind governing elites of the spoken and unspoken rules that limit and diminish autonomy. For scholars of development, it was always eminently clear that the assumption of state sovereignty that underlay realist/liberal debates ignored the relations of dependency that actually characterize the international system. Third World states have suffered from their very creation from fractured, incomplete, diminished or failed sovereignty (Sørensen 1999). Jackson and Roseberg (1982) capture this with the apposite distinction between juridical (*de jure*) sovereignty, which was a guiding principle of the inter-state system and was expressed through the power to vote in the UN or other international bodies, and empirical (*de facto*) sovereignty, the right to make appropriate and independent policies. As a result, Development Studies probed the ways in which sovereignty is, and always was, debased coinage in the developing world. As a result, it is hardly surprising that the study of global governance borrows from state debates about the imposition of external regulation and discipline from Development Studies (Grugel 2005).

The gulf between how developing states experience the global system and the global-state nexus in advanced capitalist countries may, even, have widened as a result of the series of economic and financial crises since the 1980s which have had severe costs across much of the developing world. The debt crisis of the early 1980s was followed by experiences of impoverishing growth in the 1990s, financial crisis, rising inequity and a genuine impasse after the acknowledged failure of forced experiments in neoliberal growth (Payne 2005b: 38). In this context, it is perhaps logical for some authors, especially from the developing world, to see global governance merely as a continuation of long-established practices of subordination. Chimni (2003: 897) argues:

> The network of international economic, political and social organizations established at the initiative of the first world constitute a nascent global state whose function is to realise the interests of the powerful

states to the disadvantage of third world states and peoples. The evolving state formation may therefore be described as having a neoimperialist character.

Payne (2007) makes a similar point when he writes: '. . . what purports to be global governance is really governance of the globe by the powerful, justified by protestations about the need to offer leadership to the inhabitants of the whole of the globe'. But others (Harrison 2004) have questioned this approach, pioneering something of a more nuanced interpretation that draws attention to the ways in which development processes are negotiated between external organizations and local elites. These insights are certainly useful. But they are also limited from our perspective because their concern is primarily with the formal and elite structures of the polity, not with the popular perception of governance structures in the South or with their impact on ordinary people.

Liberalism and rights in global governance

Whatever their many merits, these different approaches reveal the difficulties of constructing a macro-theory of global governance in a world characterized not by uniformity but by massive inequalities, complexity and uncertainty. Moreover, from our perspective, they do not offer a useful or nuanced path into debates about the character of particular global governance regimes outside the economic domain. Instead, we propose to take Payne's (2005a) distinction between *projects* and *theories* of global governance as a starting point. Whereas most analyses of global governance have focused on theories, we argue that there is much to be learned from a critical discussion of projects of governance. Moving to this level of analysis, furthermore, allows for focused attention on the ideas, actors and relationships that emerge within specific regimes of governance.

Projects of global governance are essentially strategic interventions or policies that aim to manage the stresses of global politics and globalization through global rule-making. They may be the work of politicians, global bureaucrats, international institutions, states or other policy actors such as NGOs. Projects of this sort have emerged in key issues in the global polity such as the environment, trade and finance; they have also been developed to offer regulatory frameworks for the management of specific communities of people – in our case, children and migrants. Such strategies typically involve the establishment of an international framework, the creation or strengthening of international institutions and the introduction of new global rules that regulate state behaviour. They take different institutional forms and have different normative underpinnings; different actors are caught up within them and different kinds of resources are exchanged within them.

All contemporary projects of global governance draw, sometimes loosely and sometimes more explicitly, on Western liberalism. Certainly, all are imbued with a belief in progress. All claim to be trying to fashion a 'better' world. In order to understand the nature and the norm-sets of contemporary governance projects more fully, we need to look at the seismic shift which took place in global politics in the 1980s and the 1990s, and which culminated in a vigorous re-emergence of liberal politics, as well as liberal economics.

In fact, this 'new' political liberalism was, in many ways, not 'new' at all, as Molyneux and Lazar (2003: 17) note:

> The debate continues over what has been termed liberal internationalism ...
> whether it represents a contemporary rebuilding of an older concern
> about the limits and the potential of liberal systems of governance to
> effect meaningful reform and to promote social justice.

But if the intellectual concerns were not new in any ideational sense, the twin collapse of statist models of development and the Communist bloc in the early 1980s, made their re-emergence possible. Part of the global transformation to what used to be termed 'a new world order' involved doubts as to whether, in fact, states should be the ultimate arbiters of global order or of what was right within national borders. This was accompanied by a global 'wave' of democratization (Huntington 1991), which seemed to suggest the emergence of a global paradigm for states and state–society relationships (Grugel 2003a, 2003b). After 1989, democracy and the importance of the rule of law were enthusiastically reconfirmed as discursive ordering principles for the international system. The 'third wave' of democratization did not always lead to the establishment of new democratic systems of rule. But it did confirm the centrality of democratic principles and the difficulty of grounding political domination in any other kind of belief system. Whatever the policies governments actually pursue, almost all states have come to mimic conformity with democracy so as to form part of the 'international community'.

A central part of the trend towards democratization, from the 1980s onwards, was a fresh recognition of the importance of human rights, understood as the minimal set of freedoms and entitlements that make acceptable human life possible. These comprise security, legal, political, social and economic rights, as well as rights to equality and some collective rights. They are laid out in UN declarations, including the 1948 Declaration of Universal Rights, the International Convention on the Elimination of All Forms of Racial Discrimination in 1965, the Convention on the Elimination of all Forms of Discrimination against Women in 1979, the Convention on the Rights of the Child in 1989 and the 1990 Convention on the Rights of All Migrant Workers and their Families. Such rights are regarded as essential for meaningful human well-being and states are regarded as having a duty to guarantee their provision. But despite the progressive codification of human rights internationally, the international human rights regime was exceptionally weak before 1989 as a result of 'conscious political decisions' to protect sovereignty (Donnelly 1989). Western states were not prepared to take economic and social rights with the same seriousness as political and civil rights. The West has continued to resist calls for economic and social rights, which are still associated with Communism, even after the Cold War (Nyamu-Musembi and Cornwall 2004). This remains the case especially in the USA, where a strong ideological resistance to the idea of economic and social rights is rooted in its political history. US opposition has serious implications for the workings of UN agencies and the extent to which they can force debates about economic and social entitlements because the UN relies so heavily on funding and staffing by the US (VeneKlasen *et al.* 2004). The result is that, while rights have become part of global discourses, the meaning of rights remains contested terrain.

Despite opposition to economic and social rights, it was possible to upgrade rights concerns and to put rights onto the political agenda, especially within the UN, in a far more vigorous fashion after 1989 than before. In the process, it initially seemed that some of the tensions between claims of sovereignty and the principles of universal and individual rights had been resolved through a commitment to strengthen the UN system and, by extension, the global system of rights-based regulation. But, needless to say, states resisted any substantive transference of power to the UN. State actors feared the full consequences of strong regimes of global rights which, if implemented, would not only have shifted authority upwards to the international level but would also have placed states under a strong obligation to deliver them in practice. Additionally, debates about strengthening the UN and human rights regimes were caught up and entangled in debates about the legitimacy of Western power. Historically, the principles of individualized human rights derive from Western political thought. In the post-1945 world in particular, they were consistently used as an instrument to beat the non-Western world into submission (Evans 1997). Not surprisingly, therefore, moves to strengthen human rights regimes encountered suspicion and opposition outside the West as well as within it.

Nevertheless, it was not possible to return to the *status quo ante*; the genie of rights would not go back into the bottle. Since the 1990s, despite hostility of the overt and covert kinds, globally active non-governmental actors and UN bureaucracies have continued to champion the codification of rights and the strengthening of rights-based regimes. Specialist globally active human rights organizations such as Human Rights Watch and Amnesty International have learned sophisticated lobbying techniques, forged alliances and been able to argue for rights protection; they have been joined by myriad other international non-governmental bodies, all of which have taken advantage of the resurgence and re-legitimization of civil action under the new liberal dispensation. In some specific issue areas, they are joined by states. To give just one example: the USA (despite its hostility to economic and social rights and to the concept of children's rights) offers considerable strategic support to campaigns against human trafficking and child labour.

It is surprising, then, that the drive for global rights remains the least examined face of the new liberalism. Far more attention has been paid to ways in which liberal ideas colonized economic policy-making in the 1980s and 1990s. Effectively, for most of the 1980s and 1990s, to talk of 'liberalism' operated as a shorthand for economic openness, not political rights. Economic crisis across much of the developing world, coupled with the collapse of state socialism, increased both the normative authority of economic liberals and the power of international financial institutions (IFIs) such as the International Monetary Fund (IMF), which has always been sceptical of the notion that states could effectively shape the market or development. As a result, the early post-Cold War witnessed the roll-back of the state in development processes and an almost global endorsement of market-led strategies of development. The new economic liberalism radically altered economies and societies across Latin America, Africa and Asia. While this is not the place to debate its achievements and failures, we should note that the experiment in extreme economic liberalization not only diminished the authority and the capacity of the state in many countries, it dramatically increased poverty. By the beginning of the new millennium, even organizations that had once endorsed the new economic agenda with enthusiasm were concerned about rising levels of poverty and social exclusion. In the process, social inequity and a lack of political rights were posited as causal in underdevelopment, even within organizations such as the World Bank and the World Economic Forum (Zurita 2006).

In the face of such dramatic impoverishment and an apparent willingness in international institutions to re-engage with rights and politics, new approaches to development have begun to emerge. Rights-based approaches to development bring together supporters from a diverse range of NGOs, development agencies and UN organizations. In effect, the re-discovery of rights, in response to the failures of markets, constitutes the second key moment in the post-Cold War period, and the new prominence of rights in development has been central to the emergence of global rights debates more broadly.

Nevertheless, what rights mean with regard to both development and governance is still unclear. There is still something of an artificial separation between human rights and development needs. Until fairly recently, there was very little dialogue between international human rights and development organizations, although both in effect championed related kinds of rights, the former limiting their advocacy to civil and political rights via a focus on state repression and legal reform, and the latter being more concerned with the promotion of economic, social and cultural rights from the perspective of community participation (VeneKlasen *et al.* 2004). NGOs such as Amnesty International have only engaged with the language of rights-based approaches to development since 2001/2002. Since then, a gradual *de facto* collaboration between human rights and development NGOs has been emerging (Nyamu-Musembi and Cornwall 2004). But the rights agenda is still loose enough to embrace a range of different meanings. For the International Labour Organization (ILO), for example, concerned overwhelmingly with the impact of economic liberalism on wages and jobs, rights are tied to campaigns for 'decent work':

> The present forms of globalization have not succeeded in making markets work for all. At the same time, a host of social problems have emerged or intensified, creating increased hardship, insecurity, and anxiety for many across the world, forcing a strong backlash. As a result, the present form of globalization is facing a crisis of legitimacy from an erosion of popular support ... It is clear that the major technological changes driving globalization are here to stay. It is equally clear that a number of specific changes to the present economic and social policies need to be adopted for the credibility of the overall process. This effort has been described as putting a human face on the global economy.
>
> (ILO 2000)

Human rights organizations such as Amnesty International and Human Rights Watch, meanwhile, although they have widened their brief, continue to work with an older concept of rights drawn from international law. And for some NGOs, rights have become a maximalist, almost utopian, demand for sweeping global and social restructuring. And finally, UN institutions have pioneered debates, largely from within a broad church of liberal internationalism, which have come to suggest that rights should provide the basis for reconceptualizing development as human well-being, social and political inclusion, and sustainable livelihoods. If realized, this approach would have massive implications for global programmes for development. Taking a rights-based approach to material deprivation such as poverty, for example, would suggest that it is caused principally by a lack of (mainly political) resources; a successful anti-poverty strategy would thus be to empower people to make appropriate claims, rather than simply to direct spending towards covering primary needs. The potential rights have to make a difference to development is summed up in Table 1.1 on page 16.

Under Kofi Annan, the UN system shifted definitively towards a firm endorsement of rights promotion. According to Annan (quoted in Cecilia Ljungman 2005: 4):

> A rights-based approach to development describes development not simply in terms of human needs or of development requirements, but in terms of society's obligations to respond to the inalienable rights of individuals, empowers people to demand justice as a right, not a charity, and gives communities a moral basis from which to claim international assistance when needed.

Table 1.1

Needs Approach	Human Rights Approach
Works towards outcome goals	Work towards outcome and process goals
Recognises needs as valid claims	Recognises that rights always implies obligations of the state
Empowerment is not necessary to meet all needs	Recognises that rights can only be realised with empowerment
Accepts charity as the driving motivation for meeting needs	Regards charity as an insufficient motivation for meeting needs
Focuses on manifestations of problems and immediate causes of problems	Focuses on structural causes of problems, as well as manifestations and immediate causes of problems
Focuses on the social context with little emphasis on policy	Focuses on social, economic, cultural, civil and political context and is policy-oriented

Source: Ljungman (2005)

Annan called on development agencies to mainstream rights within their work, placing human rights, not growth, at the centre of development. The United Nations Children's Fund (UNICEF), one of the key UN bodies in development terms, was transformed into a rights-based organization after 1996. Other UN organizations, such as the UN Population Fund, followed suit. And, partly in response, national aid donors and large development NGOs have also re-focused their work on rights.

Taking rights seriously

How far does the new embrace of rights within the UN and the NGO communities and, perhaps more tentatively, other global institutions, create a climate in which rights are now taken more seriously in global governance? In the first place, we should note that debates around rights-based development focus in practice principally on the significance of *political* claims for inclusion through the principles of non-discrimination, participation, voice and empowerment, and the importance of transparency and accountability in state policies – the core of the liberal agenda, in other words. The UN Office of the High Commissioner of Human Rights (OHCHR) suggests:

> Perhaps the most important source of added value in the human rights approach is the emphasis it places on the *accountability* of policymakers and other actors whose actions have an impact on the rights of people. Rights imply duties, and duties demand accountability.
>
> (OHCHR 2002: paragraph 23; cited in Nyamu-Musembi and Cornwall 2004: 15)

But, and this is our second point, strategies for implementing rights-based governance are rather vague, beyond an insistence on the importance of codifying rights in law. Economic and social rights in particular remain controversial. Thirdly, rights politics depends on non-governmental advocacy, and working towards cultures of rights also requires effective partnerships between state actors and non-governmental organizations over the long term and in different policy domains. Rights-based approaches call on states to become proactive in rights; but states require the cooperation of non-state actors to deliver rights on the ground (Moser and Norton 2001). Fourthly, although human rights are intrinsically universalist, rights-based approaches to development assume that rights can constitute a device for the empowerment of the poor and the socially marginalized in particular. And finally, it is not clear whether individuals or civil society organizations must first lay claim to rights for them to be made real or whether, conversely, states have responsibilities to deliver rights, regardless of social demand (Ljungman 2005).

Defendants of rights as a motor of development see them as underpinning not just individual well-being but the beginning of broader, structural reforms that can reshape power relations in society. But it is not always clear whether the reforms that are envisaged are merely political – citizenship, participation, inclusion and voice – or whether rights are also supposed to serve as a device for claim-making in the social and economic domains as well. We argue that clarity is needed here because the separation of rights into different, discrete bundles only works in the abstract. It does not capture the nature of rights struggles in the real world, perhaps especially by poor people in the South, which tend in practice to be a very messy business in which the specific nature of the 'right(s)' claimed can be unclear. Rights activists on the ground also tend to make much less of the distinction between 'political' and 'economic' rights than is traditional in Western liberal scholarship, and indeed within international institutions. This confusion is a source of both controversy and conflict.

As if these problems were not enough, Gledhill (2005) has noted that there are particular difficulties in applying a rights focus to contexts of multiple deprivation – which rights come first and can people be expected to agree on a rational prioritization of rights? How will needs be prioritized – or will states simply respond to the loudest voices or to international pressure? Moreover, it is not easy to persuade people to claim rights, given that this first requires that they conceptualize lived experiences of material deprivation or political exclusion as rights-violation. And is it reasonable to expect 'rights-deprived' individuals and communities to exist in a state of permanent claims-making? Archer (2005) has identified some practical and theoretical difficulties, including how to reconcile individual rights and collective benefits within governance strategies; how to balance the possibility of long-term gains for the many against losses for a minority, how to take developmental decisions in the context of scarcity – rights-based development, he suggests, fails to address hard questions about whether priority should be given to inequities in education or in health, for example. On the basis of these difficulties, he argues that, as yet, rights-based development makes for only a soft or aspirational approach to decision-making.

Nevertheless, despite the undoubted intellectual difficulties with regard to the rights agenda, rights have been endorsed enthusiastically by development practitioners and NGOs alike – and sometimes by ordinary people themselves. This may mean that the concept of rights has an intuitive meaning and a very genuine resonance on the ground. If this is the case – and we believe that it is – then an intellectual way forward must be found. One approach, suggested by VeneKlasen *et al.* (2004), is to move beyond the legalistic approach, which has traditionally dominated the study of human rights, and the generational approach, which rigidly separates rights into distinct packages – political, economic, cultural and so on. Instead this should be replaced with an understanding of rights as a political process, of rights as work in progress, forged and refined through social struggles. Different social struggles generate demands for different rights. The legalist approach to rights, which emphasizes only legal entitlements, judicial processes and formal compliance, tends to ignore the dynamic role of society-based movements in rights-based struggles. The idea of rights as work in progress is an important insight and it draws attention to the importance of engagement with social organizations that instigate rights claims or use rights as the basis for social action. We do not mean to suggest by this that judicial process is unimportant. But the courts are only one of several sites of rights-based struggles. Moreover, VeneKlasen *et al.*'s (2004) approach allows for a discussion of the spaces where rights-claims emerge – within civil society. For, although human rights are individual, claims are usually staked by civil society movements which regard themselves, and are regarded by states and international institutions, almost as proxies or agents for individuals and communities (Brysk 2002). The UN acknowledges this: civil society groups, as well as individuals, can now be designated 'human rights defenders' and the UN has granted a number of NGOs a quasi-official status in the pursuit of rights. Human rights defenders are those who:

> ... address any human rights concerns, which can be as varied as, for example, summary executions, torture, arbitrary arrest and detention, female genital mutilation, discrimination, employment issues, forced evictions, access to health care, and toxic waste and its impact on the environment. Defenders are active in support of human rights as diverse as the rights to life, to food and water, to the highest attainable standard of health, to adequate housing, to a name and a nationality, to education, to freedom of movement and to non-discrimination. They sometimes address the rights of categories of persons, for example women's rights, children's rights, the rights of indigenous persons, the rights of refugees and internally displaced persons, and the rights of national, linguistic or sexual minorities.
>
> (http://www.ohchr.org/english/issues/defenders/who.htm)

The growing importance of rights and the fact that rights are now central to debates about global development and human well-being is being recognized, especially by scholars of international norms, transnational advocacy movements or global civil society (Keck and Sikkink 1998; Khagram *et al.* 2002; Bandy and Smith 2005). Transnational civil society organizations play an important role in global politics and link local and national politics to organizations and norms that emerge within the global order. Keck and Sikkink (1998) trace and identify the ways in which civil society actors go 'outside' their state in order to build alliances with other activists from other states to bring pressure to bear on domestic states. In the process, activists lay claim to universalist notions of rights so as to mainstream their claims and build effective coalitions for action. In a slightly different vein, Kaldor (2003) has also made an impassioned case for the importance of recognizing global civil society within international politics. But taking rights seriously as a source of governance means identifying regional, national and local rights politics that develop in response to global rights campaigns, as well as describing global or transnational networks. This is where we feel that analysis so far has tended to stop short. The research emphasis has largely been on transnational action, even though rights politics takes place at all levels of global and national polities. The emergence of global-rights networks of civil society activists should not blind us, in short, to the persistence of rights activism in local and regional contexts. Local NGOs, we argue, can play an important role in terms of connecting the rights struggles of ordinary people to global frames of rights and regulation, and can take advantage of the structure of local opportunities and their local resources to play a role in governance chains. Additionally, they can use their connections within specific states to influence or push for implementation of policies; influence local and national norms so as to embed rights-based demands; make accountability demands on government; and frame local struggles in the global language of rights.

Exploring rights-based governance in two distinct arenas: children and migrants

How do rights-based regimes of global governance emerge and how do the different actors involved in them come together to provide a framework for regulation and/or contestation? UN human rights treaties or conventions constitute the foundations of all such regimes. But some have evolved towards more elaborate codes of conduct and firm legal rules and have been widely ratified, while others remain less institutionalized. In one of our examples, childhood, the regime has been institutionalized through an elaborate written code, supported by the apparatus of the OHCHR, UNICEF and other UN bodies. The Convention on the Rights of the Child (CRC) thus establishes a body of global 'rules' with regard to children, which are policed, at least formally, by established international bodies. It also enjoys widespread ratification.

Migration has been less successfully institutionalized. These different levels of institutional fixity undoubtedly make a difference to states' responses and the extent to which states assume responsibility for making policy changes. The global regime on migration is weaker and the room for manoeuvre by non-state actors is less. But ratification in the case of the CRC has not meant implementation; the consequences of both regimes are evaded by states. Moreover, what rights mean, in both cases, is still subject to discussion. And, in both cases, relevant actors have different interpretations of the regimes.

In both regimes, as in all regimes of governance, norms play an important overarching role. Norms frame, constitute and bring into being global 'problems' and shape policy responses. The normative/ideational dimension of governance regimes is fundamental to creating what Gamble (2000: 112) calls a new 'constitution of governance'. To be fully effective, the normative underpinning of such constitutions must be regarded as binding and legitimate by actors involved or with interests in the issue area. All projects of rights-based global governance begin with attempts to create a set of standardized code of rights across a particular issue area. Notions of what responsibilities states should take on; what kinds of tasks are best delegated to non-state actors or global institutions; what rights and duties ordinary people have; who are the appropriate and legitimate representatives of society; and what is the 'correct' relationship between society, the market and politics; these all require the development of common lens and mindsets. As we will see, both regimes are still in the process of constitution-building.

Nevertheless, institutionally, the CRC is the stronger of the two regimes. Institutions embed, justify and reproduce the norms of the governance regime. International institutions provide, in the words of Barnett and Finnemore (2004), 'rules for the world'. Regimes that are based *solely* on norms or informal rules are weaker and implementation is more difficult to achieve, compared to regimes that are encased in institutions or international law. Regimes with strong global institutions are rare and the CRC is no exception here.

The effectiveness of both regimes is subject to debate. Effective regimes demand cooperation between different kinds of, and differently situated, actors. States come to depend on civil society groups for technical expertise, monitoring, support or implementation. Civil society actors frequently find their legitimacy enhanced if they are recognized by international bodies. International organizations can do little or nothing to implement policies without states and non-state actors. But the terms and the nature of interdependence vary and the resources the various actors bring to their particular issue area vary over time. There is no single, fixed pattern of interaction that fits all governance regimes and, even within regimes, relationships can change over time.

We use our case studies both to probe the construction of governance in these two particular issue-areas and to open up debate regarding governance regimes more generally. With regard to childhood, we discuss the regime created by the CRC, which involves an array of actors, including international bureaucrats, state actors, local, national and global NGOs, journalists and researchers. With regard to migrant workers, international organizations including the ILO and the UN form part of the chain of regulation, along with states, NGOs and migrant workers themselves. Both regimes illustrate the complex ways in which states, international organizations and non-state actors combine to shape governance as well as struggling over what it should mean. But actors play their roles at different points in the policy chain. While international organizations are influential, along with NGOs and some states, in shaping the framework of regulation, implementation depends on state actors and non-state actors – often different ones from the NGOs that operate at the global level.

Since rights struggles are almost always work in progress, success is difficult to determine. Nevertheless, it is clear that some claims can be made more effectively than others. The nature of the international regime that frames the rights struggles – and sometimes codifies the legal entitlements of a particular community – is an important factor here. We hope to illustrate this through our choice of two very different kinds of global regimes: economic migration and childhood. Economic migration has always been a characteristic of human history. But the creation of a genuinely global economy established hitherto unimaginable opportunities for people to move from their places of birth to seek work elsewhere. The North–South dimension of migration has become a steadily more pronounced feature of the global political economy since the 1960s as a reflection of the intensification of the North–South divide in income, living standards and well-being. It accelerated even further in the 1980s and the numbers of economic migrants has continued to rise. Pressures have built up, particularly within industrialized states and other receiving countries, for policies to manage migration. In the process, the governance of migration has come to be seen as dominated by states and the concerns of states – security, employment, policing boundaries, controlling welfare spending – have shaped the debate about migration, especially in the North. But there are also significant pressures from some international agencies and migrant-centred NGOs for the rights of migrants to be respected. Here the struggle is to reframe a states-led agenda in the direction of rights and to transform the governance regime into one that acts to mitigate the human suffering migration entails, rather than simply responding to the needs of states to control and limit the social, political and economic spaces migrants occupy.

Our second example is very different. In 1989, the CRC endowed all children with a broad range of rights. As such, it was the result of a more liberal view of personhood than that which had previously dominated international and national laws. It aimed to address injustices done to children in general. But in practice, the CRC is viewed as a tool that can address the particular needs of poor children or children in the South. In contrast to the migrant case study, a relatively strong global constitution came first. The CRC was primarily the work of sympathetic states, in conjunction with broad-based child advocacy organizations such as Save the Children and legal activists. But the impact of fast-tracking rights in this way was completely unknown. In the past, rights have usually resulted from extensive social struggles by those who would benefit from rights charters themselves. The CRC, in contrast, exhorts states to take rights seriously for individuals and groups who have not always themselves staked claims. Moreover, the CRC uses rights in a very sweeping and broad fashion and it is not clear which rights take priority. Our case studies, then, are somewhat different. One is narrow (migrants) and one is broad (children). Within one regime, rights are not yet a firm or legitimate feature of the governance regime; in the other, rights form the core of international legislation. Nevertheless, neither poor children nor economic migrants enjoy rights in practice. Within both regimes, NGOs and advocacy movements engage in rights-based struggles to make concrete gains for socially marginalized groups, using discourses of liberal rights and the structures of liberal global governance.

Conclusion

Most debates about global governance have tended to refer either to the remaking of (Western) authority, sometimes in a more acceptable fashion, or to the issue of policy-making and delivery in an age where states promise more but seem able to deliver less. Key themes include the emergence of public–private partnerships, new forms of cooperation between states, and the reform of some international institutions and the creation of completely new ones. On the one hand, 'governance' captures the emergence of new forms of regulation and the technical difficulties of providing order in an increasingly complex and globalized world. But, on the other, global governance is recognized as a deeply political exercise, in which different actors seek to impose their vision of order and rights and make use of unequal resources to get their way. Global governance is, thus, also shaped by critical, engaged and sometimes principled opposition to it. Opposition to global governance, or to the kind of global governance projects that are emerging, is not of one piece. Some opposition entails a wholesale rejection of what is seen as an attempt to create order based essentially on updating the ideational authority of the West and of Western-dominated capitalism, while other forms of resistance call on policy actors to deliver on the promises of justice, rights and individualism in which liberal global governance is encased. For these critics, some specific projects of global governance can be justified if they address, rather than contribute to, global injustice and global social marginalization.

Different literatures have variously understood global governance as sets of norm-based regimes or global laws; a spatially tiered system of disaggregated regimes; a way for states to try and manage the challenges of 'globalization', rooted in the transformation of state capacities; forms of governance above states, in which a range of different kinds of actors are present; and a mode of regulation that can involve the extensive participation of non-state actors and which sometimes presents as a site for resistance or contestation on the part of civil society organizations. All these approaches have insights and they all suggest that global governance is a new way of doing global politics, distinct from the state-centric mode of the past, comprising sets of disarticulated regimes in which different actors engage in political contestation and different projects of governance collide. We have suggested that, whatever their merits, all these readings pay insufficient attention, theoretically and empirically, to the place of rights within contemporary governance systems. Moreover, while we share the view that global governance refers to new attempts at defining and managing global issues that do not rely exclusively on the deployment of state power, we argue that methodologically global governance is best approached via the study of specific projects of governance. Within this, we focus on projects of rights-based governance in particular.

Despite the energy, enthusiasm and expertise NGOs and rights defenders bring to rights struggles, we are aware that human rights claims can be sullied, either by their origins in Western liberalism or by the difficulties in using them as strategies for effective advocacy. We recognize – and hope to explore – the real moral dilemmas in rights mobilization in the developing world. Rights-based projects proclaim the importance of the individual – but may not pay sufficient attention to structural inequality. Moreover, the grand ideas that underpin global governance – ordered and stable politics, democracy, human rights, individualism – undoubtedly have their origins in the Western enlightenment. We recognize that, for some analysts and activists critical of the ways in which liberal thought has been incorporated into the developing world, the arguments about rights are not clear-cut. Even with regard to rights-based governance regimes, the degree of normative and material compulsion, coupled with the inequalities in power between the North and the South, means that they can come to be seen as something of a steamroller, ceding little to cultural difference. Although we are generally positive about the concept of rights-based global governance, which we see as a defensible, though limited and flawed, project of human betterment, we are also aware that rights-based interventions make a difference in only very few cases. We return to these ethical and moral dilemmas at the end of the book.

2 International migration

Throughout human history, migration has taken place as an expression of the desire to seek new opportunities and a better life. But migration is a Janus-faced phenomenon and its dark side is played out in the form of involuntary or forced migration, associated historically with the beginning of slavery in the late seventeenth century and migrant indentured labour from colonies since the mid-nineteenth century. International labour migration is, thus, clearly linked to the gradual expansion of a global capitalist economy, which was initially mainly driven by European nation-states (Castles and Miller 1993). In other words, the direction which many (but not all) migration flows take – that is, from developing to developed economies – is at the very root a response to the geographically uneven effects of capitalist development.

As much as they were involved in instigating the migration of 'others' (slaves, indentured labour), Europeans were also the main (in terms of numbers) migrants who initially populated North America, Australia and New Zealand – destinations which have since become classified as traditional 'settler' countries, disregarding the existing aboriginal populations. Since 1945, partly as a result of 'de-colonialization' processes and partly also linked to economic development, a growing number of countries have experienced in- or out-migration in addition to the classical 'settler' cases. These various 'waves' have led to the coinage of the phrase 'age of migration' (Castles and Miller 1993) or 'age of mass migration' (Hatton and Williamson 1998). Countries situated in Northern and Western Europe were among the first to experience the transition from origin to destination countries. Their attempt to solve post-war labour shortages by way of 'guest worker schemes' eventually resulted in the permanent settlement of substantial numbers of foreign workers. As with the newly industrialized countries (NICs) in East Asia, Southern European states began to make the shift from being solely migrant-sending to becoming migrant-receiving countries in the 1980s. In addition to cross-continental flows, intra-regional migration has become more significant in recent years with countries such as South Africa, Nigeria and Chile attracting increasing numbers of migrants from their neighbours (Piper 2007b). A major difference between previous ages of migration and the more contemporary era is that migration before 1914 was fairly 'free' (at least for European immigrants to the new settler countries) compared with the severely 'constrained' migration of more recent times (Hatton and Williamson 2003). Migration flows are greatly conditioned by destination countries' policies, which have over the years become increasingly restrictive, mostly in response to changing demand and supply structures. Economic downturns 'at home' have resulted in origin countries' needing to 'export' more of their unemployed or under-employed people whilst destination countries want to close their doors for fear of, or in response to, political backlashes (rising anti-foreigner sentiments in view of rising unemployment); and with more origin countries having loosened their grip on the movement of their peoples as the result of the fall of the Berlin Wall and the Iron Curtain, Third Wave democratization processes and economic restructuring processes such as the Doi Moi in Vietnam, there is more competition among labour-exporting countries. The transition of the global political economy from imperialism to a post-colonial, more globalized setting has, thus, changed the direction and complexity of migratory flows and the numbers of countries involved – so much so that there is hardly any country in the world today not affected by migration (UN 2006).

In an era of heightened economic globalization (Hoogvelt 1997), it appears that it is capital penetration in developing countries through foreign direct investment that determines much of labour migration today (Sassen 1988). This was also evident in interviews conducted by Piper in Tokyo in the late 1990s with undocumented migrant workers from Iran and Bangladesh. When asked why they chose to go to Japan rather than elsewhere (e.g. the Middle East), the usual answer was that ubiquitous advertisements of Japanese products and TV programmes on Japan raised awareness of Japan's high economic achievements and provided Iranians and Bangladeshis with the incentive to seek opportunities there. This was also observed by Rahman (2003) in his work on Bangladeshi migrant workers in Singapore. Studies on Mexico have shown how capital penetration through economic development has transformed local economic life by raising wages and consumer demands, creating a need for capital that for many people can only be gained through international migration (Massey and Espinosa 1997: 969, quoted in Briones 2006: 16). In this way, globalization has an impact on the aspirations and consumer demands of people in poorer countries, the realization of which are leading more people to choose to migrate across borders. Migration scholarship has added socio-cultural factors to these economic aspects by highlighting the significance of migrants' personal networks, which play an important role in determining the direction of migration flows.

Given these developments, it does not come as a surprise to find that international migration has become one of the key features of contemporary social, political and economic life globally in two major ways: economic migration (work), and forced migration owing to persecution (asylum). The international refugee regime distinguishes economic migrants from refugee migration, which depends on different legal instruments (most importantly the 1951 Convention Relating to the Status of Refugees, known as the Geneva Convention) and, therefore, involves different UN agencies. In the case of refugees, this most notably relates to UNHCR, which has a humanitarian mandate and, therefore, deals with migration reactively, *after* its occurrence.

Making a distinction between (involuntary) refugee and (voluntary) economic migration suited the situation of the classical refugee of the Cold War era, when defecting political dissidents were small in numbers and welcomed in the West; 'the situation, however, became problematic with the struggles against colonialism and authoritarian regimes from the 1960s onwards. It became extremely difficult to maintain a clear distinction between asylum-seekers and economic migrants from countries undergoing rapid change and crisis' (Castles and Loughna 2003: 2). Although the migration–asylum nexus is as such, not a new dilemma, what is new are increasingly restrictive and deterrence policies since the early 1990s aimed at limiting access to asylum. Such policies have been implemented in most highly developed countries with the result that more asylum-seekers move as undocumented migrants and, there is, consequently, a blurring of the two categories (Castles and Loughna 2003). Our aim in this section is simply to highlight these connections without engaging further with the issue of the linkages between migration and refugee flows since our principal concern is with economic migration.

International migration – global policy and governance

Along with ongoing economic restructuring generally associated with neo-liberalism and increased integration of regional labour markets, the scale, scope and complexity of cross-border flows have grown significantly. Given the continuing problem with human displacement and restrictive immigration policies on the part of destination countries, rising numbers of irregular or unauthorized migrants can be witnessed worldwide. Partly in response to this, 'migration issues today occupy the centre state in national and international public policy debates' (ILO 2004: 4), as exemplified by three global reports that were published by different global commissions in recent years, which have placed migration issues firmly on the global policy agenda (the Commission on Human Security in 2003, the World Commission on the Social Dimension of Globalization in 2004 and the Global Commission on International Migration in 2005). The activities and establishment of these three Commissions, and their final reports, also show that states and other stakeholders have become acutely aware of the challenges and opportunities presented by human movements.

As indicated by the names of these global commissions, they have concerned themselves with issues beyond the purely economic dimensions of cross-border migration. There are a number of reasons why it is important to understand the social ramifications of migratory processes in addition to the economic: it is the social sphere that acts like a mirror for the way in which the international division of labour is incorporated into spatially uneven processes of economic development. As a result, cross-border migration can provide new opportunities for migrants to improve their lives, escape oppressive social and political relations and support those who are left behind. But it can also expose people to new vulnerabilities as the result of their precarious legal status, abusive working conditions, discrimination based on ethnicity/race/religion/gender and exposure to certain health risks (UNRISD 2005). The majority of economic migrants work in lower or unskilled types of jobs and consequently are over-represented in marginal, unregulated and badly paid jobs where working conditions are poor and abusive practices, in form of labour-rights violations, rampant (Caron 2005; Piper 2005a; Smith and Paoletti 2005; Verité 2005). Foreign workers consequently constitute a specifically vulnerable social group everywhere.

In the context of international migration, governance assumes a variety of forms, including migration policies of individual states in their role as origin or destination countries, inter-state discussions and agreements, multilateral forums and consultative processes, the activities of international or inter-governmental organizations, civil society organizations and trade unions, as well as laws and norms. For our purposes, three levels of governance of migration are discussed over the space of this and the following two chapters. First, we consider the global normative and institutional level involved in the formation of a regulatory framework on migration. Specifically, we address the dialectics between the ILO's attempt to revive a migrants' rights framework on the one hand, and a global shift toward an overtly utilitarian (that is to say, economic) approach to migration on the other; secondly, we consider the regional level and cooperation by states in the form of intra-regional processes (Chapter 3); and thirdly, the meso level, i.e. NGOs involved in political activism with specific reference to transnational networks formed regionally (most notably in Asia and Europe) to promote migrants' rights (Chapter 4).

This present chapter aims to provide the general background to migration trends and policy concerns so as to assess how far, and in what form, a rights regime is part of the regulatory framework of migration that has been emerging.

Migration trends and policy concerns – a global perspective

Both the numerical size and patterns of migration have undergone important changes during the last few decades. Since the 1960s, the overall volume of international migrants has doubled. In 2000, the Population Division of the UN estimated their total number to be approximately 175 million. This figure has been revised in the recent report by the General Secretary to 191 million as of 2005 (UN 2006). These numbers include refugees and displaced persons, but they do not capture irregular migrants who often escape official accounting. Thus, about 2.9 per cent of the world's population, or one in every 35 persons, are moving across borders (IOM 2003). Taken together, migrants would make up the fifth most populous 'country' in the world (ILO 2004: 8). It is predicted that the volume of cross-border movements of workers in search of employment is likely to grow, especially in view of globalization having thus far failed to generate enough jobs and economic opportunities in the localities where people live (World Commission on the Social Dimension of Globalization 2004).

All regions are implicated in the rising mobility of people in the search of work and other opportunities, and the associated policy issues have correspondingly risen on the political agendas of global and regional institutions as well as national governments. Although foreign workers still represent a small percentage of industrialized countries' total workforce (4 per cent), migratory flows of workers from the developing to the industrialized countries have been rising in recent decades. The USA received the largest proportion (81 per cent), followed by Canada and Australia (11 per cent) and the EU (ILO 2004: 5). Women account for an increasing proportion of international migrants (49 per cent in 2000), reflecting their significant role as primary income earners, leading to concerns about the 'feminization of migration'. The majority of women are migrating for work as domestic helpers, in the entertainment industry, in factories and, to a considerable extent, also as nurses and teachers (ILO 2004: 10–11). Substantial migratory movements continue to occur within the South or regionally, and there is evidence of former 'sending' countries turning more and more also into 'receiving' countries – e.g. Thailand, Mexico and Nigeria.

International migration involves at least two sets of countries: those migrants originate from and those they migrate to, or their destination. A third set are so-called 'transit countries'. Although migration in the search for better opportunities has long been part of human history, the contemporary era of globalization processes has led to qualitatively different migration patterns and pressures. According to the ILO (2004), the evidence points to an increase in migration pressures in many parts of the world. Processes integral to globalization have intensified the disruptive effects of modernization and capitalist development. Many developing countries face serious social and economic dislocation associated with persistent poverty, growing unemployment, loss of traditional trading patterns and what has been termed a 'growing crisis of economic security' (ILO Socio-Economic Security Programme 2004):

> In a number of countries, accelerated trade is replacing or undercutting domestic industrial and agricultural production with cheap imports, but at the expense of many jobs in those sectors. Structural Adjustment Programmes (SAPs) imposed reductions in government spending, state budgets and state subsidies, as well as significant reductions in government employment. Job creation by the private sector in many countries

affected by SAPs has not kept up with the numbers rendered unemployed by downsizing governments. Population increases have further added to the ranks of job seekers, increasing the gaps in many countries between needs and opportunities for decent work and survival.

(Taran and Demaret 2006: 392)

Destination countries, by contrast, are commonly undergoing serious demographic changes leading to the rapid ageing of society and fertility rates below replacement level. Japan, for instance, is the world's most rapidly ageing society. The expansion of the middle classes in Asia and Latin America and the increasing numbers of women entering the labour force in the absence of adequate childcare and elderly care facilities have resulted in rising demand for certain types of migrant 'care' workers. The restructuring of (North and West) European welfare states as well as other demographic and labour market-related changes in developed countries in the West have increased the demand for skilled foreign workers in, for example, the health sector. This has revived older debates from the 1970s on the supposed 'brain drain' and raised issues such as 'ethical recruiting' in by some countries, notably the UK. Specific labour market shortages, such as the one triggered by the information technology (IT) boom in the 1990s, lead many governments to recruit highly skilled foreigners in those sectors. Germany, for instance, implemented the so-called Green Card, specifically targeting IT workers from India. At the same time, there are increasing numbers of undocumented migrants, usually those classified as unskilled, in certain sectors of the labour market such as agriculture, the hospitality sector and construction (ILO 2004). These foreign workers are typically 'needed but not wanted' by destination societies. Irregular migration is now much higher than in the 1980s and so is the rate of employment in the informal sectors, where many lower skilled migrants can be found.

With regard to the patterns and nature of today's migration flows, major policy concerns relating to international migration, which have been highlighted in the existing literature, revolve around the rising numbers of irregular/undocumented migrants (largely in the absence of legal migration channels) and the increasing shift toward temporary and circular migration, as opposed to permanent settlement. The two fastest-growing regular migration flows have been described as involving migration of highly skilled people, and temporary migration, involving both skilled and unskilled, even in traditional settler countries such as North America and Australia. Related to this is the increasing bifurcation between skilled and unskilled migration in the ease of movement between countries. Skilled migrants are typically given a preferential status and more rights and entitlements, such as family reunification (Piper 2007a).

The question which arises is to what extent migration patterns and concomitant policy responses differ in the context of movements from developing to developed countries (North–South, East–West), flows between developed countries (for example intra-EU), between developing countries or between developing and non-OECD countries representing South-to-South flows (such as migration from Bangladesh and Indonesia to Malaysia, Singapore, Hong Kong and the Gulf States). Often these flows take place between neighbouring countries where borders are the result of colonial or post-colonial partitions that artificially divided peoples of the same ethno-cultural background (Wong 2005). What could in sociological terms, therefore, be described a 'natural' flow becomes 'illegal' in political and legal terms. There is considerable evidence of irregular and undocumented movements of this sort which create specific types of problems for the individuals involved (see, for example, Battistella and Asis 2003; Piper and Iredale 2003; D'Angelo and Pasos Marciacq 2002).

Even in the destination (and typically higher-income) countries, where many undocumented migrants commonly work in the informal sector of the economy, their presence is often tacitly approved. But because these foreign workers tend to be lower or unskilled, their presence is not wanted and their contributions are officially not recognized (as evident from the reaction by NGOs and trade unions to the recent Green Paper published by the EU on economic migration, which pointed to the EU's neglect of undocumented migration).

Given their different positions within the global or regional political economy, countries of origin and destination tend to have conflicting interests in, and different ways of dealing with, economic migration. It is important to underline the fact that policies of developed countries often create stratified patterns of migration by selectively opening up their economic routes of entry and providing differential rights and entitlements according to the migrant's apparent utility to the economy and his/her social status. Hence, while in Europe, North America and the NICs, IT workers and paid domestic workers are both in short supply, the former have enjoyed a considerable array of rights, while the latter have subsisted in low-status employment with few entitlements. What is important to understand are the key axes of differentiation and stratification. Some of the crucial axes demarcating the bundle of rights are those between 'skilled' and 'unskilled', and the 'legal' compared to the 'illegal' or undocumented. The two are connected because those with fewer skills are far more likely to slip into an irregular status during the migration process. In turn, a migrant's position in relation to these axes influences access to various entitlements, such as family reunification (Boyd and Pikkov 2007; Kofman 2007). In this sense, the issue of migration relates strongly to issues of rights and citizenship.

The human rights of migrants

Historically, non-nationals have been subject to very little legal protection other than by the diplomatic services of their country of origin. Only with the emergence of an international human rights regime has a set of rights protecting all individuals, regardless of their status, brought new forms of protection. In principle, migrants are included in the coverage of the most important human rights treaties, such as the International Covenant on Civil and Political Rights (ICCPR) and the International Covenant on Economic, Social and Cultural Rights (ICESCR) (Pécoud and de Gutcheneire 2004).

The international protection of migrant *workers* was addressed by the ILO as soon as it was founded in 1919. Its mandate is built on the ideological movement for social and labour concerns throughout the nineteenth century and on the efforts of organized labour, which had become a politically stronger force in war economies (Hasenau 1991). In 1947, an agreement was concluded between the ILO and the UN 'according to which the competence of the ILO included the rights and situation of migrants in their quality as workers, while the competence of the United Nations enclosed the rights and situation of migrants in their quality as aliens' (Hasenau 1991: 693). The 1990 UN Convention on the Rights of All Migrant Workers and their Families has its origins in the work of the ILO.

The two main aims of the ILO in this field have since been to work towards first, equality of treatment between national and foreign workers, and secondly, coordination of migration policies between states, and between states and social partners, that is, workers' and employers' organizations. The latter is a reflection of the ILO's tripartite structure. To this end, the ILO has engaged in numerous standard setting activities in the form of conventions and recommendations, addressing a wide range of issues such as recruitment, social protection and freedom of association (for an extensive list of all instruments, see ILO 2004). Parallel to these standard setting activities, the ILO also undertakes a substantial operation programme in the migration field, offering technical assistance to governments, for example. The advancement of a rights-based approach to migration in the history of the ILO has, however, been subject to changing socio-economic conditions to do with economic downturns, rising unemployment and the politicization of immigration in destination countries. Its progress, as well as backlashes in this regard, has thus been mainly subject to the interests, and pressures, of the highly developed countries in the North.

On a general level, the biggest barrier to a rights-based approach to international migration lies in the difficulties of reconciling the sovereign right of states to protect their labour markets and national citizens, on the one hand, and the fundamental rights of individuals who seek life and work outside their country of birth or nationality, on the other. To illustrate this, in international law there is the clear right for individuals to *leave* their country of birth but no commensurate right to *enter* another country. This results in a tension between internal and external forces, and creates conflicting interests of a kind for which there are no easy solutions.

Academic debate

Much of the debate on the rights of migrants has focused on legalistic aspects revolving around the existing international law framework for the protection of migrants (Aleinikoff and Chetail 2003; Satterthwaite 2005; Cholewinski 1997) or on more specific rights, such as political rights (Layton-Henry 1990), and this has typically occurred in the context of liberal states' role as countries of immigration (Joppke 1998). Another angle taken by existing scholarship is citizenship, in which older debates revolved around issues such as assimilation and naturalization of first generations of immigrants. In these approaches, the level of analysis is tied to the nation-state and the starting point is again the perspective of 'proper' immigration, where acquisition of citizenship is possible and family reunification an option. This, however, does not reflect the situation of many temporary or undocumented migrant workers, nor the situation of migrant workers in the South (Piper 2006a).

Citizenship is also becoming less important for the highly skilled who obtain most rights via permanent residency (PR) status. At the same time, changing citizenship is easier for the privileged and a toleration of dual citizenship is on the increase (Dauvergne forthcoming). For the lower or unskilled, the issue of citizenship is of less immediate importance than accessing overseas employment (Briones 2006). Furthermore, temporary contract and undocumented migration entail return and re-migration, with the result that the acquisition of a new citizenship is out of reach, and even irrelevant, for many. There are, in other words, differences in priorities and also rising inequalities in access to PR status and citizenship. As a result, it has been argued that the rising incidences of temporary and return migration call for a transnational approach to the issue of citizenship and migrants' rights (Piper 2006a).

Rights as a concept easily conjure up the image of a legalistic approach focusing 'on what the law says' by downplaying the dynamic aspects of the political processes at play (VeneKlasen *et al.* 2004). Piper (2007b) addresses the limitations of traditional rights approaches that place the content of international law at the core of rights work, instead of noting the importance of starting with an understanding of rights as a political process (VeneKlasen *et al.* 2004). When rights exist on paper, the challenge lies in guaranteeing their implementation and creating institutional avenues for claiming them. When rights are not recognized by governments, efforts to advance and expand rights not yet enshrined in law constitute the first step (VeneKlasen *et al.* 2004; Piper 2006a).

By introducing a social movement or activist perspective into the academic debate on the human rights of migrants, Piper (2007b) has followed Johnston (2001) in taking a social-scientific (as opposed to a juridical) perspective on rights. This means that rights first appear not when governments recognize them, but when people begin demanding and exercising them. It is through meaningful organizations that an enabling environment can be created, leading to the empowerment of foreign workers through education, knowledge provision and collective action.

The subject of migrants' rights thus clearly emerges as an issue broader than national citizenship and typically relates to debates on international human rights. The evolving debate on 'the human rights of migrants' involves two broad levels: migrants' rights as they are already codified in existing human rights law, and the gaps in existing human rights law that have emerged with the changing reality of international migration today. Related to the latter is that gender perspectives have more recently been introduced into the debate on the human rights of migrants, reflecting the increasing numbers of women participating in all migration streams, and pointing to the fact that the experience of migrant women is often different from migrating men. It has been argued that the protective capacity of existing human rights law is inadequate in the case of certain jobs that are predominantly carried out by women. In this context, the view has been advanced that, instead of consulting migrant worker-specific international instruments (see later), it might be more useful to make use of other covenants or conventions which are not migrant specific from the outset, such as the Convention on the Elimination of All Forms of Discrimination against Women (CEDAW), and which might initially appear as irrelevant or less useful for the protection of foreign workers (Piper and Satterthwaite 2007). This is an important argument in light of the comparatively low ratification rate of migrant worker-specific instruments.

The legal and normative framework of international migration

Certain groups in society, such as children, women and refugees have been targeted by international treaty law to protect them as a category of people identified as particularly vulnerable. In recent years, considerable progress has been made in establishing an international legal and normative framework for protecting the rights of international migrants. This is related to three international agreements that came into force during the past few years: the 1990 UN Convention on the Rights of All Migrants Workers and their Families (CRM), which finally came into force in 2003 after reaching the minimum number of ratifications; and the two Protocols on Human Smuggling and Human Trafficking, supplementing the 2000 UN Convention Against Transnational Organized Crime. But in comparison to other UN conventions and covenants, the overall rate of ratification of migrant worker-specific instruments has been slow. Apart from the CRM, which has so far only been ratified by countries in the south, the other two migrant worker-specific instruments are ILO conventions nos. 143 and 97. As of April 2003, the former has 18 ratifications and the latter is ratified by 42 countries. The only exception is the Protocol on Human Trafficking, which has been ratified by 110 states, which is, however, not a human rights instrument. This supports the argument that is being advanced here: that destination countries, especially the highly developed countries, are more concerned with controlling irregular migration than with the human rights of migrants. This is evident from the fact that the provision of 'victim support initiatives' is often underdeveloped, under-funded, or absent from implementation procedures.

The rights of migrants can be categorized according to five broad classifications. They relate to (i) the pre-departure phase in the country of origin and the actual journey to the destination, revolving around issues such as information about visa requirements or other travel documents, working conditions, recruitment, contracts, medical services, etc.; (ii) the arrival, involving issues such as assistance in finding employment or customs exemption; (iii) employment, relating to wages, working conditions, job security, social security, health and safety, trade union rights, access to courts, access to other jobs, vocational training and freedom of movement; (iv) social and civil rights, for example education and culture, transfer of funds to home country, family reunification and visits, advisory services; and (v) return, that is assistance with arrangements and rights of returning migrant workers (ICFTU-APRO 2003). This clearly indicates that both countries of origin and destination are responsible for certain rights of migrants, which is also evident in migrant worker-specific instruments.

Once in the country of destination, the core principles of relevance to migrant workers are non-discrimination, equality and equal protection before the law. Migrants' specific vulnerabilities stem from the fact that they are not citizens of the country in which they work and reside. In addition, a distinction is usually made between 'legal' and 'illegal' migrants, with the latter being granted basic human rights, but not the full breadth of rights that legal migrants enjoy, although, as we show later, in practice, even these basic rights are violated. This renders irregular migrants even more vulnerable as far as international human rights law is concerned.

A note on terminology is required here. Migrants without documentation or work permits are typically referred to as 'illegal', which is misleading as it conveys the idea of criminality. Many studies have shown that migrants shift between legality and illegality for various reasons, often beyond their control or knowledge. The term 'undocumented' is preferable, but does not cover migrants who enter the destination country legally but later violate their original entry visa. At the 1999 International Symposium on Migration in Bangkok, 21 participating countries agreed to use the term 'irregular migrants', which has since become common practice.

Taken together, existing UN and ILO conventions provide fairly comprehensive – albeit incomplete (as argued by Gosh 2003) – protection but they exist in a fragmented and scattered manner, and it is sometimes not obvious that they could relate to migrant workers at all if the focus is on the single variable of 'migration status' rather than on multiple variables relevant to women and men who migrate for work – including race or ethnicity, occupation and gender (Satterthwaite 2007). It is common that destination countries single out the migration status and, by treating workers as non-citizens, especially when they are irregular migrants, the rights of states clearly prevail over the rights of migrants, with states retaining the ultimate right to set the conditions under which foreigners may enter and reside in their territory (Pécoud and de Gutcheneire 2005, see also Martin 2003).

Normative shifts

There has been a gradual shift in recent years, coming mainly from trade unions and NGOs to treat migrants first and foremost as workers once they have entered the territory where they work, regardless of their legal status. This development has become evident at the international level also, in the form of the revival of a rights-based approach even for irregular migrants, as manifested in the ILO's latest Plan for Action, the result of the International Labour Congress of June 2004. The most recent and ground-breaking development in this regard, however, is the ruling by the Inter-American Court of Human Rights that states that all migrants – documented and undocumented – are covered by the principles of non-discrimination, equality and equal protection in the host states where they live and work, and must not be excluded from the protection of labour laws on the basis of their migration status (for more detail, see Satterthwaite 2005).

Migrants' human rights in practice

Despite frequent incidences of abuse and discrimination, migrants' rights have remained on the margins of the international human rights agenda for several reasons. These include lack of data; gaps between different institutional mandates of the UN; parallel systems of protecting employment rights and human rights; relatively little reporting by human rights NGOs; the dominance of refugee protection in the migration field; and the fact that until the CMR was drafted, human rights law only made explicit reference to migrants – as non-nationals – in the context of free movement. Lack of information – about types of violation, where they occur, their frequency and characteristics – has been an obstacle to policy-making. Violations have been under-recorded particularly in the case of migrant women and of forced or exploitative labour that typically takes place in the underground or informal sectors of the economy. The result is a high degree of invisibility of certain types of migrants in human rights discussions (Grant 2005: 3–4). Much of this also relates to the absence of vigorous civil society activism and advocacy activities in the field of migration policy (Thouez 2005). This has, however, gradually begun to change – a point to which we shall return in Chapter 4.

As mentioned earlier, migrants' human rights are at stake in the country of origin, transit and destination. With regard to labour rights at the destination, lower skilled and unskilled workers, who form the majority of migrants, are more vulnerable to rights violations as opposed to skilled workers because they tend to work in the informal sectors of the labour market or in sectors where labour standards are not applied, even for local workers. Temporary contract migrants face the problem that their residential status is linked to their work permit which ties them to one employer. At the end of a contract, they have to leave immediately, a situation which employers often take advantage of by paying less than the full wages or none at all. This is even worse for undocumented migrants who fear exposure and detection by the immigration services. Problems such as non- or under-payment of wages, unfair dismissal, bondage (withholding of travel documents), long working hours and precarious working conditions are widespread. Furthermore, migrant workers' freedom of association, that is the right to join trade unions and be politically represented, is commonly violated.

Generally speaking, therefore, what remains a major problem with human rights is the gap between theory and practice, or between ratification and implementation. A number of recent studies have shown that possibly the most important root cause of non-ratification or non-implementation is political will (Piper and Iredale 2003; Pécoud and de Gutcheneire 2004). An additional problem for origin countries is that, with increasing competition on the 'labour export market', they have relatively little influence on the treatment of their nationals in the countries of destination and little bargaining power when it comes to the negotiation of bilateral agreements (BLAs) or Memoranda of Understanding (MoUs), partly because they fear losing their share in the regional or global market. There is in fact some evidence that 'troublesome' or rights conscious or otherwise more assertive migrants of a particular nationality are replaced with those from elsewhere. But not all sending countries are equally affected by this and it seems that diversification in terms of skill levels, occupations and countries of destination is one way to avoid being the victim of competition of this sort. This has been done quite successfully by the Philippines, for example (Iredale *et al.* 2005). Hence, acquisition of 'human capital' is another component which would improve the protection of migrants because the better-educated and skilled migrants are for those jobs that are in heavy demand in a variety of countries, the less they depend on a few specific destinations.

Migrants' rights – transnational and 'developmental' perspectives

The multiple interlocking networks of social relationships that are the basis of today's migration experience also have an impact on our understanding of rights – in theory (legal rights) and practice (the politics behind the granting or non-granting of rights to migrants). Placing rights within the transnational sphere points first of all to the fact that taking a simple approach to migration – as a one-way or one-off emigration and immigration phenomenon – does not hold true for an increasing number of migrants. As mentioned earlier, this has implications especially for a conventional understanding of citizenship: in view of high incidences of return and re-migration, the acquisition of citizenship in the new country of residence is often not desired by migrants or is simply out of their reach. For temporary contract workers and undocumented migrants, access to overseas work and socio-economic rights are of greater importance.

In addition, since much migration is now of a short-term, temporary or circular nature, many migrants are experiencing transnationally split family life because they are legally not allowed to bring their families or it is not practical to do so due to the nature of their work. This creates a new context in which rights have to be extended to family members who are 'left behind'. The analysis of migration has, in fact, begun to be conceptualized as something that takes place within social fields that extend beyond those who actually move to those who are connected to migrants through networks of social relations across borders. In other words, transnational communities consist of those who migrate and those who stay behind (Levitt and Nyberg-Sørensen 2004). Furthermore, in the expanding literature on transnational communities and/or diasporas, attention is now placed on celebrating migrants as 'agents of development'. States may offer dual nationality and overseas voting rights among the various strategies used by origin countries for maintaining migrants' loyalty – with the ultimate objective to ensure their contribution to national development. Other strategies include investment policies designed to attract and channel economic remittances and boost local development.

To date, the subject of migrants' rights has mainly been discussed from the perspective of the destination countries, revolving around issues to do with integration policies, settlement and the gradual acquisition of citizenship rights. Yet, in a transnational setting, rights issues take on a new dimension, leading Piper (2006a) to argue for a new transnational conceptualization of migrants' rights. Transnationalization refers to rights which migrants maintain *vis-à-vis* the country of origin when crossing borders; gain when entering the destination *vis-à-vis* the country of origin and destination; and keep or gain when returning to their country of origin. Many of these are covered by existing international instruments, but only in a fragmented manner as they are codified over several conventions.

Moreover, 'transnationalization' involves not only the simultaneous existence of rights *vis-à-vis* the origin and destination states (a principal aspect well reflected in international legal instruments), but the recognition of, and need for, 'new' rights that reflect the transnational life of migrants. Furthermore, there is the new issue area of 'portability of rights', or complementarity, as they relate to social welfare rights (Tamas 2003). A large number of migrants, typically the older generation, have accrued social rights and are beginning to raise issues of transferability upon returning to their countries of origin. A few existing studies, derived mostly from the context of Northern African immigrants in France, have shown that some rights, such as pension rights, are reduced if accessed outside the country in which they were built up. A different example of rights in the transnational sphere relates to the frequent occurrence of transnationally split families for whom conventional family unification policies are irrelevant or not applicable. The concept of 'rights to a family life' might take secondary importance compared with a different set of rights for the left behind. So far, there has been too little discussion on the rights of those left behind. Thus, the conception of 'transnationalized rights' points to the responsibility on the part of both the sending and receiving states as well as societies. Last but not least, the notion of 'transnationalization' is also meant to refer to the political process of advancing and promoting rights in the form of transnational political activism to reflect the transnational nature of migration.

In December 2005, the Office of the High Commissioner for Human Rights (OHCHR) invited the submission of discussion papers for the Migrant Committee's *Open Day of Dialogue*, which was on the theme of 'protecting the rights of all migrant workers as a tool to enhance development (see http://www.ohchr.org/english/bodies/cmw/docs/global.pdf [accessed 10 February 2006]). A few of the contributions raised the issue of 'portable justice' in the context of the violation of labour rights and the obstacles to seeking redress – while still working in the country of destination, after returning home at the end of their contracts or after deportation when detected for working illegally (Caron 2005; Piper 2005a; Smith and Paoletti 2005). This shows that employment or labour rights are also played out in the transnational sphere and require responses not only by the destination but also origin countries. States' policies, however, often focus on only migration aspects when enforcing laws and regulations, without paying due attention to labour or work-related aspects, in terms of monitoring work sites for example. Moreover, the example of the OHCHR's *Open Day of Dialogue* also shows that there is a link between migrants' rights and development.

Major concerns with regard to employment rights are breach of contract and the non- or under-payment of wages. The difficulty of claiming grievance in labour courts or labour standards offices because of the worker's temporary migration status has been raised by a few scholars (Caron 2005; Piper 2005a; Smith and Paoletti 2005). Often, when temporary contract migrants lose their jobs, even in cases of unfair dismissal, they are made to return home and thus have no channels available for recourse. This is an area where transnational networking between NGOs and trade unions gains importance (Piper 2006b) and where embassies could also take a more active role, by providing lawyers for instance.

As mentioned earlier, in the area of development in recent years, another trend has been the rising interest of countries of origin in establishing a link to their nationals who are overseas (referred to as 'diasporas' or trans-national communities). This is largely driven by their recognition or hope that migrants can advance national development from abroad through remittances or investment. To stimulate such assistance, emigrants are increasingly being endowed with special rights. Two types of such rights have political implications – overseas voting rights and dual citizenship – and countries of origin are, as we noted above, now more and more inclined to offer these. By 2000, ten countries in Latin America had passed some form of dual nationality or citizenship; only four had such provisions prior to 1991 (Jones-Correa 1998; Levitt and Nyberg-Sørensen 2004). Other countries allow the expatriate vote, including the Dominican Republic, Mexico and the Philippines (Levitt and Nyberg-Sørensen 2004). Migrant associations have been at the forefront in advocating for overseas voting rights – successfully in the Philippines and unsuccessfully in Sri Lanka (Iredale *et al.* 2005) – but often based on a different understanding of development, that is the creation of jobs and socio-economic security at home that would allow more migrants not having to migrate in the first place or at least not having to re-migrate. Here migrants' NGOs are making clear that they do not want only 'elite' migrants to have a stake in politics in the country of origin, but also the much larger number of low or unskilled temporary migrant workers.

The notion of 'transnationalization of rights' is in its early stage of conceptualization and represents an important paradigm shift in the under-standing of 'migrants' rights', highlighting more fundamental issues involved in the simultaneous responsibilities of origin and destination countries that go far beyond the conventional understanding of (legal) rights. This, how-ever, poses a challenge to the governance of migration characterized by geo-graphical, political and institutional complexities. To ensure that migration is a largely beneficial experience, it is vital to incorporate the voices of migrants themselves. There are organizational channels that function, or have the potential to function, as 'voice institutions' for foreign workers. This is the subject of the following chapter which shifts our attention to the role of social partners and civil society organizations (CSOs).

Conclusion

On the global policy level, two trends can be observed, namely the 'celebratory' discourse of the 'migration-development' nexus and the 'man-agement of migration'. This poses a serious challenge to the question of 'how to move beyond the obscure normative assertion that migration has "benefits for all" to concrete and workable solutions on the one hand; and a focus away from "migration management" on the other hand' (Thouez 2004: 7). 'Managing' migrants implies a top-down approach characterized by an 'inherent hierarchy of "someone managing someone else"' (Thouez 2004: 14) and, consequently, this term has emerged as loaded with very negative connotations.

Aiming to improve their livelihoods and those of their families, increasing numbers of migrants (and among them more and more women) seek work abroad. This is not necessarily their first choice but at times a reflection of lack of 'decent work' opportunities at home and the high demand for workers abroad in specific types of jobs. With restrictive migration policies and the prevalence of temporary contract schemes, migrants' full potential or ability to secure livelihoods and their chances for personal socio-economic empowerment and active participation in 'voice institutions' are inevitably limited. In light of this, the path towards a people-centred, participatory rights-based approach seems a rather thorny one. In the following chapter, we discuss in more detail the issue of rights from the viewpoint of the emerging governance regime of migration on our way to exploring the extent to which its architecture and instruments provide new spaces, or anchor points, for political activism.

3 The regulatory framework of economic migration

Over the past two decades, international migration has resurfaced as a prominent feature of contemporary social and economic life, as reflected in current political and academic debates in countries across the world. Global initiatives have emerged, concerned with the regulation of international migration flows (Overbeek 2002). Efforts to bring all states implicated in international migration (that is, 'sending' and 'receiving' countries) together at the global level to discuss multilateral approaches to migration policy constitute a new phase in the development of migration governance. Reaching this phase has proven to be a major challenge and the issue of international migration has emerged only gradually on the global agenda. It was not until 2004 that the ILO devoted its annual congress to the issue of migrant workers, and it took until September 2006 for the UN to hold a High-Level Dialogue on the theme of 'International Migration and Development'. In the meantime, an increasing number of UN agencies, inter-governmental institutions, international financial institutions (IFIs), donor agencies and international non-governmental organizations (INGOs) have begun to engage with international migration in one way or another, some-times with differing or overlapping mandates and objectives (Newland 2005; Thouez 2005).

As we indicated in Chapter 2, the global policy debate on economic migration has broadly been dominated by two main themes, namely manage-ment of migration and migration as a tool for development. The push towards the 'management of migration' refers to the (revived) recognition of the need for international cooperation between all countries implicated. This (re-)emerging concern with the elaboration of an international framework for migration management is related to a number of global initiatives, such as the recent Berne Initiative (for more details, see http://www.iom.int/en/know/berneinitiative/index.shtml), the establishment of the Global Migration Group (comprising representatives from the ILO, UNCTAD, UNHCR, OHCHR and UNODC), and the work and final report in October 2005 of the Global Commission on International Migration (GCIM), which was set up in December 2003 by the General Secretary (see http://www.gcim.org). The main objective of this global agenda is to promote cooperation between states in dealing with the complexity of international migration today. Clearly, therefore, this is a state-owned process.

In the attempt to improve the 'benefits of migration for all' (often expressed in terms of a 'win-win situation'), the second major theme of the global policy debate has revolved around the various linkages between migration and development (GCIM 2005; UN 2006). Although the focus is often predominantly on the developmental impact of out-migration for origin countries in the form of remittances, investment, or skill transfers, the need for enhanced development has also been discussed in terms of alleviating the pressure to migrate in the first place. This theme relates to current thinking among policy-makers and donor agencies, as well as among many academics, which views migrants as potential 'agents of development' in connection with origin countries' efforts to tap into 'diasporas' or 'transnational communities' of nationals residing overseas in order to secure remittances, that is 'transfers in cash or in kind from migrants to resident households in the countries of origin' (Bilsborrow *et al.*, 1997:321) and investment in migrants' home communities. This is also linked to reduced, or shifting, aid budgets on the part of donor countries and the search for alternative sources on the part of migrant origin countries.

In the context of economic migration, a further policy development is the recent revival of a rights-based approach to the 'management' of migration by the ILO, which is aimed at addressing the protective deficit for migrants in current policy practices by individual states. Taking a human rights perspective on economic well-being and livelihoods reflects a normative framework in the form of 'rights-based approaches' that has been emerging in relation to a number of global issues, such as development (adopted by the UN General Assembly in 1986), health (as championed by the World Health Organization), childhood (which we discuss in detail in Chapters 5–7) and migration (ILO 2006). Under its broader mandate of promoting decent work for all, the ILO's rights-based approach to migration aims to foster cooperation and consultation not only among states but also between states and social partners. This is reflective of the ILO's tripartite constituency, comprising governments and worker and employer organizations, which is a unique set-up within the UN.

In addition to the ILO's attempt to revive a human rights framework for migration, the OHCHR set up the Migrant Committee in 2004, the Treaty Body in charge of monitoring the implementation of the 1990 UN International Workers Convention on the Protection of the Rights of All Migrants and their Families (CRM) that came into force in September 2003, having finally reached the required minimum number of ratifications (for more information, see http://www.ohchr.org/english/bodies/treaty/index.htm). The procedure by which State Parties, or governments which have ratified the CRM, are required to submit reports has since started.

Although this shift in the migration-policy debate towards a focus on international cooperation is primarily concerned with control over entry and exit with the particular aim of preventing irregular migration, broader human rights issues, as well as the rights of foreign workers, have in fact entered into the discussion (GCIM 2005; IOM and FOM 2005) and, consequently, led to a concern for the basic units of analysis of migration: the migrants themselves. But it is yet to be seen whether this is a matter of paying mere lip service or whether there is indeed a serious concern with migrants' human rights and whether real efforts toward safeguarding such rights are being made, especially in terms of providing mechanisms by which these rights can actually be claimed. In other words, the important question these shifts in discourse and policy concerns raises is: are these two elements – managing migration and the protection of migrants' rights – going hand in hand or do they constitute conflicting areas of concern and policy, with rights issues being sidelined? How are these shifts reflected and played out in terms of the various governing institutions involved? For instance, do international institutions involve non-governmental or civil society organizations in their policy-making processes and are there mechanisms in place for the actual claiming of rights? To what extent are linkages between the two major policy areas which dominate the current migration debate – management and development – made? Are the two rights-based frameworks – to labour migration and development – brought together?

Global policy discourse and practice on migration – an emerging rights-based approach or an issue of control?

Management of migration

Among the key features of global governance today is the so-called management of migration (Jordan and Duevell 2003). The agenda behind managing migration has mostly been about the designing of policies aimed at regulating the entry and exit of various different types, or groups, of migrant workers, in addition to the emphasis put on the need for cooperation among states, especially origin, transit and destination countries. The main incentive is to prevent irregular migration but, increasingly, there are also concerns about long-term migration leading to settlement. The ultimate goal, therefore, is controlling the movement of people with a view to maintaining labour market flexibility and 'national security'.

This aspect of 'control' is not a new concern at all. In fact, controlling migration has preoccupied the minds of policy-makers since the 1970s, and even more forcefully since the late 1980s and 1990s, partly to do with the world's changing geo-political landscape. Although the shift from 'migration control' to the term 'migration management' indicates some new nuances at the discursive level, the policies of European and other highly developed governments continue 'to follow a philosophy predominantly concerned with restricting and controlling migration' (Doomernik *et al.* 2005: 35). The global push towards 'cooperation in controlling', consequently, seems to reflect an agenda largely driven by, and predicated upon, the concerns of the highly developed destination countries. This is also evident in the statement by the European Economic and Social Committee (EESC) in response to the recent Green Paper published by the EU outlining a possible common European approach to managing economic migration, in which the EESC commented that cooperation between states must be extended to cover the overall management of migratory flows, including the perspective of origin countries – and should not only be based on the interests of Northern governments alone (CESE 2005).

It has been suggested that the very use of the term 'management' is based on the pre-globalization assumption of state control over migration processes (Newland 2005). However, much cross-border movement does not follow state procedures and takes on its own dynamic by, for instance, relying heavily on private recruitment agencies or brokerage services which are especially prominent in Asia and, probably most commonly on migrants' own networks. There is in fact a proliferation of actors making decisions about international migration independent from, and outside, state frameworks of regulation. And, most importantly, it is the migrants themselves whose actions and behaviour defy state regulation in many ways (Ford and Piper 2007). Foreign workers are not only 'pushed' to migrate by conditions in their countries of origin, but also respond to certain 'pull factors' in specific destination countries (Ball and Piper 2006).

Being mainly concerned with combating so-called 'illegal' migration, maintaining border controls and returning deportees, it does not come as a surprise that states' actual practices in terms of managing migration are tied first and foremost to (im)migration policies and only secondarily to labour market, employment and other public policies. This is evident from the fact that individual (especially receiving) states' governance of migration is typically part of the portfolio of Immigration Departments which come under Ministries of Justice or Home Affairs, rather than as part of the portfolio of Ministries of Labour/Employment, beyond the administering of work permits. Even at the 2004 ILC, the annual ILO Congress, on Migrant Labour, some states included immigration officials in their delegations, although the ILO's structure only allows for direct relations between labour ministries and the ILO. To include immigration experts in the ILC delegations is, therefore, an indication of labour migration being treated as a matter of controlling the exit and entry of foreigners. This makes policy elaboration and implementation part of policing, internally and externally and turns it into an issue of national security, rather than a matter of labour-market regulation and employment conditions. In several Asian countries, for instance, there is outright reluctance to engage in cooperation and coordination between immigration authorities and labour ministries (Piper and Iredale 2003).

To return to the global level, concerns for the need to govern migration have gradually built up since the World Conference on Population and Development in 1994. For a long time, there was no consensus within the UN General Assembly on international migration until the former Secretary General Kofi Annan recognised the need to develop an integrated approach. To this end, he set up the GCIM in 2003 with the mandate 'to provide the framework for the formulation of a coherent, comprehensive and global response to the issue of international migration' (GCIM 2005: vii). In the meantime, a number of regional consultative processes took place in Puebla, Bali, Manila, Southern Africa, Budapest as part of the Berne Initiative. The GCIM's consultations in connection with the preparation of its final report took a similar form, namely that of 'regional hearings'.

Parallel to attempts to 'manage migration', which tend to focus more on controlling cross-border flows, are the ILO's efforts to address the protection deficit by shifting attention to the need for a rights-based approach to economic migration. Reflecting states' reluctance to enter into a new multilateral agreement, symptomatic of a general multilateral fatigue and the current critical stance *vis-à-vis* the UN by many states, but also more particularly of the highly sensitive nature of cross-border migration in general, the ILO has chosen the route of the 'non-binding framework' to promote and push for the implementation of its rights-based approach. The ILO's Governing Body took note of this framework at its meeting in March 2006 and agreed to its wider promotion and dissemination, which meant a *de facto* approval (personal email communication with Dr Ryszard Cholewinski, Migration Policy, Research and Communications Department, IOM, 19 May 2006). In choosing this option, the ILO effectively acknowledged the authority of the highly developed countries which had pushed for the soft law approach.

Resonating with the ILO's concern for a rights-based framework to migration governance and the need for social dialogue among all stakeholders on migration policy, the *Declaration of The Hague on the Future of Refugee and Migration Policy* from 2002, the product of a three-year consultative process involving government officials and non-governmental representatives aimed at shaping future policy on migration, argues that all states need to cooperate on developing a common approach to migration based on human rights standards. In the preamble it is noted in an optimistic tone that the potential for international cooperation is increasing and, together with the global advance of human rights and democratic governance, new perspectives are opening up. This Declaration further emphasizes that migration management should be treated as a 'complex process which goes beyond punitive measures and instruments of control'. To this end, dialogue and cooperation of all parties is required as well as a transparent and participatory approach to migration management, which is to be developed within the framework of international law.

What all these initiatives and declarations attempt to achieve is the promotion of a comprehensive debate among all relevant states, as well as other stakeholders, with regard to migration; the analysis of gaps in current policy approaches to migration; the examination of inter-linkages between migration and other global issues; and the presentation of appropriate recommendations to the UN and governments. Reflecting the trans-border nature of this phenomenon, the management of migration in the form of more cooperation between origin, transit and destination countries has, therefore, been supported by international, inter-state organizations and global commissions – albeit by giving less weight to the importance of the protective aspects – i.e. the human rights dimension – of a global regulatory framework.

States commonly take a utilitarian approach to migration, prioritizing their own macroeconomic interests: origin countries are often driven by the desire to increase foreign remittances and reduce unemployment; destination countries are interested in solving labour-market shortages in certain sectors by ensuring a highly flexible and compliant workforce. As a result, governments typically take less notice of migrant workers' needs and concerns as opposed to those of employers – and sometimes not even of those employers who are in favour of legal channels for the migration of lower skilled workers. This has become evident in an ILO survey on policy-making and the involvement of social partners: 'There are ... only a few examples where the formulation of labour migration policies, laws and regulations takes place through formally established tripartite structures' (2004: 112). There are, therefore, competing societal demands and supply structures at work, which are rooted in real and perceived socio-economic needs, but the economic, social, political and distributional consequences of migration at the micro level have not yet been explored and are, as a result, not fully understood. Overall, there is little evidence of a 'social dialogue' taking place as part of this policy-making anywhere in the world, which means that governments take less notice of workers' (and definitely not foreign workers') voices as opposed to those of corporations and big businesses. Some origin countries have set up special ministries dealing with overseas migration (e.g. Philippines, Bangladesh, Sri Lanka) and there are a few examples of so-called 'migrant welfare funds' or commissions. But often migrant worker associations or rights advocacy NGOs are not part of their boards of management, although, by contrast, recruitment agencies usually are represented and the migrants' own concerns find little expression. In addition, there is no transparency with regard to the spending of the accumulated fees charged by state-run recruitment agencies or government agencies, such as in Singapore and Hong Kong where a so-called 'levy' is charged for the employment of lower-skilled migrants.

On the issue of cooperation between destination and origin countries, apart from multilateral agreements or declarations, there are other options for negotiating bilateral agreements or Memoranda of Understanding (MoUs), but these are again 'state-owned' and often reflect the power inbalance between origin and destination countries, which means the latter dictate the conditions. 'Good-practice' examples with regard to the inclusion of rights clauses are, to no one's surprise, few and far between. UNIFEM in Bangkok, for example, is currently facilitating the establishment of an implementing mechanism for MoUs between Jordan–Indonesia and Jordan–Philippines that contain rights protection for migrant workers, but it is not clear what the concrete outcome of this endeavour will be. Moreover, the problem with bilateral agreements and MoUs is that they give preferential treatment to a specific group of migrants and, by not promoting universal standards across all nationality groups, a hierarchy among migrant workers emerges. This is particularly evident in the case of foreign domestic workers in Asia. Filipinas are usually given the best deal (guaranteed minimum wage, one day off per week, etc.), followed by Indonesians and Sri Lankans whose 'market price' is lower and who are often subject to worse conditions than their Filipino counterparts (Wee and Sim 2005). Also, international agreements affecting migration at global, regional and national levels are more likely to favour skilled rather than unskilled migrants (Skeldon 2004), leaving many female migrants and lower-skilled male migrants at a disadvantage.

As pointed out earlier, states typically take a utilitarian approach to migration and therefore have little concern for migrants' rights. This can be seen from the low ratification rate of the CRM and the two migrant worker ILO conventions. But even in Europe, Australia and New Zealand where one of the arguments against ratification of migrant worker-specific conventions is that those rights are covered in already ratified and implemented instruments and that, therefore, ratification of the CRM would lead to 'duplication' and wasting of resources with regard to the reporting requirements, a rights-based approach to migration is not favoured or promoted. The EU and Australia, together with the USA and Canada, were among the most outspoken critics at the ILO Congress in 2004 where the rights-based approach was formulated and negotiated. The recent EU Green Paper on a common approach to future migration policy has been criticized by trade unions and NGOs for its overtly utilitarian approach with too little concern for migrants' rights. All this reflects the politically sensitive and potentially volatile nature of this issue.

From a governmental perspective, this also raises the issue of incentives – why should states be interested in protecting migrants in the first place? Countries of origins' interest in their nationals overseas is largely driven by their increasing recognition that migrants can advance national development while working abroad through remittances and investment back 'home'. As a result, there are more and more examples of emigrants being endowed with special rights and protections to make this easier. As far as countries of residence are concerned, it is up to employers' organizations, which are, contrary to popular belief, often in favour of legal migration of lower-skilled workers, and workers' organizations to put pressure on governments to endow foreigners with rights. This raises the important question, which we will return to discuss in more detail later, of how extensive the participation of NGOs is in both the 'management' debate and the actual policy-making processes.

Migration–development nexus

Two global reports have highlighted the two main elements of the migration – development nexus: the ways in which development processes can reduce pressures for migration, and the ways in which migrants can be a resource for poverty reduction and sustainable development in their home communities (UN 2004: 24; GCIM 2005). This has also been touched upon by the 2006 UN report on migration and development which states that all countries should strive to create more jobs, and decent jobs, to allow everyone the option of staying at home. In addition, numerous national, regional and international meetings and conferences have taken place, some of which have been funded and organized by donor agencies such as Gesellschaft fuer technische Zusammenarbeit, or GTZ, and research papers and reports by IFIs such as the Asian Development Bank and the World Bank, have been published exploring how migration relates to development and vice versa.

Most existing analyses of the 'migration–development nexus' and concomitant policy prescriptions have largely focused on economic indicators of progress in the countries of origin, using monetary remittances as a yardstick. These analyses largely derive from the context of a numerically small number of 'elite' migrants moving across continents in the form of South–North migration, as exemplified by studies on Indian IT workers and Chinese businessmen, for example (GTZ 2006; Gomez 2007). The large number of semi-skilled or unskilled migrants, however, send larger proportions of their income home than their highly skilled counterparts. Semi or unskilled migrants are sometimes even required to do so by their origin countries' policies. They constitute a group of migrants who experience far more exposure to abusive and exploitative practices than the higher skilled. Studies on exploitative practices by recruitment agencies (such as excessive charging of fees) and employers (usually under- or non-payment of wages), which largely correspond with the ILO's forced labour framework, have shown the potential for double exploitation in the origin and destination countries (Verité 2005; Rahman 2003). This therefore raises the question about who benefits in development terms from the prevailing forms of economic migration.

On an individual level, not all migrants' personal development is enhanced by the migration experience, despite the recognition that migrants are not necessarily victims but can also be 'agents of change' (UN 2006: 15, with specific reference to migrant women). Respecting migrants' rights as part of economic and social development is seen by some as the best long-term solution to reduce the pressures of out-migration (GCIM 2005; UN 2006; UNFPA 2006). Measures to improve the benefits of migration include providing migrants with a proper legal status, permission to change employer and, for women, permission to work when admitted for family reunification. In cases of out-migration, it has been argued that one of the important ways to ensure protection is via skills acquisition (Piper and Yamanaka 2007) which provides a clear link to human and social capital building. The issue of 'skills' has received some attention in migration scholarship in a different context also: by pointing to the limitations to 'upward social mobility' for the lower skilled, especially in the case of female migrants due to their positioning within gender and ethnically seg-regated job markets (Piper 2007a).

What is nevertheless missing from the debate on the migration–development nexus are the broader connections between migration and development from a rights-based approach and a more fundamental understanding of the type of 'rights' at stake. Furthermore, considerations of the multiple social dimensions of migration are still lacking. In other words, a sys-tematic analysis of the linkages between migration, social development and social policy has not been undertaken, and as a result the long-term effects of migration on issues such as redistribution, social cohesion, equal-ity and rights are under-explored (Hujo and Piper 2006). Migration scho-larship, in other words, needs to engage with scholarship on social policy. In so doing, the 'three Rs' highlighted by migration scholars (Papa-demetriou and Martin 1991) at the centre of the migration–development link – recruitment, remittances and return – should be complemented, or even replaced, by a different set – regulation, redistribution and rights (Deacon 2000).

As we argue here, rights are one of the important ways in which to get at the fundamental root causes of migration. This was also high-lighted by the Migrant Committee, the Treaty Body of the CRM, in its statement to the UN High-level Dialogue on Migration and Develop-ment of the General Assembly in September 2006. In this statement, the Migrant Committee recalls 'that the human being is the central subject of development and should be the active participant and beneficiary of the right to development, as set forth in the Declaration on the Right to Development' (2006: 2). As Article 1 of this Declaration (from 1986) states:

> the right to development is an inalienable human right by virtue of which every human person and all peoples are entitled to participate in,

contribute to, and enjoy economic, social, cultural and political development, in which all human rights and fundamental freedoms can be fully realized.

This resonates with two of the important elements outlining the major differences between 'needs-based' and 'rights-based' approaches (see Table 1.1). What deserves to be especially highlighted is the emphasis of rights-based approaches on being 'people-centred' and people's 'ability to claim rights or entitlements'. And one important avenue to achieve this is via *participation* in the form of collective organizations.

On a broad level, a direct link between a rights-based approach to labour migration and a rights-based approach to development has not been established by global policy-makers. This is mainly due to the politically sensitive nature of the underlying global inequalities at play. A deeper normative and empirical analysis of the political and economic processes and linkages between migration and development is, therefore, required to address the protective deficit for many migrants. A comprehensive analysis of this sort could also assist non-governmental activists make these connections in their advocacy work, which could, in turn, lead to new or extended coalitions between various civil society organizations, nationally and transnationally. We will return to this in the next chapter.

Institutionalized mechanisms for promoting and claiming migrants' rights

UN standard setting and complaints mechanisms

Despite the importance migration now has for global politics, there is no comprehensive international legal framework governing the cross-border movement of people and, as a result and related to this, no single UN agency whose exclusive mandate is international migration. This means that various UN agencies have competences that include migration issues in that they focus on migrants in their separate roles as workers, women or non-citizens – although rarely in the entirety of these roles (see Table 3.1).

Within the UN's current structure, it is the ILO and the OHCHR that are the main standard-setting agencies with regard to migrants – as workers (ILO) or non-citizens (OHCHR). The CRM was passed by the UN General Assembly in 1990, and is to date the only migrant worker – specific UN instrument. It came into force in 2003 only after a global campaign to boost its ratification was launched in 1998 (for more details, see http://www.migrantsrights.org). Until fairly recently, no relevant institutions within the UN had made any efforts to promote the convention. Until 1996, it was even difficult to obtain a copy of the actual text. It is largely due to NGOs that knowledge about the convention has spread and that its content has been translated into local languages. After finally reaching the minimum

Table 3.1

Migrant in role as	Global norm-setting or monitoring institution	Legal instrument
Worker	ILO	ILO conventions (nos 143, 97)
Woman	OHCHR	CEDAW
Non-citizens/aliens	OHCHR	CRM, CERD, ICESCR

Note: It could be assumed that UNIFEM is a norm-setting body but this is not the case. UNIFEM is not an autonomous, fully operational agency. In fact, no agency has full responsibility related to CEDAW and the Beijing Process. This has resulted in a call for a new UN agency for women (Donovan 2006). Source: ILO (2004: 147)

number of ratifications in 2003, the Committee on Migrant Workers, the treaty body, was set up. One of its first major jobs was to specify the reporting guidelines for State Parties, in order to then call upon respective governments to submit reports on their actions towards implementation. This process has only just begun and only three reports have been received by the Committee so far (for an update on the reporting process, see http://www.ohchr.org/english/countries/ratification/index.htm). The treaty body system of the OHCHR allows the NGO community to submit 'shadow reports' to provide an alternative view to the one given by governments. The submission of individual complaints to the Committee on Migrant Workers is also possible – but only under 'certain circumstances' and it is unclear at this moment in time what these are, as this is untested ground. In this sense, the Migrant Committee offers a direct avenue for complaints voiced through civil society organizations. One serious shortcoming, however, is that concerns for migrants are not properly mainstreamed into the workings of *all* treaty bodies. Specific migrant worker issues should be incorporated into the workings all treaties since they cover migrants already in their role as non-citizens.

In addition to the treaty bodies, the UN has another system by which it monitors specific types (or target groups) of human rights: country-specific or thematic Special Rapporteurs. The mandate for the Special Rapporteur on the Human Rights of Migrants was created in 1999 and extended for a further three years in 2005 by the Commission on Human Rights which requested the Special Rapporteur to 'examine ways and means to overcome the obstacles existing to the full and effective protection of the human rights of migrants'. To this end, the main functions of the Rapporteur include the gathering of information from all relevant sources; the formulation of appropriate recommendations; the promotion of the effective application of relevant international norms and standards; and the recommendation of actions and measures. In practical terms, this can be done in a number of ways, such as 'fact-finding missions' – i.e. country visits (for which the Rapporteur, however, needs the invitation of the government in question); participation in conferences and meetings relating to the human rights of migrants; and the preparation of an annual report to the Commission on Human Rights. The budget for these activities is very small, however, and as a result the number of country visits is very limited. Civil society organizations are an important source of information for these Rapporteurs and face-to-face meetings are a good opportunity to exchange data and experiences but, because of budgetary constraints on the part of the Rapporteur, it is up to these NGOs to seek funding to make such meetings happen. One of the Asian networks, Co-ordination of Action Research on AIDS and Mobility (CARAM) in Asia, managed to do just that and organized a meeting in Kuala Lumpur in 2003 with the Rapporteur, its member NGOs and representatives from other international organizations, as well as academics.

The ILO has historically always included the protection of migrants as workers in its overall mandate, and all its fundamental core standards as well as its conventions relate to migrant workers. Its first migrant-specific convention dates back to 1949 and its second to 1975. The ILO was also the main technical advisor to the UN during the drafting process of the CRM. To address rights violations, the ILO offers a complaint mechanism based on Articles 22 and 23 of its constitution, according to which State Parties are obliged to submit reports on the implementation of the eight fundamental conventions (and every five years on other conventions, to which the two migrant worker-specific conventions belong). The violation of one of the core labour standards, the Freedom of Association, is the only issue on the basis of which a complaint can be filed when the perpetrating country has not ratified the relevant convention. Given its tripartite structure, comprising governments, employers' and workers' organizations, migrant worker-related concerns and complaints can really only be channelled through trade unions. NGOs have no direct access to this mechanism but have to seek the support of trade unions, which are generally not in favour of the formal inclusion of NGOs into the ILO governing structure (Waterman 2005). Yet unions have only recently attempted to organize and assist migrant workers and they have not therefore used this mechanism for complaint.

In the specific context of migrant *women*, it is the United Nations Development Fund for Women (UNIFEM) which runs programmes and projects to ensure gender equality, including female migrants' rights. This is especially evident in the case of Asia: from its regional office in Bangkok, UNIFEM runs a project entitled Empowering Migrant Workers in Asia aimed at the adaptation of the Convention on the Elimination of All Forms of Discrimination Against Women (CEDAW) to the protection of migrant women – a project which does not exist in any other region. In terms of technical assistance to governments, UNIFEM has been influential in persuading a few governments in Asia to include rights clauses in MoUs pertaining to domestic-worker migration. As part of the UN structure,

UNIFEM has actually no 'official' responsibilities related to CEDAW, the Commission on the Status of Women or the Beijing Platform for Action, which resulted from the 4th World Conference on Women held in Beijing in 1995. In fact, no UN agency does. Contrary to popular belief, UNIFEM is in practice not an 'autonomous' agency but is 'in most ways treated just like one of the many UNDP departments' (Donovan 2006: 32).

A recent study assessing the UN's mandate on women's rights has argued that the CEDAW Committee could be very powerful with regard to pushing women's rights and, since the adoption of an Optional Protocol in 2000, this Committee has even obtained the power to receive complaints by individual women or on behalf of groups of women. But in reality, its full potential has so far not been exercised (Donovan 2006).

Unlike CEDAW, which has been widely ratified, migrant worker-specific conventions (ILO conventions no. 97, 143 and the CRM) have the lowest ratification rate in the developed as well as developing world. Recent studies have pointed to the largely political reasons for this: the little promotional activity undertaken by the UN itself, and the obstacles to the ratification in key regions of migration (Piper and Iredale, 2003; Pécoud and de Gutchteneire, 2004). The general reluctance to ratify and implement these migrant-specific instruments is however, paralleled by an increasing interest in combating trafficking and smuggling. This is reflected in the relative success of the 2000 United Nations Convention Against Transnational Organized Crime, also called Palermo Convention, and its two protocols (in terms of the speed with which it came into force). This convention focuses on the criminal aspects of cross-border migration and is more concerned with national security and border control than the protection of trafficked victims. Thus, human rights issues are clearly sidelined in this document (Gallagher 2001).

To assess how far a rights-based approach to migration is in fact becoming the global norm and an accepted legal practice among states (who are the only members of most international organizations), a more detailed analysis of the influence and standing of organizations such as UNIFEM and ILO would be insightful, but goes beyond the scope of this chapter. UNIFEM is certainly less well funded compared with other UN agencies. It has to be pointed out, however, that its development funds go directly to women in vulnerable sectors, like migrant women, no matter how small is the amount. Despite its limited budget, it stretches funds well. But UNIFEM is a fairly minor player in budgetary terms. The $51.1 million budget in 2004 stands in stark contrast to UNICEF's 2004 budget of over $2 billion, which means that UNIFEM has 2.5 per cent of UNICEF's funds (Donovan 2006: 17).

The ILO also has a difficult stance in that it has to compete with the International Organization for Migration (IOM) in the field of migration. Many Western governments, in fact, support the IOM more and wish to reduce the ILO's mandate for migrant workers. This became quite clear in the statements made by various governments of highly developed countries at the 2004 International Labour Congress (ILC). Governments were reluctant to give the ILO a stronger mandate in the area of migrant labour and the IOM was seen as the preferable agency.

The reason for governments' preference of the IOM is precisely related to its not being a norm and standard setting international organization and the fact that it does not involve social partners in any direct way. The IOM is an inter-governmental organization which has no normative framework for the protection of migrants' rights (Human Rights Watch 2003). Related to the fact that it does not have a formal mandate to monitor human rights abuses or to protect the rights of migrants is that the IOM has no effective accountability mechanisms to answer criticism with regard to its practices and their impact on human rights.

However, this does not mean that general policy statements of the IOM do not include the mention of rights. Official IOM policy states that, despite the absence of a formal mandate, the IOM 'recognizes its responsibility to ensure that when providing assistance to migrants, its activities must obtain full respect for the rights of the individuals ... and must not diminish the human rights of others' (IOM 2002, quoted in Human Rights Watch 2003: 2). Also, the IOM took on the chairmanship of the Steering Committee for the Global Campaign for Ratification of the CRM in 2003. Furthermore, efforts by certain regional offices in promoting the CRM and migrants' rights (such as in Colombo and Dhaka) have to be acknowledged, and the commitment of certain individuals within the IOM should not be disregarded by a general critique of the IOM's overall organizational stance and policy. Moreover, it is the 'constituents' – the governments of the highly developed countries – which support the IOM more than the ILO when it comes to migrant workers. This is evident in terms of funding: Northern governments provide a huge amount of money for IOM activities, some of which appear to obstruct the rights of the very people the IOM is supposed to assist. This highlights the importance of the role of states with regard to international organizations.

Last but not least – and very importantly for our purposes here – the IOM has no official mechanism by which to engage with civil society. There is a clear lack of meaningful consultations with non-governmental and humanitarian organizations dedicated to allowing real participation and input by civil society (Human Rights Watch 2003).

Migration and trade

The analysis of these global shifts toward a global 'management of migration' and its impact on advancing migrants' rights is also crucial with regard to another development that takes place alongside those mentioned above: the ongoing negotiations at the World Trade Organization (WTO) revolving around the General Agreement on Trade in Services (GATS)/

Mode 4 which indicate a trend to subsume migration under a broader trade agenda.

GATS is the first multilateral and legally enforceable agreement on international trade in services and Mode 4 concerns the movement of 'natural persons' (In legal parlance, a 'person' is any legal entity, such as a business. Hence, reference to human persons is made by using the term 'natural' persons). Mode 4 is defined in Article I.2(d) of GATS as 'the supply of a service ... by a service supplied of one member, through presence of natural persons of a member in the territory of another member'. In this sense, the terms of Mode 4 do not actually make any reference to movement, labour migration or employment. What is certain to date is that Mode 4 targets only the highly skilled. Also, GATS does not apply to measures regarding citizenship, residence or employment on a permanent basis (Klein Solomon 2007). In fact, it applies only to a small subset of overall migratory movements. The discussion is still ongoing of the type of categories of service supplied that are covered by GATS, such as self-employed or independent service suppliers, foreigners employed by host country companies and others. For instance, whether a fruit-picker is a temporary agricultural labourer or could be defined as a supplier of fruit-picking services is still unresolved (Klein Solomon 2007). The concept of a 'service provider', however, is alien to most domestic immigration laws, which more commonly use categories of temporary or permanent economic migrants. In this sense, it would be better to move beyond the service rationale of Mode 4, but this would go beyond the jurisdiction of GATS (Klein Solomon 2007).

Developing countries are often said to have a surplus in skills in the service sector and GATS provides opportunities to earn higher wages. But the strictly temporary movement of Mode 4 of GATS, targeting the highly skilled (which also means it is more beneficial to male migrants than female), with limited commitments by developed countries, imposes serious immigration barriers and, thus, a limited set of rights. Although it has been suggested that the GATS negotiations could provide an opportunity to address human rights risks linked to migration (Dommen 2005), the WTO is not a forum that allows for inputs from social partners and other civil society organizations, and, consequently, non-governmental voices that are usually at the forefront of pushing for rights are not given a chance to be heard.

Another indication that migration is being shifted to trade agendas is the inclusion of clauses related to human mobility in Economic Partnership Agreements (EPAs). One such example is the EPA signed between Japan and the Philippines in 2006, which is phrased in the same style as the GATS Mode 4, makes reference to 'natural persons' as service providers and is geared mostly towards professional and highly skilled workers. Rights and entitlements are not part of the terminology and 'package' of such agreements. The secretive manner in which these negotiations take place, government-to-government and behind closed doors, makes it very hard for advocacy organizations to know what is discussed and to find an entry point for lobbying purposes. In the words of the Director of the Center for Migration Advocacy in Manila:

> We raised a lot of questions and serious concerns on (the) Japan EPA in terms of reference as well as the process it underwent, which was in utmost secrecy to say the very least.
>
> (email communication, 30 January 2007)

Regional mechanisms

Regional processes can offer additional mechanisms, or steps towards, achieving a global policy agenda that aims to maximize the benefits of migration and protective standards for migrant workers. At this current stage of the global debate on the governance of migration, states are often intimidated by what they perceive as open-ended undertakings that compromise their sovereignty. In these circumstances, regional agreements can be seen as less threatening and a more effective avenue to go about the advancement of a rights agenda. Globally, there are differences with regard to the current level or degree of institutionalization of regional structures, with the EU having the most developed common approach to migration (with regard to intra-European mobility but to a lesser degree with regard to new migration), followed by NAFTA and the African Union. Asia has the least advanced common approach of all regions.

Regional human rights bodies also play an important role in consolidating a rights-based approach to migration. The most progressive example here is the Inter-American Human Rights system, which offers mechanisms for investigating and promoting human rights in the Americas. On a normative level, the Inter-American Court and the Inter-American Commission for Human Rights have broken new ground in international human rights law by asserting that migrants must fully enjoy the rights of non-discrimination and equality in the host country where they reside and work. More importantly, as we noted in Chapter 2, the Court holds that 'all migrants, undocumented and documented alike, are covered by the principles of equality and equal protection' (Satterthwaite 2005). Although the Court leaves untouched the sovereign right of states to limit certain political rights to nationals, it is absolutely clear on the issue of labour rights which 'necessarily arise from the circumstances of being a worker, understood in the broadest sense' (Satterthwaite 2005). In other words, once a migrant enters an employment relationship, the migrant is first and foremost to be treated as a worker, regardless of his/her migration status, which has, so far, always been the first role or status a migrant has been judged by.

Furthermore, the Inter-American Commission on Human Rights has created one of the most flexible mechanisms to advance the promotion of human rights: that of special rapporteurships referring to 'mandates filled by individuals who are designated to investigate and report on specific thematic human rights concerns' (Satterthwaite 2005). Currently, there are seven issue areas for which rapporteurships have been established and among these are the rights of migrant workers and their families. The reports of this regional rapporteur, together with those of the UN Special Rapporteur, have documented well the failure of restrictive policies to halt irregular migration and the negative consequences of fortified borders in creating opportunities for trafficking and smuggling, leading to increasingly dangerous journeys and a rise in migrant deaths. They also record the rampant rights violations migrant workers are subjected to. In addition to the rapporteurship, the Inter-American Human Rights system offers further strategies to promote the rights of migrant workers, which include general interest hearings, petitions alleging to human rights violations, and on-site visits (Satterthwaite 2005).

Although not as developed as the Inter-American system, all regions in the world have a regional human rights body except for Asia, which is not surprising considering that statistically Asia ranks the lowest with regard to ratifications of UN human rights instruments. This is mainly due to the huge diversity in terms of political systems and levels of economic development. Many countries in Asia have national human rights commissions, and in 1996 existing national human rights institutions formed the Asia Pacific Forum as a venue to discuss and promote human rights standards in Asia. But migrant worker issues have so far not been on the agenda. NGOs, meanwhile, have set up a Working Group for an ASEAN (Association of Southeast Asian Nations) Human Rights Mechanism and have highlighted labour migration as an important dimension of human rights concerns.

With regard to broader regional agreements, trafficking seems the most dealt with and best covered issue. Unlike the management of labour migration, which has been subject to little regional cooperation in Asia Pacific, the problem of trafficking has been taken up at the regional level to some extent. A number of initiatives, however, do not directly relate to human trafficking holistically but deal with it as a subset of other issues, most importantly irregular migration. Most of these initiatives deal with the control and prevention of such migratory flows, rather than addressing the root causes leading to trafficking and putting protective measures and victim-support mechanisms in place. One exception seems to be the so-called Coordinated Mekong Ministerial Initiative Against Trafficking (COMMIT). Also, a number of bilateral agreements on trafficking are under discussion between Thailand, Lao PDR, Myanmar, Cambodia and Vietnam. Among the specific objectives, agreed standards and procedures on repatriation and victim support are mentioned. In addition, COMMIT is one of the few, if not the only, anti-trafficking initiative that explicitly includes men as potential victims. (For more information on policies and progress of this Initiative, see http://www.no-trafficking.org/content/ COMMIT_Process/commit_process.htm accessed 30 May 2007).

A fairly recent and important development in the Asian region is the holding of three ministerial-level consultations involving labour ministries by Asian labour-sending countries – in Colombo (April 2003), Manila (September 2004) and Bali (2005) – to discuss issues of common concern, including the protection of migrant workers. Concrete action has not been taken, beyond drawing up a plan for a feasibility study for the establishment of a Common Migrant Resource Centre in the Gulf Cooperation Council Countries (GCCC). The final statement of the Bali ministerial consultation, however, directly refers to the 'management of migration', which is defined as 'orderly labour movement and employment policies consistent with the welfare of workers'. Four areas of management are highlighted as essential: ensuring the welfare and well-being of vulnerable overseas workers, especially women, during recruitment employment; optimizing benefits of organized labour flows, including the development of new markets; building institutional capacity and inter-ministerial coordination to meet labour movement challenges; and increasing cooperation between countries of origin and destination countries in ensuring the welfare of overseas workers. More specifically, one area of cooperation is to aim at 'establishing minimum wage levels and ensuring safe and decent conditions of employment for contract workers, particularly women, in low skill and low wage sectors'. This constitutes a clear recognition of the rampant abusive employment practices, and the challenge that lies ahead is to translate this rhetorical statement into action.

These meetings have the same characteristics as so-called 'regional consultative processes' (RCPs) on migration. The regional level has in fact been posited as the more effective when it comes to policy development (Thouez 2004). But, as argued in the previous chapter in the case of various initiatives on the 'management of migration', it is governments or international organizations that take the lead in establishing RCPs. RCPs are state-centered activities and they exist in most regions of this world. Their objectives are to provide a forum for debate and exchange of information, improve inter-state cooperation and facilitate political will. Their outputs come in the form of non-binding recommendations or declarations, plans for action or guidelines for government action. The experience in other issue areas, such as international corruption control, has shown that regional efforts are the first step toward the internationalization of standards and approaches (Thouez 2004). There is, therefore, hope. Of concern, however, is yet again the non-inclusion of civil society and private-sector organizations in either the proceedings of the RCPs or even in some kind of pre-meeting consultation.

Bilateral arrangements are another step along the scale of multi-state agreements. The ILO has developed regional frameworks and agreements to facilitate labour migration. ILO Recommendation no. 86 contains a Model Agreement on Temporary and Permanent Migration for Employment, for example – and urges governments to negotiate BLAs or MoUs within such frameworks. In certain regions such as Asia, destination countries typically prefer MoUs because they constitute a soft option and give them flexibility, whereas BLAs are more formal and binding, and cover a range of issues, such as social security, employment contracts and conditions of work and dispute settlement, which many receiving countries do not want to be bound by. Issues of concern with existing agreements have largely to do with the non-provision of enforcement or redress mechanisms, the fact that major rights such as freedom of association are denied, lack of gender sensitivity and the non-involvement of social partners and civil society organizations in design and monitoring. In this sense, many existing MoUs do not conform to international norms on protection of migrants' rights (Wickramasekara 2006).

Mention should also be made of the most recent development at the regional level in Asia which had just taken place at the time of writing: a declaration on the Protection and Promotion of the Rights of Migrant Workers at the ASEAN summit in January 2007 in Cebu, the Philippines (see www.aseansec.org/13264.htm; accessed March 2007). This declaration was signed by all ASEAN member states, which comprise all the major labour importer and exporter countries in this region. Among the obligations of receiving states, they now should:

> Facilitate access to resources and remedies through information, training and education, *access to justice*, and social welfare services as appropriate and in accordance with the legislation of the receiving state, provided that they fulfill the requirements under applicable laws, regulations and policies of the said state, bilateral agreements and multilateral treaties.
>
> (Emphasis added)

Origin countries are called upon to:

> Ensure access to employment and livelihood opportunities for their citizens as *sustainable alternatives to migration* of workers;
> Set up policies and procedures to facilitate aspects of migration of workers, including recruitment, preparation for deployment overseas and *protection of the migrant workers when abroad* as well as repatriation and reintegration to the countries of origin; and
> Establish and promote legal practices to regulate recruitment of migrant workers and adopt mechanisms to eliminate recruitment malpractices through legal and valid contracts, regulation and accreditation of recruitment agencies and employers, and blacklisting of negligent/unlawful agencies.
>
> (Paragraphs 11–14; emphasis added)

This reflects not only the policy approach on 'management of migration' from a rights-based perspective as championed by the ILO, but also the policy concerns with underdevelopment as a fundamental root cause of migration. Although so far only a declaratory statement, this nevertheless appears to be a significant development in a region where the concept of 'workers' rights', let alone 'migrant workers' rights', is an extremely sensitive matter. Yet, in practical terms, as observed by the Director of the Center for Migrant Advocacy in Manila, this Declaration is non-binding and many of the provisions are already part of existing laws and policies on migrant workers, but are not implemented. More importantly, the Declaration is limited in scope to only documented migrants and their families who are already residing with them (personal email communication, 17 February 2007).

Civil society – organizational channels for migrant workers

One important step toward ensuring that protection and rights aspects are part of migration policies is by reaching a broad social consensus via an informed debate. To this end, the ILO has called many times for the need to engage in 'social dialogue' – that is for governments to bring employers' and workers' organizations into the decision-making process on migration policy. But as we have seen, there are very few examples where the formulation of labour-migration policies, laws and regulations is based on a social dialogue of this sort.

Having an organizational set-up through which influence on policy and the normative/legal framework can be channelled at all stages of the migration process (pre-migration, stay abroad, return migration) helps the promotion and implementation of migrants' rights. Having meaningful institutions in both countries of origin and destination to support migrants' rights is, therefore, very important. The creation of an enabling environment can be achieved through institutions that aim to empower workers through education, knowledge provision, etc. Particularly significant in this regard is participation in 'voice institutions' (ILO Socio-Economic Security Programme 2004: 339).

This raises the question, of course, of what counts as a voice institution. In the realm of work, trade unions have historically constituted an important institution for the representation of workers' interests. In addition to trade unions, there has been a rise in the numbers of migrant associations and NGOs globally advocating for migrants' rights and offering essential services to this extremely marginalized group of workers. These NGOs address protection deficits often not tackled by trade unions, by reaching out to migrant workers or a certain sub-group such as domestic workers (Piper 2003, 2005c). In order to give more impetus to the recognition of migrants' rights, recent studies have argued for a need to enhance collaboration between trade unions and migrant organizations (Piper and Ford 2006).

Organizing migrant workers poses a particular challenge in contexts where migration is characterized by widespread informalization, temporariness and/

or illegality. Migrant associations, trade unions and other civil society institutions have an important role to play in offering support services and advocating for the rights of migrants. This has been recognized by academics (Ford and Piper 2007) as well as policy-makers (ILO 2004; GCIM 2005). These different types of organizations have their respective strengths and weaknesses, based on their organizational histories and processes and offer different opportunities and limitations for advocacy. In recent years, new strategies have begun to emerge in the form of intra-organizational policy shifts – and trade unions opening their doors to migrant workers – or reform processes and inter-organizational alliances within and across borders.

Representation in some institutional form is important as migrants' own voices and inputs are typically missing when the 'management of migration' is being addressed by policy-makers or in the actual management practices. From the perspective of individual migrants, management of migration is largely about risk management and securing of livelihoods, by obtaining and remaining in overseas employment. These are areas where governments have simply not responded well enough – and, to make them respond, collective action via 'voice institutions' is crucial (ILO Socio-Economic Security Programme 2004: 339). It is in particular self-organizing by migrants themselves, or by former migrants, that is vital. This, however, often proves to be difficult because of foreign workers' legal and visa status, as well as type of job they do – and the lack of democratic space and recognition of associational rights in destination countries (Piper 2005c).

Associational rights

The right to organize or join trade unions or form other organizations is firmly established in international human rights law. Freedom of association is among the fundamental principles championed by the ILO that are universal and applicable to all people in all states, regardless of the level of economic development. In addition to the ILO norms and standards, the right to form and join trade unions is also enshrined in the International Covenant on Economic, Social and Cultural Rights (ICESCR) as well as in the CRM.

However, there are crucial differences and nuances with regard to the scope and extent to which migrants can organize politically as set out by relevant covenants, the migrant worker – specific ILO conventions and the CRM. Article 26 of the latter stipulates that all migrant workers, regardless of legal status, have the right 'to take part in meetings and activities of trade unions and of any other associations established in accordance with the law', and 'to join freely any trade unions and any such association as aforesaid'. The explicit right to *form* an organization, however, is confined to *documented* migrants.

The ICESCR in its Article 8 refers to the 'right of everyone to form trade unions and join the trade unions of his [*sic*] choice, subject only to the rules of the organization concerned'. Unlike the CRM, this Covenant, however, only refers to trade unions and not to 'other associations', which would include civil society organizations.

Because of its tripartite structure, the clauses on 'freedom of association' championed by the ILO relate to trade unions only. Unlike the CRM, the two migrant worker-specific ILO conventions (nos 97 and 143) restrict the equality of treatment and opportunity in respect of trade union rights to those migrant workers *lawfully* within the territory of the destination country. This means the CRM goes the furthest with regard to 'rights to institutional representation' in terms of *types* of organizations, but the ICESCR takes associational rights one step further by extending this to all workers regardless of legal status, even though this right to self-organizing remains restricted to trade unions.

This reflects two major issues: the dominant recognition of trade unions as *the* institution to represent workers as far as international law is concerned, and the widespread reluctance to allow *all* foreign workers the right to organize regardless of migration status. This confirms general comments made on migrant worker-specific instruments as well as other UN conventions: they tend to reflect the situation and concern of *Western* countries more than of countries in the global South (Piper and Iredale 2003; see Davies 2004 on the 1951 Refugee Convention); and in the South the trade union movement has never had the same influence as in the North. Moreover, this also underpins the argument that priority is given to controlling migration rather than the protection of all migrants in their capacity as workers.

On the issue of protecting *undocumented* migrants, there has been a gradual shift in recent years, coming mainly from trade unions and NGOs, to treat migrants first and foremost as workers once they have entered a country and are working at their destination, regardless of their legal status. More and more national trade unions take steps to offer some kind of protection to irregular migrants (Piper 2005c). This development has become evident at the international level also, in the revival of a rights-based approach to migration, including irregular migrants, within the ILO. As mentioned above, the most recent and ground-breaking development in this regard, is the ruling by the Inter-American Court of Human Rights that clarifies that all migrants – documented and undocumented – are covered by the principles of non-discrimination, equality and equal protection in the host states where they live and work and must not be excluded from the protection of labour laws on the basis of their migration status. This, however, still leaves unaddressed the issue of organization and the impediments to associational rights – questions we will return to in the following chapter.

Conclusion

The level of attention given to international (economic) migration reflects the fact that both the volume and patterns of migration have undergone important changes during towards the last few decades. Global policy on migration has most certainly shifted towards a greater recognition of the need to push for human rights, indicative of the convergence of labour rights and human rights (Adams 2001). However, the most important standard setting institution with regard to workers' rights, the ILO, has chosen, or was made to choose by Northern governments, the path of a 'non-binding' framework that reflects states' reluctance to engage in multi lateral commitments. In addition, the UN mechanism for promoting and claiming migrant worker-related rights is a highly under-used system.

In the current political climate, the role of the regional and even bilateral levels is, therefore, probably more significant. Most states at this stage are intimidated by what they perceive as open-ended undertakings that compromise their sovereignty. Although they may be wrong in this, it remains a fact that regional and bilateral agreements are perceived as less threatening and might, therefore, prove a better starting point for the recognition of migrant rights, as part of a 'step-by-step' approach.

To date, social dialogue, or consultation with social partners and other civil society organizations, has been absent from most international, regional and national migration policy initiatives. As a result, the 'management of migration' tends to take place outside normative frameworks, social dialogue and labour-market institutions. In Western liberal countries, migration is simultaneously approved of and yet combated. As a result, the distance between policy pronouncements and de facto arrangements reflects a major contradiction in governments' practice. In addition, there is increasing unease with, if not outright hostility towards, trade unions (Adams 2001).

In existing scholarship and policy-making approaches, migration has not been sufficiently analysed as an integral part of global development and transformation processes. Instead, migration is conceptualized as a problem to be 'managed', with the underlying assumption that there is a 'solution'. The highly developed countries' agenda is to prevent migration by tackling especially the problem of 'undesired' migrants. The global redistributive function of migration is not taken into account (Taran and Demaret 2006). At the same time, a deeper political analysis of policy-making processes and the identification of good practices in specific countries is needed to inform relevant policy developments and political advocacy elsewhere (Poniatowski and Jimenez 2005).

Discourses on management and development both emphasize cooperation and partnership but still tend to be state-owned processes and exclude civil society from policy-making. Rather than simply trying to 'manage' migrants, a better approach would be to involve them in the making of policies that affect them (ILO 2004: 127). Related to this, migration should be treated as a global social phenomenon which is not merely economic in nature. It cannot be understood outside the context of a complex web of often conflicting interests in which migrant workers find themselves entangled. In particular, the conceptual and normative linkages between migrants' social and economic rights as related to migration need further exploration in specific geographic or cultural settings.

This requires in turn, a close examination of the normative linkages between a rights-based approach to migration and development and the implications for policy and political activism. Migrant worker issues could become a revitalizing force for the labour movement where it has become weak, for example in Europe and North America, or has never been strong, as in Asia. This is the subject of the next chapter, which addresses the other side of the coin to 'state-owned management': the nature of civil society organizations and their input into, and influence on, rights-based approaches to migration.

4 The governance of migration in Southeast and East Asia

In this chapter, we explore the relevance of recent policy shifts within global structures governing international migration and how the control-protection-dynamics are played out in the specific case of cross-border economic migration in Asia. In other words, our focus here is on intra-regional migratory flows, in particular between Southeast and East (SE/E) Asia. The Asian region is comprised of origin, transit and destination countries, and the sub-region of SE/E Asia hosts the world's largest labour-exporting country – the Philippines – which has in recent years overtaken Mexico as the country with the highest number of workers deployed overseas. Furthermore, the Filipino overseas migrant population is the most widely dispersed – in close to 200 countries and territories depending on the sources. It has the most diversified migrant population in terms of skill levels, type of migrants and destination countries. The feminization of migration is also clearly pronounced: of all newly deployed and land-based overseas migrant workers, women represent between 61 and 72 per cent for 1998–2002 and between 69 and 72 per cent for 2000–02 (Asis 2005). Twenty-five per cent of the world's seafarers are Filipinos, working on foreign-owned vessels. If seafarers and rehires were included, the gender distribution would be about balanced.

Asia also hosts the largest Muslim country in the world, Indonesia, which constitutes a significant exporter of labour, female and male, mostly to destinations within Asia mainly the Gulf countries, Malaysia and Singapore. If 'Asia' is taken in its entirety, inclusive of the Gulf States, Saudi Arabia becomes host to the largest number of foreign workers: migrants constitute at least a fifth of its population (UN 2006). In SE/E Asia, Singapore constitutes the destination country with the highest percentage of migrant workers (30 per cent of its population). In terms of absolute numbers, Malaysia has the largest foreign worker population in this part of the world (Piper 2006b).

In terms of regional governance structures, Asia stands out for the lack of regional integration in institutional terms. ASEAN is less formalized than the EU, the North American Free Trade Agreement (NAFTA) or the Economic Community of West African States (ECOWAS) and lacks developed regional human rights mechanism (see previous chapter). At the same time, there has been a mushrooming of migrant worker associations and unions, many of which are integrated into regional non-governmental networks and operate transnationally. This is the setting in which we now explore the opportunities and obstacles to the promotion of a migrants' rights agenda and civil society participation in establishing a rights-based approach to migration in the area of SE/E Asia.

Migration policies and migrants' rights in Asia

Intra-regional migration dynamics

According to the ILO, Asia constitutes the region with the second largest volume of migrant workers after Europe (22.1 million or 27 per cent as opposed to Europe's 27.5 million or 34 per cent) (ILO 2004: 7). In terms of contemporary cross-border flows of economic migrants, what distinguishes Asia from other regions is the rapid growth of a market-led intra-regional migration system (IOM 2003). As a result, the regional level can be treated on its own, based on considerable intra-regional migratory flows rather than across regions. This type of cross-border movement tends to involve migrants who are from the poorer strata and, therefore, lesser skilled as the costs are lower for migrating to nearby destinations (Rahman 2006).

The vast majority of migrants are workers participating in regional migratory systems with specific characteristics. Although worldwide figures show that the percentage of migrant workers of national labour forces is relatively small (1.2–1.5 per cent), at the regional level their importance, and impact, has grown considerably. In the case of Asia, a shift of direction in destinations has occurred from the Middle East to East and Southeast Asia, with migration to Malaysia, Hong Kong and Singapore now indispensable to these economies (ILO 1999).

With regard to policies, Asian destination countries practise temporary contract schemes as the norm, with settlement of economic migrants being rare, as far as official policy is concerned. Labour migration is mediated by employment agencies. This has the effect of ever-increasing costs for cross-border migration due to enhanced competition within the regional labour market, with more countries appearing on the 'export scene', pushing recruitment fees up. Because it is, officially, strictly temporary, migration in Asia is restrictive in that it ties foreign workers to one specific employer and sector. The high number of undocumented migrants, who are not necessarily illegal entrants but often turn into 'illegal workers' after entry by changing employers or overstaying their visas is a result of all these features. Overall, the entire migration process creates a situation in which abuse and rights violations inflicted by agents and/or employers are common.

In terms of type of work or sector, most male migrants find occupation in the construction sector, in the manufacturing sector of small firms and subcontracting companies, in agriculture such as plantation and rice mills, as well as fisheries and services. In Singapore, many migrants also work in the shipping sector. Migrant women are typically confined to traditional roles in the labour market, mostly in the health, entertainment and domestic service sectors. In addition, they can also be found working in factories, especially in the garment sector. As entertainers and domestic workers, they are inadequately addressed by labour legislation, and so are the so-called 'trainees' (mostly men), a system commonly used in Japan and Korea to get around official government policy of not allowing the employment of unskilled foreign workers. But it has to be said that, even in those sectors covered by labour laws, lower-skilled migrant workers often have their employment and associational rights violated.

The number of undocumented migrants is especially high in certain countries. In the case of Malaysia they amount to about 50 per cent, with the highest percentage being in Japan at about 68 per cent. This has either to do with porous borders as, for instance, between Malaysia and Indonesia, or with the absence of legal channels for lower-skilled migrants despite local demand for such workers, as in Japan. Partly as a result of the high levels of irregular migration, wage discrimination and violation of labour rights are common (ICFTU-APRO 2003).

The feminization of labour migration is prominent in SE/E Asian countries, where the share of independent women in all labour migration flows has increased sharply since the late 1970s (ILO 2003a: 9). In some cases, women clearly dominate over their male counterparts. The countries of origin sending higher percentages of women than men are the Philippines, Indonesia and Sri Lanka, which is the only South Asian country that officially dispatches lower-skilled women workers. Bangladesh policy, by contrast, allows only the emigration of skilled women and imposed a ban on the migration of less-skilled women (Piper and Iredale 2003), which was only very recently lifted. If undocumented migrants were accounted for, the share of women among Thai migrant workers would also be much higher than official statistics indicate (Asis 2005). The increase in women's participation has to do with men's increasing inability to find employment locally and the demand for female-dominated jobs overseas, in domestic service, care work, nursing and in garment factories.

Migration policies

Government policies in Asia (as elsewhere) have focused on regulating the 'departure and entry' dimensions of migration by neglecting work or employment related aspects, labour standards and rights of foreign workers' lives. As a result, abusive and exploitative employment practices are widespread (Asis 2005). Asia contrasts with Europe and traditional immigration countries in that Asian governments practise temporary migration schemes only and, therefore, officially prevent migrants in lower-skilled categories from settling and reuniting with their families in the host country. According to Parreñas (2004), this common. Many European countries prohibit migrant domestic workers from reuniting with their families at their destinations also. Many Asian governments tacitly allow the presence of migrant workers longer term (often whole families) without officially recognizing that settlement is taking place and without responding by way of integration policies.

As a consequence of the lack of integration policies and recognition of longer term migration as a reality, the acquisition of permanent residence status, let alone citizenship, is out of reach for most migrants in Asia. Unlike the government-to-government arrangements in Western European guest-worker programmes of the 1950s and 1960s, the system that evolved in Asia did not involve governments as such. Rather, recruitment has largely been left to private agencies and a dense network of brokers and intermediaries, a practice that exposes migrants to human and financial exploitation at all stages of the migration process (Asis 2005). This also entails high levels of collusion between members of business and government circles (Piper and Iredale 2003).

Comparisons of migration policies and their implementation among Asian host countries reveal that, despite many similarities, there has been some variation regarding aims and policies for dealing with lower-skilled foreign workers. Broadly speaking, there have been two types of migration policies in SE/E Asia. The first can be found in Singapore, Malaysia, Taiwan and Hong Kong, where migrants enter to work on contract at well-defined jobs for a specified number of years. This can be called a 'front-door' policy (Yamanaka 1999). Under this policy, governmental regulations designed to manage immigration flows require employers to pay a levy upon hiring each employee, and a security bond to ensure his/her exit upon completion of contract. Governments also determine quotas for the numbers of workers per industry and for each country of origin (Wong 1997; Huang and Yeoh 2003). Moreover, governments adopt strict exclusionary policies through which lower-skilled migrants are prohibited not only from obtaining social welfare services and from establishing permanent residence, but also from integrating with the local population through marriage (Huang and Yeoh 2003).

The second type of immigration policy has been operative in Japan and South Korea since the 1990s. In contrast to Singapore, Malaysia, Taiwan and Hong Kong, these two East Asian countries do not officially admit lower-skilled migrants to work on contract; they encourage skilled foreigners to work in selected occupations. However, the rhetoric and official policy notwithstanding, both countries have been the destination for many years for up to 200,000–300,000 lower-skilled migrants (Cornelius 1994; Lee 1997). Through the many 'back' or 'side' doors (Yamanaka 1999) available to entrants, migrants arrive legally as residents, students, industrial trainees, entertainers, tourists, etc. and many remain to work without authorization.

In the absence of family reunification policies in Asia, migrant households often constitute transnationally 'split households', with either one or both parents working abroad and, in the case of the latter, often in different countries. Because legal schemes are strictly temporary, the numbers of return migrants are relatively high. Since temporary contract schemes are the norm, phenomena such as transnationally split families, high numbers of 'left behind', children, elderly relatives and return migration pose challenges but also provide opportunities for the expression of migrants' rights and political organization.

Migrants' rights and protection issues

As stated earlier, migration policies in this region have yet to extend to guaranteeing basic conditions affecting migrants, such as a minimum wage, working hours, days off, safety in the workplace, freedom to seek better wages/employers and to form associations. Of course, it has to be noted that a minimum wage often does not exist for local workers either, as in Singapore and Malaysia. Some NGOs have, however, argued for special treatment of foreign workers in this regard (by implementing a minimum wage for them) because of their specific vulnerability.

This has implications for the organizational form and issue focus of political activism. Citizenship and integration-related issues are rarely touched on because of their remoteness; instead, it is basic labour and social welfare rights that activists focus on because of the immediate urgency (Bell and Piper 2005). With regard to political rights, overseas voting rights have been part of non-governmental activism as, for instance, in the Philippines (successfully) and Sri Lanka (unsuccessfully) (Iredale *et al.* 2005). As temporary and/or undocumented migrants, the rights issues at stake are related to broader human rights, such as international labour standards stipulated by the ILO and the human rights standards established by the core UN conventions.

Lower skilled temporary migrant workers, who form the majority of labour migrants in Asia, are more vulnerable to rights violations than skilled workers because they tend to be located in the informal sectors of the labour market, or in sectors where labour standards are not applied or not applicable even for local workers. Problems such as non- or underpayment of wages, unfair dismissal, debt bondage, withholding of travel documents, long working hours and precarious working conditions are common, and affect both male and female migrants. It has been noted, however, that on the whole abusive and exploitative practices in male-dominated sectors are better documented and more visible because men usually work in groups, in construction, agriculture or sectors that are organized by trade unions (Piper 2007b). Since women migrant workers often go into individualized and unregulated work environments, for example domestic service, or entertainment, data on migrant women in these invisible occupations are not readily available (Esim and Smith 2004: 8). This often results in practices of exploitation, violence and harassment. In Singapore, however, the recent high-profile report by Human Rights Watch on foreign domestic workers (FDWs) (2006a) has gained a lot of public attention and there has been considerable media coverage of domestic worker-related problems.

The key issues and concerns for foreign workers that centre upon workplace grievances can be broadly classified under two headings: employment-related, and welfare, occupational health and safety issues. Employment-related issues are mainly about non-payment or under-payment of wages and unauthorized deductions. Issues to do with welfare, occupational health and safety are concerns pertaining to accommodation, long working hours and workplace hazards. The latter includes work-related injuries and accidents as well as physical and sexual abuse of FDWs. Official statistics on numbers and types of the various workplace grievances are rare, as are systematic studies or recording activities by NGOs.

Reflecting the significance of domestic work as an important source of legal employment for foreign women and the continuing demand for such services, their specific situation has been highlighted by the UN Special Rapporteur for the Human Rights of Migrants, (see http://www.ohchr.org/english/issues/ migration/rapporteur accessed April 2006) the ILO and UNIFEM as well as a number of NGOs, for example CARAM Asia, Migrant Rights International and Human Rights Watch. Some of the UN treaty bodies, most notably the CEDAW and the Convention on the Elimination of All Forms of Racial Discrimination (CERD) Committees, which are in charge of monitoring the implementation of human rights conventions, have also called attention to human rights violations against FDWs (Satterthwaite 2005; Piper and Satterthwaite 2007).

There are differences between countries as to the extent of which they recognize the domestic sector as an area of employment. Some countries and territories, such as Hong Kong, Singapore, Malaysia and Taiwan, recognize domestic work for visa purposes, while others, such as South Korea and Japan, do not. However, legal status (via a work permit) does not mean recognition by labour laws. In fact, domestic work is widely excluded from national labour legislation. In Singapore, FDWs are not covered by the Employment Act. According to Yeoh *et al.* (2004), this is not because they are non-citizens, but because of the nature of the work they perform. Similarly, foreign workers in industries such as construction and manufacturing in Taiwan are covered by industrial relations legislation (in Taiwan's case, the Labour Standards Law), but women working as domestic helpers or carers are not (Loveband 2004). National employment acts or labour standard laws do not recognize domestic work as a legitimate form of labour, effectively excluding domestic work from legal protection (Chin 2003; Huang and Yeoh 2003; Lan 2003). In Singapore, for example, the government is concerned about 'productivity' and 'welfare' of male construction workers while neglecting the same concerns for FDWs (Huang and Yeoh 2003). Moreover, some receiving states, most notably Singapore and Malaysia, in their attempt to exert control over their populations, officially prohibit FDWs from marrying citizens or permanent residents of the host society. This is, by the way, the same for un- or semi-skilled male migrant workers. It seems, therefore, to be an issue of class rather than gender. In an extreme form of control of female bodies, some states require migrant women to take periodic pregnancy tests and to leave the country immediately if they become pregnant (Wong 1997).

A very complex and controversial issue is the human rights of migrant women in the sex and entertainment industry. Feminists approaches to this issue take two forms: the abolitionists who argue that all prostitution is a violation of women's human rights, and the defenders of 'sex workers' rights, who advocate for their recognition as workers. It is an ideologically charged debate that often overlooks the multi-layered structure of this 'industry', as well as silencing the voices of those most directly affected (Augustín 2005; Piper 2005b).

According to leading NGOs in Malaysia, in 2004 the top violation of labour rights was the non-payment of wages, followed by unfair dismissal in the construction and small and medium industries, linked to the sub-contracting labour system. There are so many loopholes in this situation that it is next to impossible for undocumented workers to claim unpaid wages ('no redress'), leaving employers unpunished for illegal practices. The Malaysian Trade Union Council (MTUC) and NGOs have begun to call for the right of all workers to be able to seek redress to put an end to such abusive practices. Tenaganita, a migrant NGO based in Kuala Lumpur and supported by the MTUC, has recently published several press statements calling for the need to create a 'culture of payment of wages'.

According to a recent report (Verité 2005) that covers Vietnam, Indonesia, the Philippines, Thailand, Taiwan, Jordan and Malaysia, the list of common abuses against foreign contract labourers included excessive overtime, improper wage payments and withholding pay. Despite the widespread existence of legislation limiting fees, service, placement or recruitment charges were nevertheless found to be excessive in two regards: they exceeded legal limits and often accounted for a large portion of a worker's earnings. This discrepancy between law and practice has to do with the absence of formal legal mechanisms for governing the payment of placement fees across the area, with the exception of Vietnam. The report concludes that the level of indebtedness of foreign contract workers is such that it constitutes 'debt-bondage', consistent with the UN definition of human trafficking.

Non-governmental organizations and the promotion of migrants' rights

In this section, we raise the issue of demanding or voicing rights for and by migrant workers. We make a somewhat arbitrary distinction between the 'human rights of migrants' as stipulated by international law and 'the rights of migrants' as a socio-political process of ongoing struggle. The latter reflects a more comprehensive approach to rights by addressing the root causes of migration, whereas the scope of the former is narrower.

The 'demanding and voicing' of rights typically occurs in the form of collective action and through an organizational framework. What types of institutions or organizations are involved in formulating and pushing for the recognition of migrant rights, and what kind of rights do they focus on? This depends very much on migrants' legal and employment status as well as the political space given to political activism at the destination and origin end of the migratory movement.

NGOs and migrant associations

Civil society organizations (CSOs) at the local, national and regional level have for quite some time been actively involved in providing concrete assistance to foreign workers and, since the early 1990s, civil society action around a rights-based approach to migration has grown exponentially. This has largely occurred outside the trade union movement (Taran and Demaret 2006). NGOs have, therefore, come to fill an important gap left by traditional labour movements by assisting non-citizen workers who are largely represented in the informal sectors of the economy or in jobs socio-legally not recognized as 'proper' work, such as domestic and entertainment-related work. Furthermore, NGOs rarely make a distinction between documented and undocumented migrants, except in the context of giving legal advice and legal assistance.

The only global survey of civil society activity in the area of migration to date was conducted under the auspices of the UN Commission on Population and Development in 1997 (UN 1997). Although this survey does not make a distinction between 'migrant workers' and 'refugees or forced migrants', it demonstrates the array of CSOs and the range of activities these organizations have been involved in, including the promotion of international standards and improved national legislation and policy. A clear distinction between the different types of migrants, however, would have most certainly resulted in a more balanced picture of CSO activity: in Europe, for instance, many NGOs had either long neglected migrant workers and focused almost exclusively on refugee and asylum seekers, or their focus was on ethnicity and anti-racism work, the latter especially in the case of subsequent generations of former guest workers who arrived in the 1950s and 1960s where advocacy largely revolved around fighting racism. Recognition of the plight of newly arrived economic migrants, especially the rising numbers of undocumented migrants, is a relatively new development. In SE/E Asia, it is exactly the other way round: there is very little CSO activity in the area of refugees, an even more politically sensitive issue than economic migration in SE Asia and a negligible issue in numerical terms in much of East Asia, but rising engagement with economic migrants.

Due to a lack of political space for human rights activism and/or a non-legal status, it is sometimes impossible or very difficult for migrants to set up their own organizations. In such circumstances, migrants depend on local citizens to take up their concerns. In SE Asia, this has been happening in countries such as Singapore and Malaysia, where self-organizing is legally impossible (Piper 2006b). In countries where it is difficult but not impossible, such as Japan, South Korea and Taiwan, migrants have been more actively involved in setting up their own organizations. A particularly well-documented example in this regard is Hong Kong (Law 2002; Wee and Sim 2005; Yamanaka and Piper 2006).

The availability, or lack of, political space for rights activism partly explains the different types of groups involved in migrant labour advocacy and service provisioning. A special issue of the *Asian and Pacific Migration Journal* provides a discussion on this, based on Singapore, Malaysia, Indonesia, the Philippines and Korea (*APMJ* 15(3), 2006). These articles provide a detailed mapping of existing organizations and their strategies to promote and protect migrants by making a clear distinction between migrant worker associations, run by migrants or former migrants, and other NGOs. Self-organizing has been identified in these studies as particularly effective, and this underpins not only the importance of freedom of association but also of the 'freedom to form political organizations' of any kind, an issue we return to later.

Trade unions

The point just made might give the impression that the labour movement has been completely absent from the 'migrant labour scene', which would not be quite right. Most Europe-based trade unions have gradually established special departments dealing with migrant worker issues since the 1950s and engage in active recruitment (Taran and Demaret 2006). Based on a global survey, Johansson (2005: 2) observes that the union movement as a whole considers 'reaching out to the unorganized and vulnerable' a key part of ensuring the future relevance of trade unions. He goes on to describe unions as 'one of the most progressive actors in the migration debate' and as 'active in organizing them and defending the rights of migrant workers'. It is debatable, however, whether unions are in fact at the forefront of the struggle to protect and advance a rights-based approach to foreign labour. There might of course be regional, and also national, variations but empirical evidence from Asia shows that it is migrant worker associations and NGOs that have played a vital role, not trade unions. It is also important here to distinguish between different historical periods and different types of migrant workers. In countries where long-term residence and proper immigration are an option, such as in North America and Europe, trade unions were more active in reaching out to migrant workers as they became long-term residents or even naturalized citzens.

The dominant patterns of migration today, characterized by temporary-contract schemes and high numbers of undocumented migrants, however, pose a particular challenge to trade union organizing in a number of conceptual and structural ways Ford (2006) summarized these as: challenges posed by the importance given to citizenship rather than shared worker identity, by unions operating at the national level; and sectoral apartheid whereby temporary migrant workers and the undocumented are viewed as 'unorganizable' because they work predominantly in the informal sector or the private sphere.

In terms of organizational make-up, the union movement is characterized by a complex structure at the international, regional and national levels. At the global confederation level, the International Confederation of Free Trade Unions (ICFTU) held a world trade union conference on migrant workers in 1974 and has advocated for migrant rights in many venues ever since. It was a crucial participant, and driver during the organizing phase, in the 2004 International Labour Congress by the ILO in Geneva. In 2003, the ICFTU argued in a policy paper that a discussion among affiliated organizations was needed to deliberate on 'mainstreaming' migrant workers into unions' broad activities.

The ICFTU's Regional Organization for Asia and Pacific (APRO) also organized a few regional consultations on the role of trade unions in protecting migrant workers (ICFTU-APRO 2003). Its Action Plan includes two major recommendations for national centres: the establishing of a migrant workers' desk or committee; the active recruiting of migrant workers as union members. The first has been realized by some national centres, such as Singapore's NTUC and Malaysia's TUC. According to a recent questionnaire by the ILO sent out to trade unions around the world (to which 42 trade unions responded, among them NTUC Singapore), 16 unions replied affirmatively to the question of whether they have a designated migration officer, two of which were in Southeast Asia: Hong Kong and NTUC Singapore. The main responsibilities of such migration officers were mostly training and information, followed by policy advocacy, individual assistance and lastly recruiting members. NTUC Singapore's designated migration officers are part of the 'Migrant Workers Forum' (MWF), which was set up in 2002. To what extent these officers engage in these four main responsibilities is, however, questionable. Often there is very little funding for sufficient full-time staff to exclusively address migrant labour-related issues, let alone offer legal assistance in cases of unpaid wages or unfair dismissal.

The second recommendation by the ICFTU-APRO still constitutes an underdeveloped aspect of trade union work in Southeast Asia (as elsewhere), even where the *legal* right for migrants to join trade unions is recognized. Without active recruitment, however, this right is not usually turned into practice. In August 2005, Thai trade union leaders formulated the so-called Phuket Declaration, following an ILO workshop on migrant labour, in which they declared, among other items, that 'Thai Trade Unions should be committed to organize and recruit migrant workers'. It remains to be seen how this rhetorical statement will be translated into practice.

Despite some laudable developments with regard to NGO and union activities, there are still huge (legal and practical) barriers to the organizing of migrant workers in many regards. We would now like to highlight one fundamental issue in connection with one of the core labour standards: the freedom of association.

Associational rights in practice

While temporary migrant workers often have the legal and, therefore, theoretical right to join trade unions, this is widely violated in practice. Moreover, despite the legal right to join trade unions, unions rarely actively seek migrants as members, which often leaves them unaware of this option and of their labour rights. In Asia, migrant workers are often not unionized in their country of origin either.

As a result of these factors, in many destination countries in Asia, organizing foreign workers is a precarious matter. In the Malaysian case, for instance, migrants' employment contracts typically contain clauses prohibiting (even legal) foreign workers to join an existing union or be politically active in any other form. The exact wording in one contract for a Nepalese worker is 'The Employee shall not marry with any Malaysian and shall not participate in any political activities of those connected with Trade Unions' (copy shown to Nicola Piper during interview, June 2005, Kuala Lumpur). This violates Malaysia's national employment law. The Industrial Relations Act and Trade Unions Act govern the formal industrial-relations system and the law allows migrant workers to become members of trade unions, albeit not hold office, but in practice migrants are prevented from joining unions through their contracts. The moment a foreign worker joins a union, the employer can sack him/her without being punished. Thus, the formal labour/employment system is weakened by the existence of informal practices. For Malaysian trade unions, this poses an extraordinary obstacle.

In addition, in Southeast Asian countries, migrant workers are legally not allowed to set up their own organizations, with the notable exception of

Hong Kong. In Singapore, for example, any organization engaging in 'political activity' is strictly scrutinized. Intentions to advocate 'rights' issues have to go through a lengthy registration process where citizenship is an important criterion. An entirely non-citizen group attempting to register a rights-based organization is unheard of (Lyons 2005). Malaysia has a more vibrant NGO sector than Singapore, even in the area of human and workers' rights, but there are no NGOs set up by migrants themselves, partly a reflection of the large number of undocumented migrants. In such circumstances, migrants depend on concerned local citizens to extend support to foreign workers through existing NGOs.

This situation is different in East Asia where migrant workers are legally allowed to set up their own organizations. The irony in much of East Asia, however, is that many lower-skilled migrant workers are 'illegal' (often by overstaying their visa or absconding from an employer they are tied to) and it is this illegal status that renders self-organizing a difficult, if not impossible, task. The issue of legality aside, trade unionists also lament the temporary nature of migration, which makes foreign workers less inclined to join unions on a fee-paying basis. They might seek assistance when a problem occurs, but as soon as it is solved they tend to move on. Under such circumstances, conventional collective bargaining does not make sense; neither does an exclusive focus on the *national* employment situation.

Rights-based approaches

In the context of cross-border migration, international NGOs such as Amnesty International have argued that the starting point for the management of migration should be the rights of migrants. Together with other NGOs and regional NGO networks in Europe and Asia, they argue that the ratification of the CRM by more origin, but especially by migrant receiving, countries, of whom to date not a single one has acceded to this Convention, is paramount. NGOs in Asia, however, are acutely aware of the fact that many rights set out in the CRM are out of reach or irrelevant in the current political and economic climate and, although they support ratification campaigns in principle, they devote the bulk of their time and energy to addressing a narrow range of concrete protection issues (Piper and Iredale 2003).

The implementation of rights-based approaches is a difficult task in regions such as Asia for a number of reasons. Broadly, transparency and accountability issues are a problem in more authoritarian countries such as Malaysia and Singapore (Piper 2006b). Liberal principles of equality and non-discrimination are hardly promoted or legally codified, and are often depicted as Western-centric values. Such principles pose a particular challenge in the multi-ethnic and multi-religious societies of Southeast Asia. Indeed, the socio-cultural dynamics of contemporary labour migration and policies in the case of the multi-ethnic and multi-religious societies in

Southeast Asia deserve a more detailed discussion that goes beyond the scope of this chapter.

What type of rights have been championed or prioritized by CSOs? Minimum rights as defined by international NGOs and the ICFTU as well as European NGOs differ from those prioritized by Asian NGOs. According to Amnesty International, for instance, minimum rights involve freedom of association and family unity, as well as access to education, housing, healthcare and other social services. Social rights are particularly highlighted and so is the right of workers to resign and change employers as a crucial labour-market principle. The right to change employers and sectors, and the possibility of switching migration status, are seen as paramount. Such issues should be relevant to advocacy in Asia also, but are not the main focus of the CSOs' advocacy campaigns.

Broadly, the main issues fought for by migrant worker associations and NGOs in SE/E Asia revolve around employment-related rights and improved working conditions. Advocacy does not address the temporary nature of prevalent migration schemes as such. Family unification, settlement and integration-related issues are, therefore, non-issues. It was only very recently, in fact, that Asia's regional migrant NGO network, the Migrant Forum in Asia, mentioned 'the right to family life' in an official statement.

In the specific case of domestic workers who are locked into informal interactions within the home, much of the activism in Singapore and Malaysia has a moral appeal as reflected in campaigns such as 'Dignity is Overdue'. NGOs have called for standard contracts as a minimum protection and are also demanding the inclusion of domestic work in national labour laws (more vocally in Malaysia; in Singapore, there is disagreement among NGOs as to whether a uniform contract is to the benefit of all FDWs). In Malaysia, the trade union council and NGOs have begun to jointly call for the right of all workers to seek redress to put an end to under- or non-payment of wages and to create a 'culture of payment of wages'. This includes a call for the right to issuing foreign workers with not just social pass visas but work permit visas to allow them to earn money while waiting for labour disputes to be resolved. It indicates that a huge problem is the non-existence of functioning complaints structures. A notable exception in this regard is again Hong Kong, and also the activism by Filipino organizations, as we discuss later.

Transnational and trans-institutional politics – the importance of networking

Transnational politics

As shown earlier, organizing transnationally and political activism are paramount in addressing rights issues for temporary migrant workers and the undocumented. Much of the literature on transnational advocacy networks has focused on CSOs. In the case of protecting migrant workers, the meaning of *transnational* networking and organizing reflects the nature of cross-border migration involving at least two countries and refers to at least one of the following phenomena: local citizens campaigning on behalf of non-citizens; activists following their compatriot migrant workers and campaigning on their behalf from the destination country; migrants campaigning on their own behalf, challenging the destination, and often also the origin country's government; and migrant workers or their compatriot activists campaigning on behalf of all migrant nationalities, not only their own nationality group (Piper 2006a).

Unlike NGOs, trade unions' involvement has not been analysed from a transnational perspective in the specific area of international migration and protection of migrants' rights. Instead, in the small but gradually expanding literature on migrant worker support organizations, it is the rise of NGOs and other voluntary associations committed to addressing the basic needs and alleviating the most serious problems of migrants in general, and migrant women in particular, that have been the subject research (see, for example, Piper 2003; Piper and Yamanaka 2003). The extent to which migrant worker associations are able to form alliances, especially within destination countries, and assert sufficient pressure on governments to achieve change has, however, been questioned (Wee and Sim 2005). Domestic work emerges again as a particularly vulnerable job category where forming alliances with women's organizations is hampered by the fact that local women activists are the employers of domestic helpers.

What is, however, missing in the existing literature on transnational networking is labour activism and the role of traditional worker organizations – trade unions – in responding transnationally to the situation of vulnerable foreign workers. This 'missing link' to trade unions has partly to do with the low level of engagement by trade unions for three main reasons: trade unions either regard migrant workers as better off and, therefore, in no need of attention (sending perspective); the migrants work in sectors that are regarded as impossible to organize (receiving perspective) or in jobs that are not recognized as 'proper' work, as reflected in the explicit exclusion from national labour laws of domestic workers; the transnational/short-term nature of many of today's migratory flows, which means that political activism is not only directed against destination governments' policies, but also origin governments' policies. This makes it difficult for unions, which tend to operate within a national framework, to engage. The political void left by the unions has to some extent been filled by NGOs.

Trade unions and networking

An interesting argument, which is emerging among social movement scholars, is that the labour movement can only achieve its full potential today in alignment, or merger, with other democratic social movements. Members of unions need to be enabled to express themselves and act not only as workers but as members of a community (Johnston 2001). In other words, struggles for labour rights are feeding into a larger citizenship movement that is concerned with women's issues, the future of children and family relations across borders. This links up with another argument about the root cause of trade unions' loss of power in recent years: unions are urged to reflect upon their form of operating, which is still primarily organizational/institutional, at a time when both capitalism and the global solidarity movement are assuming the form of networks. The conception of 'social movement unionism' has, therefore, been suggested as a way forward by Waterman (2003) who, to be precise, argues that social movement unionism should be reconceptualized in 'Class+New Social Movement' terms.

The notion that trade unions should open themselves up to networking is significant in terms of practical political mobilization and corresponds with arguments made for a broader social movement unionism based on inter-organizational networking between trade unions and NGOs, and intra-organizational networking between unions across countries ('unions without borders'). In this way, new approaches to international human rights law and transnational political activism come together to provide an impetus to ensuring better and more effective protection for migrant workers. Migrants' rights in this case can be understood both as a projection from new experiences of social struggle, and as a theoretical synthesis of trans-nationalism and human rights discourse. In this way, the issue of 'the human rights of migrants' has merged with a broader discussion of 'the rights of migrants', at least theoretically.

New initiatives by unions can in fact be witnessed in the attempt to cooperate transnationally in order to offer better protection to temporary migrant workers. The Phuket Declaration, mentioned earlier, includes in its 'Action Plan' the promotion of close cooperation with unions in sending and receiving countries. A recent document by the Malaysian Trade Union Council (MTUC) recommends that sending countries should 'develop a system for networking and information exchange between sending and receiving countries'. As laudable as these statements are, it is yet to be seen whether resources will be made available for transnational cooperation of this sort.

One form of transnational organizing is the hiring of an activist from the migrants' country of origin (to overcome language and other cultural barriers) or the dispatching of an activist to the country of destination. Trade unions in the UK and Sweden are said to have hired trade unionists from Eastern Europe to organize Eastern European migrant workers at their destination. Philippine-based trade unions have also sent organizers to Hong Kong to assist with the setting up of domestic worker unions there.

International unions such as Public Services International (PSI) and the International Union of Food Workers (IUF), which have branch offices in many countries, have come up with another idea: a transnational membership card. This provides workers who are members in their country of origin and migrate to work in another country where the union has a branch with automatic membership on their arrival.

With regard to trans-institutional networking, there is rising consciousness among CSOs and trade unions about their own respective strengths and weaknesses, and attempts to collaborate have started. There are country-specific differences as to the depth and strengths of such collaboration and the extent to which this results in 'proper' alliances, with Hong Kong and the Philippines standing out as the most advanced in this regard.

Case study – the Philippines

In the Philippines, a vibrant and broad community of NGOs and networks emerged to address and advocate for migrants' rights earlier than elsewhere in SE/E Asia. This reflects the relatively long history of state-led 'labour export' practices or policies since the 1970s, and the overall volume of overseas workers as well as a vibrant civil society in general (Piper and Uhlin 2002). CSOs have over the years pursued the task of working for the recognition and protection of the rights and welfare of overseas Filipino workers (OFWs), regardless of legal status, through direct services, organizing, education and advocacy at all levels – local, national, regional, international. Their advocacy efforts do not solely focus on the migrant worker, but also include the families of OFWs and returned migrants (Alcid 2006). In other words, rights-based activism includes not only the rights of migrants when abroad, but also the rights of family members left behind and rights to economic security 'at home', as well as absentee voting rights – a campaign which resulted in the passing of the Overseas Voting Bill in 2004. To assist returned migrants with reintegration has also become part of their advocacy agenda.

From an activist perspective, Filipinos have emerged as the most widely and best organized group of migrants, to the extent that they are even engaged in 'training' other groups of migrants to become 'good' activists, as in Hong Kong for example. They have the most extensive networks 'at home' and 'abroad', which means that the issue of 'migrants' rights' is addressed by Filipino activists from the origin country *as well as* the destination country perspective. This is not only a reflection of Filipino migrants being the most dispersed workforce in the world, but also of long traditions of an activism in general. Furthermore, Filipino NGOs have been able to work within a more open political system and have managed to gain access to elite allies within the government structure (Piper and Uhlin 2002).

Perhaps the most successful of the networks run by Filipinos, in terms of its widespread grassroots support as well as overseas networking, is MIGRANTE International which is a global alliance of overseas Filipino organizations. Membership-based, staffed by activists who were formerly migrants themselves and supported from the grassroots level, MIGRANTE has been vital in organizing Filipino migrants on a large scale. Among its objectives are strengthening unity and organization among overseas Filipinos and their families in the Philippines, and defending the rights and welfare of overseas Filipinos. It has 95 member organizations in 22 countries across the globe. By trying to address the root causes of migration in the Philippines, the NGO and its networks are addressing migrant workers' rights 'at home'. Another Philippine-based, but more regionally oriented, network is the Migrant Forum in Asia (MFA). With a membership of more than 260 organizations covering the whole of Asia, it includes NGOs from sending and receiving countries (for more information, see http://www.mfasia.org). Its member-NGOs support any migrant workers of any nationality in Asia. They hold regular regional meetings, exchange information, usually via email, and engage in lobbying activities. They make use of a human rights framework in their advocacy work.

Another development among migrant associations in the Philippines, which seems to be unique as far as Asia is concerned, is the establishment of return migration programmes by NGOs. According to the Economic Resource Center for Overseas Filipinos (ERCOF), migrant NGOs have traditionally focused on programmes for the protection of migrant rights. But the search for solutions to migrant problems has evolved into mobilizing migrant communities for economic empowerment, particularly in terms of providing a viable economic alternative to returnees. The long term aim is to reverse the migration cycle through the development of a vibrant local economy, the lack of which is one of the main reasons why people migrate, both to cities and overseas. Ground-breaking work of this sort is being done in Asia by, for example, the Asian Migrant Center in Hong Kong, which has implemented a savings programme for migrants (Gibson *et al.* 2002). What needs to be tested by future research, however, is what this new role as 'agents of development' means for the individual migrants involved and the impact it has on them.

Evolution of civil society activism in the Philippines

Non-state actors in the migrant sector comprise: non-profit NGOs, membership-based organizations of OFW families and returnees, church-based organizations, women's organizations and labour unions. Over time, their approaches and strategies have evolved, due to the changing conditions and character of labour migration. There are ideological and political differences between them but networks have nevertheless been formed.

The work to promote and protect the rights and interests of OFWs began in the early 1980s, almost a decade after the institutionalization of the labour export programme in 1974. It was undertaken as part of the broader nationalist, democratic and anti-imperialist movement that took shape in the 1960s. In the 1980s, organizing work among Filipino workers in Hong

Kong, Japan, Saudi Arabia and Western Europe began, facilitated and coordinated by the Hong Kong-based NGO, the Asia Pacific Mission for Migrant Filipinos. The most successful coordinated campaign by OFWs in the early 1980s was the opposition to Marcos' Executive Order no. 857, which required all overseas workers to remit a specific percentage of their wages through the banking system (Alcid 2006).

The 1990s witnessed the increasing feminization of labour migration. The execution carried out by the Singapore government of the domestic worker Flor Contemplacion for killing her employer in 1995 resulted in huge protest actions by Filipinos, highlighting the plight of female migrants. This public outburst forced the Philippine government to hasten the passage of Republican Act 8042, which paved the way for the ratification of the CRM. During this period, the migrant sector intensified its policy and legislative advocacy and networking became a critical strategy. The first regional network for the defence of migrant rights, the MFA, was formed, which initiated a regional campaign for the ratification of the CRM. The arena for migrant rights advocacy began in this way to include the use of UN instruments (Courville and Piper 2004).

The other priority concern in the 1990s was the reintegration of overseas workers and the first NGO with economic reintegration as a core programme was founded in 1996 – Unlad Kabayan Migration Services Inc. Its Migrants Savings and Alternative Investments (MSAI) framework evolved into MSAI for Community Development and Reintegration. Since 2000, sustained engagement with international organizations and active participation in world conferences has taken place. A major campaign was launched for the passage of the Absentee Voting Bill through mobilization of overseas Filipino communities via the internet (Alcid 2006).

NGO–labour unions

The Philippines has some of the most militant and dynamic trade unions in Asia but ideological and organizational inertia prevented them from getting involved in labour migration issues for a long time (Alcid 2006). The Trade Union Congress of the Philippines (TUCP) largely engages in 'economistic' issues such as wage increases, job security and labour standards, and only three labour organizations adhere to what could be seen as 'social movement unionism' (SMU) (Alcid 2006). The youngest among the labour centres is the Alliance of Progressive Labour (APL), established in 1996 as an alternative labour centre with SMU as its strategy. Most unions have not taken up the issue of OFWs for a number of reasons, including prioritizing other issues, lack of staff and lack of funding. Those working closely with migrant associations, such as Kilusang Mayo Uno, May First Movement and MIGRANTE, have decided to 'job share', leaving the domain of labour migration to the NGOs.

The possibility of strengthening NGO and labour union cooperation within the frame of SMU have been recognized by a few Filipino unions and NGOs (Alcid 2006). According to the Alliance of Progressive Labor, SMU is a strategy to recognize, organize and mobilize all workers and unions, and is not limited to organizing trade unions only. In this sense, SMU addresses not only the economic and political rights of workers, but also 'the social costs of oppressive economic and political systems' (APL and LEARN 2001: 74, cited by Alcid 2006: 337). This means that the 'arena of engagement is not only in industrial relations but in society as a whole' with the ultimate goal being 'social transformation' (Alcid 2006: 337).

At the destination end, examples of cooperation between migrant NGOs and trade unions (Filipino and local) around advocacy, education and live-lihood programmes, and union organizing are a more recent development. The case of Hong Kong deserves singling out as a particularly successful example of union organizing among Filipino domestic workers in coopera-tion with NGOs. This began in 2002 but came together in 2005 when the APL deployed a woman organizer to Hong Kong to expand the Filipino Domestic Helpers General Union with the aim of becoming a federation of Filipino unions that would affiliate with the Asian Domestic Workers Union (with a multi-national membership), which was set up in 1989 and was the first migrant worker union to affiliate with the Hong Kong Con-federation of Trade Unions (HKCTU).

As a partner in promoting migrants' rights, NGOs have come to see the involvement of trade unions as 'adding value' for a number of reasons: unions can enter into bilateral agreements with their partners in destination countries in connection with concrete programmes or projects; and they are represented in international and regional partnership bodies such as the ILO, WTO and ASEAN. Furthermore, part of the SMU strategy are two approaches in unionizing OFWs: unions in destination countries recruit migrants to be members (common in Europe); and migrants set up their own unions in the destination countries. In the framework of SMU, unionized migrant work-ers should not only view themselves as collective bargaining agents but also as instruments for societal change in *both* the destination and their country of origin. This understanding of SMU thus reflects the transnational and temporary character of much of today's international migration.

As for current flaws and gaps, Filipino union organizing among land-based foreign workers faces several challenges, such as sustainability (the costs of maintaining organizers overseas) and the integration of a gender perspective in union organizing in a female-dominated care economy (Alcid 2006).

Implications for citizenship

Citizenship has so far mainly been discussed in the context of destination countries – i.e. from the viewpoint of citizenship in the new country of set-tlement (Piper 1998). From this perspective, citizenship is not the most pressing issue in the case of temporary migrant workers, such as those in SE/E Asian societies, where the largest proportion of workers are given short-term contracts without any realistic hope that they will ever be equal members of the political community. Rather, the liberal-democratic theorists' ideal of extending citizenship after a certain period of time, usually around five years, ignores the actual needs and interests of migrant workers (Bell and Piper 2005). As outlined earlier, NGOs campaign for labour or employment rights, improved working conditions and, in the case of domestic workers and informal interactions within the home, for good relationships with the employer. In fact, NGOs campaign for labour or employment rights, and citizenship is not seen as the key to alleviating the type and level of abuse that migrants often experience (see Bell and Piper 2005 for a more detailed discussion).

In the case of temporary migrant workers, citizenship can take on a 'transnational' meaning, referring to politically active citizens in origin as well as destination countries advocating for migrants' rights (Ball and Piper 2002; Rodriguez 2002). Citizenship in this sense is understood as a practice rather than simply a legal status (Oldfield 1990). This is different from 'external citizenship', referring to the right to seek diplomatic assistance and protection when abroad from one's native country, and the issue of reformed and improved consular services abroad in response to overseas migrants' needs. What the conception of 'transnational citizenship' does refer to is the complex and multi-scalar nature of political struggle for migrants' rights, with solidarity being built across borders.

Addressing rights violations – linking the local and the global

With regard to global governance, the UN system is highly important for CSOs in Asia because of the absence of regional mechanisms. As mentioned the previous chapter, unlike other regions, Asia has no regional human rights body. This also means that there is no forum where origin countries' governments can legally contest the practices of another state (as in the recent case of Mexico *vis-à-vis* the US at the Inter-American Court of Justice; see Satterthwaite 2005). Related to this is the fact that Asia constitutes the region with the lowest rate of ratification of all UN covenants and conventions.

The extent to which trade unions and NGOs make use of national and international complaints structures to address the violation of labour or economic rights is an area that requires in-depth research. Nationally, labour courts offer the possibility of addressing wage claims and other types of contract violations. For this, however, coverage by the labour standards law is a prerequisite, from which FDWs are excluded. In Singapore, the only option is the mediation structure offered by the Ministry of Manpower. Malaysia does not even have this kind of informal mechanism. Certain types of legal foreign workers can be represented by trade unions in labour disputes and the Malaysian Trade Union Council (MTUC) has begun to assist individual migrants by representing them. In Japan, local labour standards offices assist any foreign workers, legal or 'illegal', but the problem here is the threat of deportation undocumented migrant workers face, or think they face, if they report to any government offices.

In the case of domestic workers, Wee and Sim (2005) report that, because they are covered by the Employment Ordinance, breaches against this law can be enforced via civil claims and criminal prosecution. In practice, most cases are adjudicated as civil claims by the Labour Tribunal, which results in financial settlements rather than the full amounts owing. The Labour Department is reluctant to take out criminal prosecution against deviant employers for breach of employment laws. Of the 31,698 cases handled by the Labour Department in 2001, most were related to wage arrears, holiday pay and wages in lieu of notice (Wee and Sim 2005: 193). Labour disputes not resolved by the Labour Department are referred to the Labour Tribunal. In 2001, 10,500 cases were filed with the Labour Tribunal (Wee and Sim 2005).

On the international level, the ILO and OHCHR offer mechanisms by which human rights violations are addressed. The ILO's complaint structures would be relevant in terms of rights violations in the destination countries. Its tripartite structure, however, means NGOs' cannot file any complaints because the only organizations representing workers that are part of this structure are trade unions. Unions are not in favour of the formal inclusion of NGOs (Waterman 2005) and their attempts to organize and assist migrant workers seem to be too recent a policy change to have resulted in concrete usage of the ILO's mechanism. It appears that the ILO's complaint mechanism is highly under-used with regard to migrant rights' violations. But there is one precedent: the case of a coalition of Hong Kong-based NGOs, which filed a formal complaint with the ILO through its member-unions, the Indonesian Migrant Workers Union (IMWU) and the Asian Domestic Workers Union (ADWU). In this complaint, they accused the Hong Kong government of violating ILO Convention 97, of which Hong Kong is a State Party. During its meeting in 2004, the ILO's Committee of Experts did not, however, pick up this case, arguing that it would fall under Convention 111 (Discrimination Convention). For this, a new complaint has to be submitted by July 2007. It remains to be seen, therfore, what the final outcome will be (Migrant Forum in Asia, email communication, 24 March 2007).

As mentioned in the previous chapter, unlike the ILO, the Treaty Body structure of the OHCHR requires State Party governments to submit regular reports on their implementation duties and NGOs are given the opportunity to submit shadow reports, pointing to any gaps or inconsistencies in governmental obligations. The CRM relates to obligations by origin and destination countries and would therefore offer the opportunity to address rights' violations at both ends of the migration process. With the CRM coming into force only in 2003, however, the treaty body structure for this Convention is still very new, with the OHCHR having to date only received two governmental reports from among the 37 State Parties and no shadow reports by NGOs yet. A recent impact study has shown that NGOs are often not even aware of this possibility (Iredale *et al.* 2005).

Conclusion

Overall, the major problems foreign workers are facing have to do with inconsistent or non-existent migration policies, employers' illegal practices and contract violations. In addition, they are denied due process of law, and abuse of the right to freedom of movement and freedom of association. Government policies tend to target visa and immigration related issues, but rarely employment rights and illegal practices by employers.

Research has shown that it is more through NGO activism that migrant workers' rights have been advocated for in Asia than via trade unions. It is in particular transnational networking among NGOs that has led to some small 'success stories' on the local level (Ford and Piper 2007). The involvement by trade unions is a more recent development and their level of their engagement is uneven across the region. With regard to destination countries, Korean and Hong Kong-based unions are more actively involved than elsewhere. As for origin countries, it is the Philippines where union engagement seems most advanced.

Migration associations and trade unions have key leadership roles to play in generating strategies and common approaches, and in mobilizing societies to ensure the implementation of a rights-based approach to the management of migration, as well as to development issues that address the very root causes of migration. The increasing levels of international labour migration and the political activism surrounding foreign workers – especially when seen from a transnational perspective – have the potential to reinvigorate labour activism in general by highlighting the global connections between local and foreign workers.

Apart from transnational networking, however, it is equally important for the various organizations involved in worker advocacy to form alliances trans-institutionally and trans-ethnically (that is across the various nationality groups of migrant workers). Stronger collaboration and alliance formation between the broader human rights community, migrant associations, trade unions and other influential actors, such as lawyer associations, are needed. Social-movement unionism in a transnational context seems the way forward. International migration poses a new challenge in the subject area of migrants' rights and development, for research and policy-makers alike, and the conceptual and normative linkages between a rights-based approach to development and migration, and how to translate this into concerted political action, have yet to be worked out.

5 Children's sphere in a globalizing world

Especially in recent years, knowledge of where children 'fit' in the global political economy has increased exponentially. Much of this new knowledge confirms children's exclusion and invisibility (UNICEF 2006), a sense of which provided the impetus for campaigns for rights-based international legislation to protect children in the period leading up to the Convention on the Rights of the Child (CRC). Partly as a consequence of the CRC, we now have a much more accurate picture of children's sphere in a globalizing world, the ways in which they are socially and politically marginalized, and their relative absence within global policy debates. There is, in short, a more complete and statistical mapping of where children fit and the lives they lead than ever before although, as we will show, there remain considerable deficits in our information about children. This chapter aims to describe in broad-brush strokes some of the spaces children occupy and the roles they play. One of its central themes is the extent to which poor children are positioned, increasingly so, as losers in processes of global change. We show this through discussion of children in war; in processes of migration; and in the world of work.

We also outline the ways in which states have tended to conceptualize children, which, we argue, has magnified their invisibility and led to the adoption of public policies and social practices which are frequently at odds with their well-being. In some cases, government interventions actually intensify, rather than relieve, childhood poverty and the isolation of children. We note the gradual reframing of many issues to do with children's well-being from a rights-based perspective, a theme we take up more fully in the subsequent two chapters. We begin with some preliminary comments on the traditional difficulties of gathering children-centred data, a problem which has contributed to adult lack of awareness of children within their own societies and within the global political economy.

Mapping childhoods in the real world

Since 1989, there has been a much greater focus on identifying spaces children (understood as people under the age of legal majority, usually 18) occupy, mainly due to the fact that the CRC has acted as a catalyst for gathering technical knowledge about them across a range of issue areas. Large NGOs, sometimes in conjunction with states or international organizations such as UNICEF and the ILO, have actively sought to deepen adult understanding about the varied life experiences of children and young people. This stands in sharp contrast to the fact that child-centred knowledge was very poor indeed until the 1990s and largely consisted of generalized and unsubstantiated stereotypes in which the complexities and detail of children's lives were not subject to serious debate. With regard to the developing world, Glauser (1990: 144) described the situation as one in which 'international agencies, policy-makers, social institutions and individuals ... feel entitled to intervene in the lives of children with problems ... on the basis of obviously unclear and arbitrary knowledge about the reality of those children's lives'. Strikingly, this was almost as true for developed countries. Even in Western Europe, official information about children was mainly indirect. Qvortrup (1993: 5), describing his efforts to compile data on children in developed countries, commented:

> The extent to which children [are] not covered in available research, statistics, government reports etc [is surprising]. In most cases they were virtually absent; while on the other hand we could find information about adults who one way or another surrounded them ... the best which could be done was to make a patchwork of bits of information which, in most cases, was not collected with the purposes of telling about children but in which children were somehow involved. Children were, in other words, split up into categories that [are] not really relevant for our understanding of their life conditions; they were actually described according to adult categories.

Needless to say, deducing information about children in this way was seriously misleading. As Hernandez (1993: 43) (see also Ennew 1986) explains:

> For example in the USA in 1988, 18 per cent of parents lived in relative poverty but, unless the data were collected, it would not be possible to discover that 27 per cent of children lived in relative poverty. Similarly, in 1991, 41 per cent of families with children had only one child and 20 per cent of families with children had three or more. But when the situation is viewed from the perspective of children, only 22 per cent of children lived in families where they were the lone child and 36 per cent lived in families with at least three children.

Children are now subjects of a considerable volume of research in their own right (Valentine 2004) and non-governmental actors have been important in creating a new agenda of child-based knowledge-gathering. International centres of knowledge about children have sprung up, including the Innocenti Library, opened in 2001 at UNICEF's Innocenti Centre in Florence, and the Defence of Children Centre, Geneva, established in 1987. There is also increasingly fluid cooperation between relevant NGOs, academics and policy-making bodies, stimulated by information-sharing though the internet, discussion groups and networks such as the Children's Right Information Network (CRIN). This has led to considerable advances in some areas, although knowledge still remains patchy and reliable data are notoriously difficult to gather. Many sources of information – national household surveys for data, for example – remain child-blind or rely on information gathered through adult heads of households. This is often problematic and, as a result, the numbers of children working, for example, is usually seriously under-estimated. Indeed, it is not always clear what constitutes children's 'work'. As George (1992, cited in Ennew 2000: 174), for example, noted with respect to government data in Malaysia:

> The collection of information on children's work is confined to participation in wage labour and little or no recognition is made of the fact that most of the work children do takes place outside. Also, the purpose of the data collected by these agencies is to estimate other aspects like labour force and education participation and not to actually look at children's labour as such.

The UNDP's Human Development Index still does not disaggregate data by age, although it does by gender and ethnicity, mainly because '"knowledge" about children is [still] derived from unreliable statistics that depict the situation of the child's family or main caregiver' (UNDP 2004). Another major handicap is that the impact of gender on child poverty remains unclear (Feeny and Boyden 2003).

Nevertheless, we certainly know more about children than in the past, and that knowledge challenges established ideas about the nature of their lives. It makes evident too, if there was any doubt, that there is no single model of global childhood. There is now an abundance of evidence testifying to variety in children's lives, depending on geography, income, culture, etc., to the agency children exercise and the reasoned choices many make, as well as to the multiple patterns of adult and institutional interactions with children. Of course, a full statistical mapping of children is still unavailable. Nevertheless, the picture is certainly clearer than in the past – and what we know points to extensive and widespread social and political exclusion.

Exploring the global marginalization of children

The contemporary cultural construction of childhood dates from the nineteenth century and implies that childhood is, or should be, a space of innocence and learning, separated from the adult world of responsibilities and work. Of course this idealized state did not describe the lives most children led at that time – most were engaged in different kinds of paid and unpaid labour, and many lived in conditions of considerable precariousness and vulnerability. Nevertheless, this kind of childhood has gradually come to be seen, in the developed world at least, as the norm even though only the children of affluent families actually stand any chance of living a life in accordance with this rosy view. These myths of childhood as a universal experience of cosseting, pleasure and learning have served to reinforce the differences between the lives of some children in the North from most of those in the South, and the children of poor families from those of the well-off or rich. Along with material processes of impoverishment, they have contributed to the global social marginalization that now characterizes the lives of most children in the developing world.

Morton (2006) defines global social marginalization as both a defining characteristic of contemporary processes of globalization and a form of social injustice produced by situations of structural inequality. The extent of children's contemporary experiences of global social marginalization can be illustrated by looking at how they labour in the global economy, the suffering they endure in contemporary forms of warfare and the failure of adults to offer adequate protection to them when they migrate, whether for economic or political or humanitarian reasons.

Children and work

It has become an established view in the West that children below a certain age (which shifts over time) should dedicate themselves to full-time education and not to labour, that they should have a gradual introduction to paid employment, working fewer hours than adults, and that they should be excluded from the harshest and most risky kinds of work. Of course, despite these assumptions, some children and young people in the developed world have always worked, according to their social class, gender and position within the family and society. But for poor children in the developing world work is and always has been an accepted part of daily life. It is remarkable, then, that only in the last decade have researchers begun to construct a full picture of the role children and young people play in circuits of global and local production, and in global and local service sectors.

Poverty is undoubtedly the main reason why children work (Ahmed 1999; Neumayer 2005). Gender is also an important factor (Bhalotra 2007). Extreme poverty can normalize what have come to be seen as deviant practices such as child-selling. UNICEF research on trafficking in West and Central Africa points to child-selling as a common, established and locally acceptable strategy of family resource management, rather than the shameful affair it would be constructed in the West (CRINMAIL 2006). UNICEF cited:

> a father in Benin who negotiated a 'good price' for his three 10-year-old sons. He received 10,000 Centrale Franc Africain (CFA) (about $20) as a down-payment from a trafficker for the boys to leave their village to go

to work in Nigeria, and was told he would get 90,000 CFA ($180) for his sons' labour for a year ... the father explained: 'It is what is done around here. I was promised good money for the boys for one year. We are very poor.'

(http://www.unicef.org/infobycountry/nigeria_34868.html)

ILO data suggest that around 250 million children in the developing world aged between 5 and 14 are engaged in paid work (not household work), of which 122 million are in the Asia-Pacific region. Around half of these are estimated to be working full time and not in education, working nine hours a day or more (Ashangrie 1998). It is estimated that 126 million children are working in what are described as particularly hazardous conditions – where children are at risk chemically, biologically or environmentally. More boys than girls are employed in paid work although girls, especially in rural areas, tend to work longer hours because they also take on domestic and household labour tasks (Ashangrie 1998). The ILO estimates that children's wages can be as little as a sixth of the local minimum wage and that many work without pay. Working children are also identified as being more at risk of injury or death.

Understanding what these figures mean, in terms of the kind of lives children lead, is difficult. The statistics represent a huge variety of life experiences and the range of work children undertake, and their social and working conditions vary enormously. All working children seem to have in common, in fact, is that they mainly (but not exclusively) come from the developing world, and that they are born into poor communities and families. While some work, and sometimes live, separated from their families, whether on the street, in factories, in agriculture or in the sex industry, others live with their parents. Many work to contribute to family income. Some combine paid and unpaid labour with education. Some, mainly girls, work in domestic environments, often without pay. Many 'street' children also work in a variety of occupations, although some live on the street because they have been abandoned or have made a choice to do so because their home life is so difficult. Children work in factories, sweatshops, mining, restaurants, hotels, agriculture, domestic labour and the service sector. In times of warfare or disruption to normal social patterns, children can find employment as messengers, nurses or cooks. Contrary to popular assumptions, then, most child labour does not take place in factories that assemble clothes or make soccer balls and trainers for the export market, or in the commercial sex industry. UNICEF estimates that only 5 per cent of children in the developing world work in assembling goods for export – still a considerable number of children, but far fewer than those engaged in agriculture or domestic work (Toor 2001).

Many of the tasks children perform, especially in the developing world, fall into a category defined by the ILO as particularly exploitative and harmful. Few children have control over the conditions in which they labour or what – indeed whether – they are paid. At its most extreme, children work as slave labour or exchange their work for shelter; many are trafficked by adult intermediaries. At least one million children have been sold by their families to work in agriculture, the sex industry, mining or factories (http://www.ilo.org/public/english/standards/ipec/themes/trafficking/index.htm).

Agricultural work is often as damaging and dangerous to children as factory labour. By way of illustration, the ILO points to research that reveals that the children under 15, who make up around 30 per cent of the labour force in export agricultural commodities such as cocoa, coffee or tea in Kenya, Brazil and Mexico, are regularly exposed to dangerous pesticides. Moreover, many are not paid for their work because they are contracted as part of a family group. Equally, domestic labour, which may appear superficially safer, often takes place out of sight of society at large and is completely unregulated. It is regarded by the ILO as hazardous because it places children in positions of extreme vulnerability. Rahman (1995, quoted in Blagbrough and Glynn 1999: 52) describes the plight of the domestic worker in the following way:

> They wake up before anyone else in the household and are the last to go to sleep. From the employer's perspective and in existing social practice, this does seem to be inhuman. Domestic workers must always be prepared to undertake any chore, light or heavy, at any time of the day or night. When the working child is going out ... away from the daily grind, ... employers perceive that she is going on an outing while in reality her role of domestic servant is the same. 24 hours a day, 365 days a year, the domestic worker's status remains unchanging.

Many child domestic workers are also subjected to physical and sexual violence. One child in Indonesia described her life in the following way:

> Sujatmi told me that I would take care of her children and would be paid Rp.300,000 [U.S.$33.33] a month. I worked at Sujatmi's house for three months. Sometimes I did not get any food. I woke up at 4:30 a.m. and slept at 10:00 p.m. I would sweep the floor, wash the clothes, and take care of the children. Sujatmi shouted at me, 'You are a poor person. You have to know your position, you are here to work.' I was not allowed to go out of the house. I had not seen my family since I left home. I was not paid any salary. Sujatmi would say to me, '[Asma], I have your Rp.300,000 [U.S.$33.33] with me and I will take you back ... to see your family.' She was lying. She never took me home. She hit me when she was angry. Three times she hit me. Once she slapped my face and then kicked me above my right hip. It hurt and swelled up. I did not go to the doctor. She laughed when I asked that I wanted to see the doctor.

> (Human Rights Watch 2005: 7)

The numbers of children, mainly girls, living this kind of life is hard to quantify but it appears to be rising, due to steadily increasing family poverty, easier transport and rural to urban migration. In Haiti, for example, it is estimated that around 10 per cent of all children live as domestic servants, with placements arranged by intermediaries. Children working on the streets, meanwhile, as hawkers, scavengers, car-parkers, shoe-cleaners, prostitutes, etc., are usually outside education and exceptionally vulnerable to violence and abuse.

The ILO and development agencies have focused most attention on the issue of children working in the developing world. But it is clear that poor children also work in the industrialized countries as well, though not in such large numbers. The number of children and young people who have migrated to the industrialized world is rising, creating a fresh pool of child labour. As a result, the number of children working in the economies of the industrialized world is also on the increase. UNICEF has carried out some pioneering work into labour practices in EU countries. Within the UK:

> Even in innocuous cases, the vast majority of children are working without a permit ... There is no minimum wage ... one child reported that he was paid just 50p an hour ... Between 1993 and 2002, four children were killed whilst working on farms ... one 10 year old boy in Oxfordshire worked for 40 hours a week in his father's shop as well as going to school ... It is unlikely that such a wide-scale breach of adult employment law would be tolerated.
>
> (UNICEF 2005a: 85)

The number of children working in very vulnerable conditions across the EU is undoubtedly on the rise, although the problem remains largely one that it is hidden and ignored by member states:

> Restaurants, nails bars and food processing factories are staffed by foreign national children ... some, particularly children from China, will be bonded workers ... they are, in effect, slaves ... the hardest to find are the children used as slaves in peoples' houses ... The most alarming cases are those children given a false passport and brought into the country by adults for the explicit purpose of exploitation.
>
> (http://www.eldis.org/cache/DOC17940.pdf)

Similar problems can be found in other developed cores of the global economy. In the USA, for example, where the government takes a strong line on the use of child labour in production in factories in the developing world, child labour can be found across the agricultural sector. US governments traditionally exempted family farms from the national labour code so that children could work on family farms. This legislation has created a loophole, which has allowed export agricultural producers to use adolescents as labourers. The availability of cheap, sometimes migrant, labour, especially in California and Florida, now means that considerable numbers of children and young people are employed as helpers or wage workers on farms that produce for global markets:

> The United Farm Workers Union estimates that there are 800,000 child farmworkers in the United States. Virtually no state is without child labor in agriculture, and certainly no state is without its fruits, as the produce that is harvested and packed by youngsters' hands may travel thousands of miles to grocery store shelves ... Laws governing child labor in agriculture are inadequate and out of date, enforcement is lax, and sanctions against violators are insignificant ... Reports of children as young as four or five working alongside their parents are not uncommon ... During peak harvesting seasons, children may work fourteen, sixteen, or even eighteen hours a day, seven days a week. Whether paid by the hour or on the basis of piece-rates, they are not paid overtime wages – the law does not require it.
> ... Children working in agriculture face an alarming array of dangers. On a daily basis they may be exposed to carcinogenic pesticides, dramatically unsanitary conditions, heat-related illnesses, and hazardous equipment. Their immature and still-growing bodies are more vulnerable than adults' bodies to systemic damage, and their lack of experience makes them more susceptible to accidents and work-related sicknesses. Despite their greater vulnerability, children are afforded no more protection than adults – to the contrary, they essentially receive *less* protection, in that health and safety standards now in place have been formulated with adults in mind.
>
> (Human Rights Watch 2000: 3)

To sum up this section, we can conclude that, while children have always worked, some of the ways in which they are caught up in the global political economy are qualitatively new and possibly more hazardous than earlier kinds of predominantly family-based work – in both the North and the South. More children are now exposed to hazards in the workplace, whether through machinery, chemicals or abusive adults than ever before. All this presents a real issue of how best to establish rules governing the work of children and young people, an issue we return to in the next chapter.

Children in migration

Widespread internal and international migration is one of the primary characteristics of the contemporary global political economy. Around 191 million people, nearly 3 per cent of the global population, are now estimated to live outside their country of birth and almost seven million people are classified as internally displaced, although neither of these figures include the significant numbers of people who remain hidden from official statistics. Whitehead and Hashim (2005) note in a report for the UK's Department for International Development (DFID) that:

> Estimating the *number* of individuals and families that have migrated and/or are affected by migration is extremely difficult due to a range of methodological problems, including: the paucity and poor quality of the data sources; countries differing widely in the extent to which they document migration; figures not being collected in any standardized way and the illegal and/or undocumented nature of some movement.
> (http://www.livelihoods.org/hot_topics/docs/DfIDChildren.doc)

Most migrants live in the South although there are rising numbers entering the industrialized countries, which accounts for the emergence of migration as a global policy issue (see Chapter 3). Children are affected by this rising trend in different ways. In the first place, they may experience a transformation in their family structures as growing opportunities for transnational migration have led to an expansion in the numbers of transnational families, where one or both parents live temporarily or permanently in different countries from their children (Parreñas 2005). The impact on their well-being in these circumstances is unclear and there are few studies or official mechanisms of support. Some may benefit from the increased financial resources a parent working abroad may provide; but equally others are more vulnerable to abuse, especially if cared for by distant family members or outside the family. Some parents also send their children to family members living in the developed world, in the hope that they will have a better life. The enquiry in the UK following the death of one such child, Victoria Climbié, in London at the hands of members of her extended family led to revised guidelines in the UK in terms of how social services should respond to and implement the 'Every Child Matters' agenda for care (DFES 2003). But it did not lead the government to trace the other children living in the UK in similar circumstances or to offer support to them. And it has not led to the emergence of a regional debate or policy push for such children at the European level, for example.

Children are also – and increasingly so – migrating themselves, although it is, in fact, very difficult indeed to find a reliable estimate of how many independent child migrants there are. The International Organization of Migration (IOM) offers a gendered breakdown of migration but has no detailed statistical analysis of child migrants, internally, within the South or in North–South terms. In contrast to media-inspired images of migrant children and young people trafficked to the Northern countries in particular, qualitative research suggests that many children opt to leave their homes and the communities of their birth independently. Such children move, for the most part, within their own countries or, at best, to neighbouring ones – only relatively small numbers come to the North. In these cases, children may leave in order to seek work, attend school or even out of a sense of adventure. In many areas of the South, migration of this sort is often an established social practice. Hashim (2005) suggests that it can be an independent choice even in cases of children as young as 11. Independent migration of this sort may be positive for both the children and the communities, she argues. Nevertheless, however voluntary and whatever the aspirations of independent child migrants, migrating children are vulnerable. Children who leave their home communities in order to work are rarely paid well and sometimes they are paid only in kind. Like other working children, they enjoy little in the way of formal legal or rights protection. They may even enjoy less formal protection than other kinds of children in need, as Whitehead and Hashim (2005: 187) explain:

> The policy space to make recommendations with respect to independent child migrants is very narrow. It is squeezed by the international conventions and protocols which are key elements of child protection policies. It is also squeezed because the success of advocacy with respect to particularly abused and vulnerable children (bonded child labour, 'street' children, 'trafficked' children, etc.) has lead to this being a potential good source of development funding for national governments. International advocacy has focused much needed attention on exploited and abused child migrants, but has also made it difficult to address the very real needs of other child migrants.

A growing tendency within both the IOM and UNICEF is to associate the rise in the international migration of children with the problem of trafficking. The dominant image of the migrant child is that s/he is forced against her/his will to work abroad, often in the sex industry, in slave conditions or as 'mail order brides' bought by men. ECPAT, for example, links trafficking to the rise of a global sex industry (see Chapter 6). Certainly, child trafficking has become a major focus of advocacy and international campaigns. Nevertheless, we should be wary of assuming that all child migrants who are in the North without their parents are brought against their will or are trafficked. There is growing anecdotal evidence, for example, of significant numbers of independent children, some as young as 13, in the waves of African boat people who have been arriving in their thousands at the Canary Islands since 2001 (Human Rights Watch 2002a; Alder 2005).

But the result of rising North–South migration, whether people are trafficked or not, is that there are increasing numbers of unaccompanied children in the asylum systems of European countries. And here a number of problems arise. Across Europe, the management of migration takes precedence over the welfare of migrants themselves. In so far as children are concerned, this means that they are frequently housed in detention centres or prisons, education facilities are poor and there is little sensitivity to their human needs or rights. Member states make little provision for appropriate care for young people, fail to deal with them according to the 'best interests' formula prescribed by the CRC and do not seek to re-unite separated children with their carers (http://www.savethechildren.net/alliance/where_ we_work/europubs/Dublin_II.pdfren). Human Rights Watch gives the example of how Moroccan child migrants are treated in Spain:

> When apprehended in Spain, [children] may be beaten by police and then placed in overcrowded, unsanitary residential centres. Some are arbitrarily refused admission to a residential centre. The residential centres often deny them the health and educational benefits guaranteed to them by Spain and in these centres children may be subject to abuse by other children and the staff entrusted with their care. If they are unlucky, they may be expelled to Morocco where they may be beaten and eventually turned loose to fend for themselves. All this takes place in two countries that have undertaken to provide all children within their jurisdiction the rights specified by the Convention on the Rights of the Child ... Children ... failed to receive the temporary legal residency status they were entitled to under the law because their legal guardian, the Department of Social Welfare, did not apply for it.
>
> (Human Rights Watch 2002b: 176)

Within the UK, 6,200 applications for asylum were made by children separated from their parents in 2004. In 2006, there were around 9,000 children seeking asylum either as a family group or alone. Many are housed in detention centres, some are separated from their families and all are uncertain as to whether they will be allowed to stay – according to Save the Children, only 2 per cent are given long-term leave to remain. Few have access to appropriate kinds of support. Their situation is particularly critical in that, although the CRC was ratified in 1991, the UK government's decision not to apply the Convention to children and young people who are subject to immigration control means that little legal pressure can be brought to bear to improve their situation (Crawley 2006). Meanwhile, even the existing child protection measures are rarely applied to asylum-seeking children (Crawley and Lester 2005).

The failure of the UK government has led to its being severely criticized by the OHCHR. In response to the 2002 government White Paper *Secure Borders, Safe Haven*, which confirmed the government's determination to maintain its management approach to migration, the OHCHR pointed out:

> Children can achieve the protection and care they need in an environment where their special psychological, religious, cultural and recreational needs are met, and their physical safety, emotional stability and overall development are safeguarded. For these reasons, OHCHR is unequivocally opposed to the detention of children who are seeking asylum. Consultations on the White Paper should be an opportunity to

review the extent to which the present asylum regime is generally con-
ducive to the proper development of children who are asylum seekers.
OHCHR recommends that the impact of dispersal on families and
children – not least in terms of community ties, physical safety and
psychological development – should be re-appraised. These factors
should be key to any discussion regarding the placement of separated
asylum-seeking children.

(http://www.unhcr.org.uk/legal/positions/UNHCR%20Comments/
comments_WP2002.htm)

In short, children affected by migration – whether migrants themselves or
not – are extremely vulnerable to abuse and mistreatment. They can rarely
claim or demand appropriate treatment. Nevertheless, given how many
children are affected by it, it is striking that the impact of migration on
them is rarely a focus either of research or policy.

Children and armed conflict

In Chapter 1, we showed how the changes within International Relations (IR)
debates, specifically the shift away from state-centric IR, alongside the changes within global politics, have created a greater sensitivity to actor-ness and
agency in making international rules. This has changed how warfare is
understood and regulated. It has also created a fresh awareness of how children are caught up in and affected by armed conflict.

The multiple ways in which children become victims of war led in 1919 to
the creation of Save the Children, which was organized to respond to the
needs of displaced children after World War One. A sense that children are
innocent victims of war remains and the changing nature of warfare means
that children are now more likely to be affected by warfare than in the past.
According to the report by Graca Machel for the UN (1996), around 90 per
cent of the fatalities in violent conflict are civilians, many of whom are children. This stands in contrast to 5 per cent of civilian fatalities before 2000.
The UN estimates that at least two million children have been killed, more
than a million orphaned and six million disabled in armed conflict over the
last decade (Machel 1996). In certain armed conflicts, such as Sierra Leone
and Rwanda, children were directly targeted by armed forces and became the
main victims of the fighting. The consequences of contemporary conflict and
warfare on the health, well-being, and mental and physical development of
children are also apparent. As well as the obvious damage to the individual
child – loss of life, limbs, etc. – war destroys communities, disrupts services
such as education and transforms established social roles. It changes children's lives in massive ways, as Boyden *et al.* (2002: 25) note:

> Armed conflict entails many transformations and hazards at the macro,
> meso and micro levels, with major implications for children's survival,

development, health and overall well-being ... the many impacts on children [include] ... social disruption, loss of service access; impoverishment; civil and political violations; threats to the physical integrity of the child, transformations in children's roles and responsibilities; and differentials in children's vulnerabilities.

Nevertheless, despite rising concerns about the impact of conflict on children, longitudinal studies that map the socio-cultural and community impact of conflict on young people are extremely rare. Instead, most studies paint only a snapshot picture of children caught up in war. Consequently, we understand very little about how civil conflict and its consequences, such as forced migration of communities, affect them over time, even though these kinds of civil conflicts are becoming more common. Close to two million children have been displaced into camps from the Darfur region of Sudan, for example, with little prospect of returning to their land. Many have witnessed horrific atrocities; and their community's independent economic survival is in doubt. Moreover, as Jesse Newman (2005: 15) shows, while basic interventions by NGOs and international agencies to protect children under the ages of five from the worst consequences of armed conflict are in place, this is not the case for young people: 'youth and adolescents are generally absent from the agenda of donors and humanitarian agencies', Newman maintains. If we examine UNICEF's response to the humanitarian crisis created in the Darfur region of Sudan by the armed conflict between the government and the rebel forces, for example, it is clear that most intervention is aimed at supporting the under-fives (http://www.unicef.org/infobycountry/sudan_darfuroverview.html). Such is the psychosocial and material damage done to communities and individuals through violent conflict on this scale that families may not even be places of safety for children.

As well as showing how children and young people suffer in war, contemporary research into children and war also attempts to push beyond the assumption that the child is simply a victim of warfare waged by adults. Watson (2006: 232) explains:

> Children are indeed victims of violent conflict, but they may be participants in a variety of ways too, and during wartime they may assume roles within a conflict society that are different from those they assume during peacetime. Children may engage in the peripheral, if provocative, activities of demonstrating, or stone-throwing or rioting; they may provide logistical support roles such as transporting supplies and conveying messages; or they become involved in the more violent activities conflict engenders. Children have of course always been involved in a variety of activities during times of conflict, but arguably their contribution may become more significant in a post-Wesphalian environment. In particular, as state apparatuses collapse, the political vacuum

such collapse leaves behind becomes filled with a variety of actors, of whom many contribute to warfare in any number of ways.

As Watson (2006) indicates, children may feel themselves old enough to make a reasoned choice and may, therefore, choose to fight; they are not, in other words, always coerced into doing so. The Coalition to Stop Child Soldiers estimates that more than 300,000 children and young people under the age of 18 are actively engaged with military organizations. But we must be wary of assuming that 'voluntary' membership of armed groups implies somehow a thought-through and reasoned choice; a Human Rights Watch study on Colombia's 11,000 child soldiers indicated that many join because they need protection from other groups, and because they are hungry and the armed groups control access to food (Human Rights Watch 2003b). They are not motivated by a desire to fight.

The numbers of child soldiers has increased since the 1980s as armed conflicts have proliferated. Although the most common media images of child soldiers are from sub-Saharan Africa, children are regularly recruited into armed forces across the developing world. The long-term effects in terms of education, health, psychosocial damage and trauma are considerable. Central America provides a good example here since the conflict was, formally at least, brought to an end 15 years ago. The Central American countries of Guatemala, El Salvador and Nicaragua all experienced sustained conflict in the 1980s and children sometimes participated in armed guerrilla groups openly and willingly. In the case of El Salvador, Claudia Ricca notes:

> Children's participation in the FMLN [one of the rebel groups] is openly acknowledged ... Throughout the armed conflict, the FMLN enjoyed wide popular support ... Children's lives were severely affected and many joined the rebel group for a number of reasons: government repression, lack of opportunities and also revenge at the killing of a friend or a relative. Many 'grew up' with the FMLN, helping with food preparation, sanitation, nursing, messenger service and support functions. ... As the conflict worsened, the number of child fighters increased and their age diminished.
>
> (Ricca 2006: 12)

But, despite their visibility as members of the rebel forces, the needs of children and young people were ignored when the conflicts ended and peace accords were signed. Despite international intervention to promote demobilization, there was little concern over how to integrate child soldiers back into society, or how to provide educational or financial compensation for the years they had lost. At the same time, although the conflict ended, the extreme economic and social inequality, that had caused by the armed conflict in the first place, continued. The result has been that conflict and violence have shifted to the social arena. Some young ex-combatants joined the *maras* or the youth gangs, and other young people who have no memory of anything other than conflict, fear and violence are also caught up in gang culture. For all these young people, the wars normalized violence, making it almost impossible for them even to conceptualize social peace. The proliferation of firearms as a result of the years of conflict has made matters worse (Winton 2004). In sum, the experiences of conflict in Central America on children indicate the needs of children in peace-building are rarely properly considered despite the risks of long-term damage both to them and to the fabric of society. This remains the case whether children fight voluntarily or not.

As a result, there are vocal demands from NGOs and international agencies for greater regulation of children in situations of armed conflict and more effort to keep children out of fighting, as well as for limiting the abuse of children during war and putting in place effective mechanisms to care for children displaced or orphaned through conflict. These struggles are now couched in the language of rights. In particular, they draw on the Optional Protocol on the involvement of children in armed conflict which is attached to the CRC and has been widely signed and ratified. Nonetheless, like ILO Convention 182 and indeed the CRC itself, most states continue to ignore the obligations they have signed up to with regard to children and warfare. The Coalition to Stop Child Soldiers (2004) notes that, although the number of children in official armed forces appears to be declining, their numbers are increasing in informal militias and government-backed para-military forces.

Explaining children's marginalization

Until the 1990s, it was largely assumed that the differences between children's lives could be explained as a result of whether they came from the developing or the developed world. The North–South paradigm certainly retains some explanatory power: it is clear that life experiences for children are generally much harsher in the South and changes to the global political economy have exacerbated these differences. But this approach ignores the fact that children everywhere experience poverty and exclusion relative to adults, even in the developed world. Moreover, it misses the pivotal role of the state; good policy-making can make a difference to children while bad policies or a failure to act undoubtedly deepen their exclusion. Children's marginalization, therefore, is due to complex sets of overlapping causes. Material deprivation lies at the core of social and political exclusion for many children that will continue into adulthood; global forms of social injustice, embedded within local societies and economies as well as the global political economy, positions poor children, and especially poor girl children or poor disabled children, in situations of extreme vulnerability; and states all too frequently neglect the needs of children. Equally, badly thought-out interventions aimed at correcting injustices may sometimes serve to make marginalization worse.

Material deprivation and vulnerability

Poverty is the material deprivation of resources and goods that are regarded as essential for a reasonable life. According to the UK-based Childhood Poverty Research and Policy Centre (CHIP), more than 600 million children worldwide live in absolute poverty, which means that they are severely deprived of even the basic building blocks of life – food, clean and safe drinking water and shelter. Children experience poverty usually as part of a family or a community but its impact on children is different from adults. Poverty experienced in childhood has lifelong consequences in terms of health, education, employment prospects and political voice and it prevents around a third of children in developing countries from completing even four years of primary school education (UNICEF 2001). Rachel Marcus (2003) argues:

> The 'window for human development' of childhood is relatively short ... While adults may be able to withstand periods of poverty and deprivation without serious long-term consequences, for children that is often not be the case.

Despite the ubiquity of poverty globally, we are only now beginning to understand how it constrains and shortens the lives of millions of children. Part of the difficulty has been an absence of firm, uncontested knowledge. Mapping how poverty affects children has required challenging established modes of understanding poverty based on income, measured in terms of household. Measuring poverty at the level of the household generally says very little either about income distribution within the household or about access to goods and services – or indeed about relative deprivation in the developed world. Instead, UNICEF has developed a deprivation index for measuring child poverty which tracks access to a basic set of services and capabilities, including food, clean water, sanitation, healthcare, shelter, formal education and information. Its authors describe it as the 'first ever scientific measurement of the extent and depth of child poverty in all the developing regions of the world' (Gordon *et al.* 2003). As a result, there are now much clearer, and largely consensual, understandings of what poverty means for children and the scale of deprivation they experience (UNICEF 2000, 2002a, 2005b; Muinujin *et al.* 2005). In fact the extent of deprivation in childhood is truly extraordinary – and very shocking. Twelve million children die annually under the age of five from easily preventable diseases, 130 million children, mainly girls, do not finish primary education, 700 million children live in conditions of absolute poverty (that is, without the building blocks of a sustainable livelihood) and over one billion children are severely deprived (http://www.unicef.org/crc/crc.htm; UNDP 2004). Children, it is now recognized, comprise by far the largest group of people living in poverty. 56 per cent suffer one or more severe deprivations, rising to 80 per cent in sub-Saharan Africa and South Asia and 90 per cent in the rural areas of those two regions.

Changes in the global political economy have intensified the vulnerability many children face. These include the creation of factory employment in the South for goods exported to the West, mentioned earlier. But, more generally, globalization has meant the triumph of free market capitalism as the primary strategy for development. For ex-Communist or planned economies, this has meant a rapid and painful economic and social transformation in which the position children occupy in families and in society shifts and their image of what constitutes the 'good life' changes. At least in the short term, this can intensify pressures on children to enter the market economy, increasing their vulnerability. This can be illustrated by an ILO (2002) report on child prostitution in Vietnam (see also ILO-IPEC 1999):

> By the mid 1980s, the country embarked on a new development path, transforming its centrally planned economy into a market-oriented one. While the new economic order has created opportunities for economic growth, other challenges have arisen in the social realm, the most destabilizing being the widening gap between the rich and the poor ... at the same time, rising expectations create real and perceived needs among a growing segment of the population ... not all children participate in the sex trade to help their families escape poverty; a considerable number do it for the ... purpose of achieving personal material goals.

The report goes on to note that, whatever their reasons for entering the sex trade, children find themselves subjected to considerable heath risks and violence and abuse from customers and from pimps. They enjoy almost no legal protection, are unable to return to education and suffer social stigmatization because of their work.

Contrary to the commonplace assumption that children suffer deprivation only in the developing world, it is also prevalent in industrialized countries. Childhood deprivation in the West, which persists amid excesses of consumption, problems of over-production and vistas of plenty, is rooted in the longstanding failure of industrialized states to respond adequately to problems of urban and rural poverty, cultural forms of social exclusion and changing family structures. But it has been exacerbated by the ways advanced capitalist states have responded to the challenges of competing in the global political economy (UNICEF Innocenti Research Centre 2007). In many cases, poor families have found their living standards collapsing as states have sought to shed social responsibilities and increase competitiveness. In the UK, for example, the drive to make the economy globally competitive has created insecure, part-time and low-paid jobs at the expense of secure, well-paid jobs for working-class people and, as a result, the number of low-paid jobs doubled between 1977 and 2005. This has had an inevitable and considerable impact on levels of child poverty (End Child Poverty Once and For All 2006): almost 3.5 million children in the UK experience poverty. In 2004, Crisis, a UK housing NGO, revealed that more than 500,000 people were homeless in the UK (Hetherington 2004) while a report commissioned by another housing NGO, Shelter, in 2006 revealed that 1.6 million children and young people in the UK live in grossly over-crowded conditions, affecting their health, their education and their family relationships (Rice 2006). As Rice shows, transnational migration and social conflict elsewhere in the world has led to an increased number of migrants in the UK seeking work, shelter or protection, many of whom live in conditions of extreme deprivation (see also Crawley 2006).

State failure

Children's social marginalization is rooted in the fact that states have tended to make them invisible by identifying them as minors, subject mainly to regulation within the private sphere of the family. Families were seen as safe and secure spaces in which adult members were able to interpret and provide for children's needs. States saw children as subject to benevolent parental control – exercised legally, until recently, by fathers – and as non-citizens. They were certainly not regarded as bearers of independent rights. In social-democratic societies, which are profoundly paternalist, it was usually assumed that if children's material needs could not be provided by families themselves, then family-focused, rather than child-centred, welfare policies would be best. Cases of 'deviant' children – where parental authority had failed – tended to be the only full exception to this rule. As a result, even in Western 'welfare' states, children have been marginalized in social and political debates. Although this is changing, according to Schuurman and Sutton (2002) of Save the Children UK, children are still considered in at best an *ad hoc* manner across the EU. Indeed, Schuurman and Sutton suggest that animals are given more extensive formal rights than children under the current European treaty arrangements.

Children whose lives do not fit the idealized pattern of family-based care find themselves particularly in danger of being overlooked, whether in the West or the developing world. Child migrants or refugees, as we argued earlier, are particularly invisible in both the North and the South. Feeny's work on Rohingya (part of Burma) child refugees living in Bangladesh reveals that, although they make up more than 50 per cent of the refugee population, they are almost universally ignored in official assessments of need (Feeny 2004). He argues that governments and NGOs fail to 'adequately recognize or allow for the differential needs of children beyond the most obvious lines of gender' (Feeny 2004: 2) or to take steps to allow children educational, developmental and personal opportunities.

Their lack of visibility, then, combined with their junior status in society, contributes to the failure of states to respond adequately to their needs, which, in turn, deepens the material deprivation experienced by many children described earlier. Poor children, even more than poor adults, confront huge barriers when it comes to accessing the political and social arenas where policy discussions take place, at all levels, local, national and international. The role of poverty in limiting political access is increasingly recognized within the international system (UN 1995). Poor children thus find themselves and their needs doubly excluded from policy debates by their status as children and by their poverty. Yet, when states do take the needs of children seriously, there is evidence to show that they can make a huge difference to their lives. Appropriate child-welfare programmes, even when they are not based directly on children's rights, can limit or reduce material deprivation experienced by children. Despite significant pockets of poverty in Western European states, state action has been instrumental in improving the lives of children. In the developing world, this is also the case. The Childhood Poverty and Policy Research Centre (CHIP n.d.) argues that sensible policy-making and sustained social investments for children can mitigate deprivation caused by markets, and shows how governments in Costa Rica, South Korea, Malaysia and Mauritius in the 1980s, in contrast to most developing countries, chose to maintain high rates of social spending:

> Social investment made by [these] high-achievers was then sustained at relatively high levels – even during periods of economic crisis in the early 1980s and the resulting periods of structural adjustment. In contrast to most developing countries that experienced these periods of economic crisis and structural adjustment, the high-achievers maintained government expenditure on health and education as a proportion of GDP. When crisis forced macro-economic stabilization and adjustment, the high-achieving countries went through a relatively unorthodox adjustment process – which helped to protect government expenditure in the social service sectors. It is also notable that defence expenditures in the high-achieving countries was lower than the average for developing countries between 1978 and 1993, thus freeing up more government resources for social investment.

The result is that in these countries levels of material deprivation are significantly lower than in neighbouring countries.

But even when state actors acknowledge the importance of making investments for children and wish to do so, carrying them through successfully requires implementational capacity and effectiveness that is often lacking in the developing world. Developing states have fewer resources at their disposal and are more likely to be captured by special interests. Despite the much better record of industrialized countries in terms of deprivation, even here bad policies can damage children or contribute to their social and economic exclusion. In the UK, for example, despite a much vaunted set of policies to reduce child poverty since 1997, poor children continue to suffer from failures in the delivery of education, health and culture and to be stigmatized, along with their families, by the introduction of means-tested welfare benefits. Poor children are also disproportionately affected by the government's decision to take a hard line on anti-social behaviour, which has led to the introduction of punitive anti-social behaviour orders or ASBOs. 81 young people received custodial sentences for breaching the terms of their ASBOs between June 2000 and December 2002, in clear violation of Article 37 of the CRC, which requires that custody can only be used for children as a matter of last resort.

In sum, states can be held responsible for much of the social marginalization faced by children. And even though much more is now known about how states *should* act toward children, Marcus and Wilkinson (2002: 38) suggest that debates about how best to integrate children into politics and society have yet to shift from the academic terrain to policy-making circles. With regard to poverty, for example, they argue that 'children [still] feature more prominently in ... analysis than in policy or action'.

Rights deprivation

The rights focus on development suggests that, beyond state neglect and material deprivation, children's social marginalization can fundamentally be explained because their rights are not being upheld. Children have not traditionally been regarded as rights-holders and they have, because of their age, been excluded from full membership of all societies and communities, although the age at which childhood ceases is of course culturally determined. Even the testimonies of children have been open to question. They are not regarded as reliable witnesses to their own lives. Their complaints are often not taken seriously and they are sometimes seen as innate fantasists. In all societies, it is remarkable how few institutional spaces exist where children are treated as full persons. Rather than offering them protection, this has merely contributed to their marginalization. As Human Rights Watch (2006b) comments:

> Children's physical and intellectual immaturity makes them particularly vulnerable to human rights violations. Their ill-treatment calls for special attention because, for the most part, children cannot speak for themselves: their opinions are seldom taken into account and they can only rarely form their own organizations to work for change.

The historical weight of long-standing and cross-cultural processes of exclusion, coupled with the continued resistance to the notion of children's rights, explains why poor children suffer such extremes of vulnerability. It also explains why they have experienced poverty and material deprivation; their lack of voice and the failure of adult societies to recognize their entitlements mean states have ignored and demeaned them and been able to engage in violence against them with impunity. The logical assumption is that giving children legal entitlements and encouraging process of voice and empowerment will act as a remedy to their marginalization. As a result, following the passing of the CRC in 1989 discussed in the next chapter, development NGOs including the Save the Children Alliance, the largest international alliance of children's NGOs, and UNICEF, adopted rights-based approaches to development. Their work is now rooted in demands for rights and in advocacy strategies that focus on the importance of implementing internationally agreed principles of rights for children. At the same time, other human rights organizations, which had tended to ignore children as rights-bearing people before 1989, also began to campaign for children. Human Rights Watch, for example, set up a children's department in 1994.

Nevertheless, the rights approach to development in general has been subject to criticisms, as we noted in Chapter 1. These criticisms have been particularly acute with regard to children. The legitimacy of rights-based approaches to the governance of childhood has been the subject of wide discussion (O'Neill 1989; Archard and Macleod 2002; Franklin 2002). O'Neill (1989) forcefully rejects the entire edifice of children's rights with the argument that dependence is an intrinsic feature of being a child and equality with adults, which she suggests the right focus implies, is therefore impossible. This argument implies that children require protection; they cannot make use of rights because they have neither the resources nor the rational capacity to do so. Others have suggested that there is a risk of the interests of children becoming subordinated to what adults believe to be correct. Pupavec (2002: 64), meanwhile, criticizes the concept of rights for children with the argument that it 'derives from the contemporary Anglo-American social risk-management model of childhood whose conceptualization of social justice stresses normative/psychological causations and therapeutic interventions'. For Pupavec (2002), in other words, the rights focus inherently establishes the child as victim of the adult world and serves as a form of familial oppression. From the libertarian right, meanwhile, the rights-based movement has created concerns that it represents an intromission of the state in the private world of the family, undermining the authority of the parent.

Moreover, because this debate focuses on *children's* rights – whose innocence and beauty are beyond dispute, at least in Western discourses of childhood – it can become especially heated. Richard Horton's influential critique of UNICEF's rights focus, which he attributes to an unfortunate attempt to follow the 'zeitgeist of international development policy' – namely, that it does not put food on the table or provide nourishment or medicines to needy infants – encapsulated the critique that rights politicize debates while ignoring pressing questions of survival (Horton 2004: 2). Put brutally, this medicalized critique suggests that the rights focus leaves infants to die: 'the language of rights means little to a child stillborn, an infant dying in pain from pneumonia, or a child desiccated by famine. The most fundamental right of all is the right to survive.' Horton's view contributed to forcing UNICEF to tone down, though not abandon, its rights-based rhetoric after 2006. But away from the drama of Horton's stark and somewhat unreal dichotomy between survival and rights, it is clear that children and young people have a range of significant needs beyond mere survival, most of which will not be met unless they are able to claim rights to education, security, social inclusion, voice and participation, as well as survival.

Conclusion

Although there are considerable areas where we simply cannot map or understand where children fit in the world, an extraordinary wealth of new evidence has been built up over the last 15 years about childhood. We now know the extent to which children's experiences deviate, sometimes to a painful extent, from the idealized Western version of childhood that has for so long dominated the social imagination. Children's lives vary enormously but they are united in experiencing institutional neglect and, especially if they are poor or from the developing world, social marginalization. Nevertheless the very richness of the new knowledge about childhood, while it provides us with a much more complex picture of children's lives, also presents difficulties for children's advocates. When their needs are so complex and different, how can they be met and how can the lives of all children improved? One way forward is to present children as rights-bearing subjects. We examine in the next chapter the nature of rights-based regulatory frameworks that are emerging in the field of childhood.

6 Governing childhood

Children did not figure prominently in international human rights treaties in the twentieth century. Although there were attempts to create minimum international standards of welfare for children in extraordinary situations of war or devastation, it was generally thought that parents, especially mothers, would provide for the well-being of children. Children, it was assumed, could safely be left to the private sphere of the family. By the 1970s, however, a greater awareness of the complex roles children play within society and the economy, coupled with a more critical understanding of the family, led to a loss of faith in the notion of the all-sustaining family. The myth that the day-to-day well-being of children could be left to the family – and the family would be able to provide appropriately for children – gave way under pressure from child-centred civil social movements that focused on the needs and entitlements of children themselves. The view that children might have rights or that that they enjoy full personhood began seriously to influence debates for the first time. The Convention on the Rights of the Child (CRC) in 1989 marked the triumph of the children's rights-based approach.

The purpose of this chapter is to examine how this new model of rights-based governance has gradually come about and to describe how it works. We pay detailed attention to the CRC in particular, which we treat as a global bill of rights for children. We also note the ways in which the emergence of rights-based governance has transformed the role of international agencies such as UNICEF and the ILO. Rights-based governance, and the CRC in particular, have been presented variously as a tool of cultural oppression or a global public good and an instrument that radically improves the lot of children. Although it has inspired some changes in international organizations, advocacy strategies and development policy, its direct impact on children has nevertheless been rather less than either of these arguments would suppose. The CRC establishes a global model of childhood based on rights; but it has serious deficits in terms of implementation. As a result, it has not addressed many of the manifold injustices or the social marginalization to which poor children and young people are subject, and it has certainly not standardized the lives children actually lead. It has given them legal entitlements; but these have not been made real. We nonetheless suggest that rights-based governance has transformed the global politics of childhood in crucial ways. It has established the first global regime of childhood, in which states no longer have the sovereign authority to decide the spaces children and young people should occupy in society, nor their rights and duties; moreover, it has created a (weak) mechanism of global accountability above states. Perhaps more significantly, it has also provided a regime through which non-governmental actors can seek accountability and press for reform on behalf of children.

Rights-based governance for children

As we noted in Chapter 1, the new liberalism which triumphed after the Cold War brought with it a complex set of competing values, ranging from a belief in the triumph of the market to convictions around the importance of human rights. For NGOs and development practitioners, in particular, the new liberal climate offered opportunities to push forward an agenda of rights-based development. Of course liberal concerns about the power-lessness of children *vis-à-vis* the adult world, the predation of the market and over-weaning states were not new. Children's rights have been on the international agenda since the formation of Save the Children in response to the refugee crisis after World War One. From then onwards, children's rights activists have sought international regulation. Partly as a result of international campaigns, the apparatus of international human rights law and migratory protocols that emerged after the World War Two recognized to some extent the separate status of children. The Universal Declaration of Human Rights in 1948 linked childhood to motherhood and argued that both had entitlements to 'special care and assistance' (Article 2[1], cited in Ennew 1986: 19). This was followed in 1959 by the non-binding Declaration of the Rights of the Child, which set out a ten-point plan for children. Twenty years later, 1979 was declared the UN Year of the Child. Although the impact of these initiatives outside the world of international organiza-tions was slight, they nonetheless created a momentum for more binding reform within the UN. The Year of the Child in particular set in train negotiations between states, NGOs and working groups from within the UN Human Rights Commission for what would become the CRC. These achievements notwithstanding, however, it was the new international climate that explained not only the passing of the CRC but, more impor-tantly, its impact. It was greeted with a wave of enthusiasm and rode the liberal tide about the possibilities of a post-Communist liberal 'new world order'. It captured, almost by chance, something of the spirit that global politics were being fundamentally re-shaped in the direction of liberal rights. As a result, it was passed quickly and without demur by the General Assembly of the United Nations (resolution 44/25) on 20 November 1989, entering into force on 2 September 1990 and going on to become the most ratified international treaty ever.

The CRC represented more than a decade of detailed discussions at the international level. It is the first substantive attempt at setting globally applicable standards with regard to the treatment and care of children. Unlike earlier legislation, the CRC is informed by maximalist ideals of what *should* be, although in practice it establishes minimum levels of care. Its ambition is the regulation of childhood across a broad range of issue areas through the principle of rights. It works by insisting that states recognize and act upon the extensive set of individualized entitlements, political, social and economic, for children contained within the CRC. It establishes standardized global rules for the treatment of children and it affirms their existence as individualized rights-bearing subjects, independent of family or other adult carers. As such, it marks a shift that is genuinely paradigmatic in the ways in which childhood is conceptualized and governed.

The liberal orthodoxy of individual rights, which was greeted trium-phantly in the post-Cold War climate of 1989, has shaped the CRC in indelible ways. For example, the CRC rests on the fundamental premise that to individualize children is to protect them. Children are viewed as unique individuals; the Preamble to the Convention, for example, speaks of chil-dren having the right to 'live an individual life in society'. A particular sig-nificance of liberal individualism in this context is that it is understood to constitute the basis of appropriate policy responses both to protect children and to address the massive material differences in how childhood is experi-enced globally; the CRC was informed and inspired by attempts to better children's lives. Clearly reflected in some of the underlying assumptions about childhood within the CRC, this liberalism undoubtedly also globalized 'once localized Western constructions of childhood', as Stephens (1995: 8) suggests. Overall, the CRC is infused with Western procedures and stan-dards, from its emphasis on legal process, freedom of thought, conscience and religion (Article 14), freedom of association and assembly (Article 15); the view of personal development though formal education (Article 28); and the belief that 'scientific and technical knowledge and modern teaching methods' will combat 'ignorance and illiteracy' (Article 28.3).

But Western ideals were not the only influence on the final document. A considerable effort was made to accommodate and respond to the needs of children in developing countries in particular. In the Preamble, reference is made to the 'importance of the traditions and cultural values of each people'; Article 17 speaks of the importance of 'a diversity of cultural' sources in education and information supplied to children; and Article 29c states that education must reflect the child's 'cultural identity, language and values'. With regard to economic, social and cultural rights, for example, the CRC calls upon states to 'undertake such measures [as required] to the maximum extent of their available resources'. Article 24 calls upon states to ensure the provision of medical assistance and healthcare, and to combat disease and malnutrition; Article 26 speaks of the child's right to 'benefit from social security, including social insurance', and Article 27 refers to children's right to 'a standard of living adequate for ... mental, spiritual, moral and social development'. It is particularly notable in this context that child labour is not outlawed under the Convention. Instead, State Parties are called on to protect children from economic exploitation and hazardous employment, as well as to implement a minimum-age policy and ensure that work is compatible with schooling. Moreover, it should be remembered that the concepts of children as rights-bearing subjects is also novel and challenging to Western societies. Ultimately, the pro-Western bias of the CRC is, we would suggest, evident less in the conscious desire to mould children into norms of the West and more in the intrinsic faith in the concept of human rights, the underlying assumption of childhood as a discrete stage in the life cycle, with different needs and entitlements from adults, and a very Western vision of implementation via the state.

Above all, the CRC rests on the notion of inalienable rights that are designed to be the 'engine' of change. The CRC decouples rights entirely from the concepts of rationality and responsibility, assuming instead that children have rights simply because of their humanity. Because the CRC establishes children as rights-bearing subjects enjoying full humanity from birth, it presents their well-being and welfare as a question of entitlements; they are no longer to be considered only as subject to their parents/carers or as objects of charity (Veerman 1992; Freeman 2000). This is a hugely important shift in terms of child welfare and well-being, in the West and elsewhere, for traditionally adults have simply imposed their views of what constituted well-being for children through the frames of parental authority and familial or community obligations or, in so far as Western charities or religious organizations are concerned, via an alternative ideology of 'child-saving'. Under the CRC, all children are regarded as possessing individual and inalienable human rights.

Children's entitlements under the CRC include the right to a name, nationality, culture, identity, shelter, education, adequate food and clean water, expression and association. States have an obligation to protect them from exploitation, violence, neglect and abuse, and must guarantee them freedom to develop and participate in all decisions which affect their welfare. These rights are set out around what UNICEF describes as four core principles: non-discrimination; the best interests of the child; rights to survival and development; and the importance of paying attention to the views of the child (http://www.unicef.org.crc). The rights to voice and participation are novel in the West as well as the developing world, and they challenge traditional global modes of welfare delivery. The CRC insists that states should 'assure to the child who is capable of forming his or her own view the right to express those views freely in all matters affecting the child'; it enshrines the right to be heard and consulted. Children are entitled to participation in decisions that affect them, alongside their parents, carers and the state, in accordance with their 'evolving capacities'. So, although the family is still privileged as the principal source of protection for children – as with the

1959 legislation – the notion that children are persons in possession of inherent and inalienable rights positions them legally in a far less authoritarian relationship with parents, carers and states than in the past.

The debate about the appropriateness and efficacy of the rights approach with regard to children is complicated by the fact that the CRC bundles together a very comprehensive set of different kinds of entitlements. Other human rights conventions tend to have more specific goals – the elimination of torture and the worst forms of state violence, or the elimination of discrimination against women, for example. Arguably, one result is that there is not really enough detail about what rights mean in the CRC and there is little guidance as to how they might be brought into being. This is particularly problematic with respect to cultural, social and economic rights. Such rights open up difficult definitional issues and complex, and sometimes conflictual, discussions about standards, realization and process, especially in the developing world, as well as the role of the UN in pursuit of them. With regard to culture, there was an additional challenge facing the framers of the CRC: how to define rights in sufficiently broad terms so as not to offend non-Western state elites and, at the same time, retain the individualized rights focus that is, above all, the hallmark of the CRC. Finding meaningful standards for social and economic rights, meanwhile, was also difficult. Economic and social rights appear as something of an add-on to the CRC, although for many in the developing world this is where the rights debate actually should start. It is hard, in the end, to escape the view that the CRC fails to define realistically how economic and social rights can be realized for poor children. Concessions made to states at the drafting stage means that Article 4 acknowledges that states have varying capacities to deliver welfare. Article 4 also differentiates between states with reference to their socio-economic responsibilities, implying, in fact, that poor children in the developing world have fewer *de facto* entitlements than poor children in the developed world. Reference is made to the importance of development aid in helping states meet their obligations and in breaching this gap – but, again, no targets are set. The result, in short, is that these rights are loosely defined and remain extremely open to interpretation.

Finally, we should also note that there is something of a confusion as to whether children have entitlements under the CRC extrapolated from the familial or community context in which they live, or whether their entitlements should be realized within the community context. In a literal sense, the CRC seems to suggest that children have rights, discursively at least, that their parents and carers may not have. Yet it is difficult to imagine a real-life context in which children can meaningfully enjoy rights – political, civic, social, economic or cultural – when the adults closest to them do not. Can the interests of child migrants, for example, be served if the interests of their carers, adult migrants, are not? Can a child have access to clean water when her carers do not? Do child combatants have more rights to protection in war than adult combatants – and can these rights be made real if they are not extended to adults? In other words, if children are given rights, should not those rights be extended and made real for the wider community?

These questions have been raised, and the utility of the CRC most fully discussed, within debates about development where rights-based approaches to development have become the vogue. Rights have now become the dominant theme in discussion of topics as diverse as policy budgets for disabled children in Vietnam (Nguyen Thi Van *et al.* 2000) to the drive for global models of child protection (NSPCC 2005). But there are concerns that echo the more general critiques of rights-based development outlined in Chapter 1 as to whether rights can reasonably act as a tool of empowerment for children in situations of poverty, exploitation and abuse. Moreover, Sarah White (2002:15) points out that the rights focus, whatever its merits, is particularly difficult to implement effectively with regard to children. It has, she argues:

> ... three major challenges. The first is to relate the universalist ideals of child rights as inscribed in international conventions to practical policy and programme outcomes. The second is to strike a balance between considering children as individuals or social groups in their own right and recognising their embeddness within the key relationships which sustain them ... The third is to bring a general approach which can be applied to diverse contexts in a way that brings out the specificity of each within an overall common framework.

There are, in other words, huge difficulties is trying to make an abstract concept like rights for children relevant for policies on the ground. It is far from clear how, indeed whether, the principles of the CRC – participation, the best interests of the child, etc. – can be translated into a common policy matrix, especially in the very varied cultural contexts and the very different issue areas in which they are to be applied. Moreover, it is not even clear exactly what 'rights' mean in specific policy domains. Who will determine the meaning, especially the policy meaning, of the right to education and to health? How are concepts such as voice and participation to be interpreted?

The appropriateness of the rights focus is, in sum, subject to debate. We explore in the final part of this chapter how some NGOs are nonetheless trying to use the rights approach, not only to try and make policy on the ground but, perhaps more pertinently, as a device for advocacy politics. We argue that this is, in fact, its most immediate utility – it provides a platform from which NGOs can enter the rights debate and offers sound support for their demands to put child-centred politics on the global agenda, at least in very general terms. This role is particularly important in view of the slow, creaky and partial processes of formal implementation.

The formal monitoring mechanisms

Despite its ambiguities, the CRC has become the principal plank in a regime of governance based on the attempted imposition of a set of globally applicable principles and norms which international institutions, all ratifying states and non-state actors are expected to move towards and uphold. It has become an incipient international regime. Its rest on the established authority of international human rights conventions to set global standards, combined with a sense of growing deterriorialization, with regard to decision-making, described by Scholte (2000) as a feature of globalization. But the operational capacity of the regime, as with all human rights regimes, depends on the capacity and the willingness of states. Although standards are globalized, the nation state is still envisaged as the principal agent of reform. In fact, rather than representing a wholly globalized world, the CRC was born of an agreement between states. As such, the regime depends upon a close working relationship between international bodies and State Parties, in which, moreover, states clearly have more capacity to shape outcomes. The CRC provides the framework and the UN has an important monitoring role. But policies can only be delivered through and at the level of the state.

The OHCHR

At the apex of the monitoring process is the Office of the United Nations High Commissioner for Human Rights (OHCHR). The OHCHR also advises states on steps to take to move towards compliance. As with other UN institutions, the OHCHR worked according to a Cold War logic until 1989 and lacked strong international credibility. But, like the UN itself, the OHCHR has become a more independent player in global politics in recent years and has attempted to act as an international standards-setting organization, a global conscience and a force of coordination in humanitarian emergencies. For Barnett and Finnemore (2004), the authority of post-Cold War international organizations now derives from their capacity to act as norm entrepreneurs above states. They can no longer be seen simply as instruments of dominant states, they argue. International organizations such as the OHCHR:

> can have authority both because of the missions they pursue and because of the ways they pursue them. [They] act to promote socially valued goals such as protecting human rights, providing developmental assistance and brokering peace agreements. [They] use their credibility as promoters of 'progress' toward these valued goals to command deference, that is, exercise authority, in these arenas of action. In addition, because they are bureaucracies, international organizations carry out their missions by means that are mostly rational, technocratic,

impartial and non-violent. This often makes [them] appear more legitimate to more actors than self-serving states that employ coercive tactics in pursuit of their particularistic goals.

(Barnett and Finnemore 2004: 5)

The problem is, despite its new humanitarian norm-setting trajectory,
the UN system still lacks sufficient bureaucratic autonomy and authority
to defend human rights effectively. Even through the OHCHR has
increasingly taken a principled line about human rights violations since
the 1990s, it has proved repeatedly unable to prevent or even sanction acts
of genocide, torture, gross abuses of human rights and everyday acts of
exploitation. With no independent capacity to intervene, OHCHR action
has been confined to naming and shaming in the hope that a fear of
reputational damage will hold states in check (Lebovic and Voeten 2006).
The gulf between its lofty aims and its actual achievements is very wide
indeed.

   This pattern is repeated with respect to the regime of childhood. The
OHCHR is at the centre of a global monitoring system that has little or no
authority to force states to deliver on their promises. The regime works in
the following way. Upon ratification of the CRC, states parties agree to
bring national procedures and laws into line with the Convention. States are
required to submit an initial report on progress within two years of
ratification and thereafter report every five years. State compliance is
checked via periodic meetings between a committee of ten experts,
representing the OHCHR, and state representatives; designed initially to
be every five years, the timescale for these meetings has now slipped to
seven or even eight. But the problem with the system is not simply this
backlog. The Committee in Geneva is toothless either to sanction or to
condemn. Moreover, it has no power to gather independent evidence or
authority to investigate individual cases of abuse. The Committee has to
rely on NGOs, which can submit independent reports although not formally assist at the sessions, for independent information. Inevitably, the
information provided is patchy, incomplete and open to criticism on the
grounds of bias. In addition to these problems, the Committee has only a
limited time for discussion of each case or for the detail of policy and
rights violations. In practice, states get away with talking up cosmetic or
legal changes rather than being forced to depict or discuss the situation in
which children within their jurisdiction actually live. Finally, because monitoring is intended to be overwhelmingly supportive, constructive and
encouraging, overt or harsh criticisms are rarely made. It is tacitly accepted
that progress towards achieving conformity with the CRC will be partial,
slow and states will be obstructionist. As a result, although the OHCHR
sets specific goals for each state to work towards, and these are codified in
National Action Plans, all advice is broad and there is no real follow-up
until the next hearing.

State Parties

For the CRC to work, states must become 'party' to it through ratification. In the past it was assumed that states would usually avoid ratifying international laws because of sovereignty costs. Such costs are generally regarded as particularly onerous with regard to human rights treaties. But this seems to be no longer the case, for human rights treaties are increasingly ratified. With regard to the CRC, ratification has been almost total. All UN member states have signed up with the exception of Somalia and the USA – and even in the USA arguments are now being made that the government is bound by the CRC despite non-ratification, because of the USA's express commitment to the principles of international law.

It would be logical, perhaps, to expect ratification on this scale to signify broad-ranging and enthusiastic state support for the principles of the CRC (Chayes and Chayes 1998). But in fact the CRC, like other human rights treaties, is honoured more in the breach than in terms of state compliance (Hathaway 2002). States have become party to the Convention but they are moving very reluctantly and only partially – at best – towards implementation. In order to explain why this should be so, we need to return to our discussion of state responses to rights-based global governance in Chapter 1 where we suggested that states accept principles of global rights-based regulation principally because of a perception that there is no real option of opposition or of staying outside global regimes. Ratification of rights-based international regimes, therefore, reflects a desire not be excluded from the 'international community', along with reputational concerns as to how states are regarded. Regional pressures can also be influential especially where regions have strong traditions of cooperation – if some states within the EU or Latin America, for example, endorse human rights treaties, then it is likely that others in the region will follow (Simmons 2000). All this suggests that ratification is only the beginning of a struggle to press states towards implementation – and one in which the main institution overseeing compliance is, as we argued earlier, very weak. Paradoxically, the weakness of the international regime may even allow more states to ratify because they are aware that there are no sanctions or penalties for non-compliance. Ratification of the CRC is, in other words, what Hathaway (2002) calls a 'costless signal'. States sign up knowing that they will be obliged to make few, if any, real changes in policy.

On a closer examination, the imprint of state resistance to strong global legislation is evident from the beginning. Debates about what the CRC should contain were shaped by state preferences and state veto, which explains why a number of articles are less specific than they might be and others weaker than originally intended. This lack of definition has created considerable leeway in terms of what constitutes implementation; it is not always clear, for example, the scale of reform that is required before states can claim compliance. States can – and do – offer very small initiatives as major steps forward because firm and specific goals, even on infant mortality, child health and levels of children in primary education, were deliberately left out of the text. State interests at the drafting stage also meant that the Convention skated over some of the deepest fissures between UN member states, and between the North and South in particular, with regard to nature of childhood and children's rights. Some extremely sensitive issues such as female genital mutilation were left out completely. Other thorny issues which were omitted include the role and rights of children in warfare and the sex industry, although these have been addressed through optional protocols to the CRC. A conflict with African states over the notion of children's responsibilities, as well as rights, was only resolved by the approval of a separate Charter for Africa, which spoke of such responsibilities – and which are now apparently unique to African children (Lloyd 2002). Finally, states can seek exemption from those clauses of the CRC that they feel impinge upon sovereignty – and many have done so, some extensively. Just to give two examples: the UK sought exemption from 37(c), which means that no UK commitment has been given to end the detention of young offenders in adult detention facilities, or to reform criminal justice procedures so as to alter the practice of applying the adult penal law to young people. The UK government has also excluded children involved in immigration procedures from CRC protection. Indonesia, meanwhile, effectively does not recognize Articles 1, 14, 16, 17, 21 and 22, and will only apply them in accordance with the existing Indonesian constitution.

Beyond the legal question of implementation and exclusions, there is the issue of state capacity to implement rights for children. State compliance with the CRC depends on states having the capacity to implement child-centred reforms. States that are too weak or too poor to guarantee rights for adults are unlikely to be in a strong position to be able to guarantee them for children. Moreover, state policy is inevitably shaped more by lobbying, pressure and embedded forms of power than by need. In this sense, children fare badly. They are not voters and they depend mainly on adult advocacy organizations to put forward demands on their behalf. This makes it difficult to move their concerns up the policy agenda. Additionally, in the developing world in particular, children compete for scarce resources, making prioritizing reform for children very difficult to achieve. Yet the CRC assumes a world of efficient, sovereign states, able to implement rights for children; and one, moreover, where states act in good faith and mean well towards children. Even this assumption, that states mean well to children, is not always the case; as children's activist Jo Boyden (1997) has pointed out, the state itself plays an active role in many cases in violating children's rights. Problems caused by state bias, state lack of interest and state (in)capacity are exacerbated by the fact that violation or the failure to improve standards carry no sanction for states. As a result, for many governments, complying with the CRC begins and ends with the introduction of some minimal reform following ratification.

International institutions

The CRC has had a far more unambiguous impact on the work of international institutions, and the rights-based approach codified in the CRC now informs the approaches of all international bodies concerned with regulating childhood. The ILO, for example, notes with respect to children in the 1998 Fundamental Principles and Rights at Work:

> Children enjoy the same human rights accorded to all people. But, lacking the knowledge, experience or physical development of adults and the power to defend their own interests in an adult world, children also have distinct rights to protection by virtue of their age. One of these is protection from economic exploitation and from work that is dangerous to the health and morals of children or which hampers the child's development ... In any effective strategy to abolish child labour, provision of relevant and accessible basic education is central. But education must be embedded in a whole range of other measures, aiming at combating the many factors, such as poverty, lack of awareness of children's rights and inadequate systems of social protection that give rise to child labour and allow it to persist.
> (http://www.ilo.org/dyn/declaris/DECLARATIONWEB.static_jump?
> var_language = EN&var_pagename = ISSUESCHILDLABOUR)

The ILO, indeed, has taken a leading role in seeking to identify and eradicate the worst forms of child labour, using the CRC as part of the justification for the extension of its role.

With regard to international law, the CRC has also had an impact. The provisions of the International Criminal Court created in 2002 recognize that children may be victims of international crimes in their own right and identify genocide (the transferring of children from one ethnic group to another), trafficking in children and the recruitment or use of child soldiers in armed conflict as specific crimes against children that lie within the jurisdiction of the court.

But the body most directly affected by the CRC has undoubtedly been UNICEF, the principal UN agency concerned with implementing polices for children. UNICEF enthusiastically embraced the rights approach in 1996 and explicitly linked development with rights for children – and rights for children with those of women. UNICEF's mission statement, indeed, indicates that the protection of children's rights is its primary objective. This was followed in 1998 by an explicitly rights-based approach to programmes within UNICEF. This meant, in effect, that UNICEF field missions were restructured in accordance with the rights approach. It was involved, for example, taking on an active role in monitoring the implementation of children's rights on the ground. Rights for children, moreover, were effectively bundled with rights for women and families, as UNICEF sought to overcome the literal extrapolation of the child from her/his familial context which the CRC implies. At the same time, UNICEF also adopted a new role as an advocacy body, moving away from its original mission to provide immediate poverty relief and primary healthcare. It began, in other words, to try to influence public policy debates in favour of social and economic rights for women and children (Rozga 2001). Local UNICEF offices began to campaign in favour of the introduction of legal reforms following ratification of the CRC, and organized training sessions for government officials so that they understood exactly what the CRC entailed. This new role has earned it criticism and politicized the agency in ways hitherto impossible to imagine. In response, Ann Veneman, who took over as Executive Director in 2005, has moved towards a 'balanced' approach that combines rights advocacy with the deployment of more resources for rapid intervention in acute humanitarian emergencies.

The informal mechanisms: civil society organizations

The blockages and biases in the formal system of implementation certainly raise the question as to whether global standard-setting and rights-based governance for children is simply a discursive veneer over a reality of the embedding of Western ideals and continued child exploitation. Perhaps with this in mind, Harper and Marcus (unpublished, quoted in White 2002) suggest that the CRC has so far failed to have an impact on 'business as usual' development policies that impoverish and disenfranchise children. In the same vein, we should note that some international NGOs, although strongly committed to the principle of rights, find themselves having to defend their policies of cooperating with the official monitoring procedures, against internal voices arguing that the opportunity costs of participation in global monitoring with the OHCHR are greater than any potential benefits from the process. But it is also the case that to treat the liberal rights movement merely as a rhetorical cover for exploitation is as erroneous as to imagine that it will work as a magic bullet that can, almost overnight, accomplish sweeping policy change and transform institutional practices. Bringing state practices into line with children's rights takes time and depends on agency and struggle; it would be foolish to imagine that rapid compliance will be an inevitable corollary of the CRC. It is better, and more realistic, to ask whether the CRC and the rights claims it legitimizes have made advocacy work more effective. Has it established a more effective basis for rights-claimants and rights-claims? Put differently, does the CRC create possibilities for informal processes of accountability or make advocacy on behalf of children more likely?

We suggest that, overall, it does. We also suggest that it shapes advocacy, sometimes in unintended ways. The new global regime has created opportunities for non-state actors concerned with children's rights and entitlements to press claims on their behalf and, sometimes, to place them on the political agenda of states and international organizations. In particular, by creating networks of non-governmental actors that cross the public/private frontier, transnational NGOs concerned with children's well-being and rights can have an impact on global policy. As a result, beyond the calendar of meetings in Geneva and the formal mechanisms of monitoring and implementation, NGOs work continuously within transnational advocacy networks and campaigns to raise the profile of rights for children. This does not mean, of course, that their campaigns are necessarily successful – or necessarily even in the best interests of children. But it does explain the range of transnational campaigns that have emerged around children in the global political economy since 1989. Moreover, the visibility of at least some of these campaigns reflects the undoubtedly more fluid structures of international governance, which means that NGOs are no longer straightforwardly 'outside' systems of power. NGOs, in other words, do not now simply engage in 'protest' work. Many, including some of the most established children's NGOs, which already have a long history of international campaigning, have been able to use the opportunities provided by the new structures of governance to good effect. They have become adept at speaking the language of liberal rights and framing social conflicts as rights struggles.

A case study is the most effective way to demonstrate some of the ways in which NGOs use the CRC in their international work, and the ways they use liberal rights-claims to structure global advocacy. We have selected as an example the campaign to End Child Prostitution, Child Pornography and Trafficking in Children for Sexual Purposes (ECPAT) because of its explicit application of the rights framework. We show how the campaign to take children out of the globalized sex industry has been successful in terms of capturing media attention and in framing debates about trafficking – and in linking these demands to the CRC and rights for children. The campaign is having a policy impact, especially in the USA and Europe, and has raised levels of international awareness about child trafficking. But using the liberal rights language to frame campaigns also has costs. In particular, presenting children and young people as 'trafficked' – deprived of their right to make meaningful decisions and effectively enslaved by traffickers – may overlook the fundamental conditions that bring children and young people into globalized labour networks in the first place, and it may ignore the agency they exercise in trying to make a living and support themselves and their families. This issue, in other words, takes us to the heart of the ambiguities of applying global rights claims and entitlements in some issue areas.

The rights focus and the campaign to stop child trafficking

Along with campaigns to take children out of warfare, the campaign to end the participation of children in the sex industry and to close the market for sex tourism, or at least for sex tourism that depends on the sale of minors for sexual services, is the most visible of the 'new' post-CRC transnational campaigns. ECPAT was formed in 1991. It was initially set up in Thailand to combat the international tourist trade based on bringing men to the country for the purposes of buying sex with minors. Thailand had emerged as a centre of under-age prostitution as early as the 1960s and, initially at least, the industry counted on the covert acceptance of the government (Ireland 1993). ECPAT moved quickly beyond Thailand, however, and there are now local ECPAT networks in 70 countries, including the USA, Canada, the UK and other European countries, post-Communist countries, most of Asia, Latin America and Africa. The focus of campaigns is no longer simply to stop tourists buying sex with minors abroad. Instead, ECPAT campaigns to end global trafficking for sexual purposes and to put a stop to international networks of child pornography. ECPAT's campaigns are high profile and bring in a range of development NGOs concerned with children and their well-being, as well as local personalities and sometimes even businesses. ECPAT UK, for example, is supported by leading children's charities such as Barnardo's, the NSPCC and The Children's Society, development groups such as Save the Children UK, UNICEF UK, Jubilee Campaign and World Vision, the human rights movement Anti-Slavery International and the Body Shop. Prominent journalists, such as the newscaster Jon Snow, have also lent their support.

The CRC is the corner stone of ECPAT campaigns. Articles 34 and 35 call for State Parties to take appropriate action to prevent children being coerced into sexual activity and to protect them from abduction, sale or traffic. International and national-specific campaigns tend to point out the inconsistency between states' ratification of the CRC and their failure to act to take children out of the local sex industry or to prevent children being trafficked or, once trafficked, working in the receiving country. Such campaigns undoubtedly draw on a view of poor children and young people as having entitlements to education, health and a 'childhood', understood as a space free of adult responsibilities. But they also rest on less trumpeted, but perhaps more embedded and long-established, notions of 'child-saving' and Western concerns about paedophilia. The spectacle of children selling or being purchased for sex is particularly emotive because it challenges deeply held views that children or young people should not engage in sex, voluntarily or otherwise. And, as if that were not enough, the campaign raises sensitivities because it tends to depict abuse of children along the relatively simple dichotomies of North–South and male–female. The sex industry, it assumes, is made up of predatory men from the industrialized world preying on and exploiting (mainly) poor girls from the developing world. Moreover, campaigns to end child prostitution embody many long-established moral concerns about prostitution itself. The result is that ECPAT is entering a policy arena where there are already established ideas, some of them based on simple moral positions, about how to conceptualize the problem and 'solve' it (Anderson and Davidson 2002). Inevitably, therefore, ECPAT's campaign to eradicate sex trafficking was always open to abuse by governments, in the USA and Europe in particular, keen to police female sexual agency and/or eliminate unwanted migrants. Over time, sex trafficking has also come to be framed by governments in the context of transnational crime rings. To some degree, concerns about trafficking in the developed world feed into the rising tide of racism in the West, frequently fed by sensationalist media reports. For these reasons, other rights-based organizations that work to try and ensure delivery of rights for workers in the sex industry and other marginal occupations have offered sometimes only ambiguous support for ECPAT and its all-out focus on sex tourism and use of children as a tool in sex-profiteering.

Nevertheless, by picking up concerns of governments and abolitionists, and arguably those of (some) children themselves, ECPAT has been able to push sex tourism and trafficking onto the international agenda. As a result, there has been progress in terms of international action to define and control the trade in children for commercial sex purposes, and there have been moves in a number of countries to take action to reduce or eliminate the presence of children in the sex industry. The Stockholm World Congress against the Commercial Sexual Exploitation of Children in 1996 represented the beginning of a serious international debate about child trafficking, and was partly responsible for linking trafficking with commercial sex work. As ECPAT (undated and unpaginated) itself reported:

> The emphasis was rather on drawing attention to the problem and raising public awareness that this was a global phenomenon, affecting both the developed and the developing world. In 1996 the use of the Internet to abuse and to lure children was only beginning to be recognized. Child sex tourism was thought to be an enterprise solely for paedophiles; the 'ordinary' man and woman as tourist abuser was revealed in the Congress background papers for the first time. In this way, the Stockholm event helped change perceptions of commercial sexual exploitation of children.

The commercial sexual exploitation of children, meanwhile, was defined as:

> sexual abuse by the adult and remuneration in cash or kind to the child or a third person or persons. The child is treated as a sexual object and as a commercial object. The commercial sexual exploitation of children constitutes a form of coercion and violence against children, and amounts to forced labour and a contemporary form of slavery.
>
> (ILO 1996)

Since then, trafficking for commercial sexual purposes has come to be seen as a sub-set of the more generalized issue of trafficking in people, who then go on to work in different parts of the global economy. Trafficking is understood to refer to:

the recruitment, transportation, transfer, harbouring or receipt of persons by means of the threat or use of force or other forms of coercion, of abduction, of fraud, of deception, of the abuse of power or of a position of vulnerability, of the giving or the receiving of payments or benefits to achieve the consent of a person having control over another person for the purpose of exploitation ... Trafficking in children shall mean the recruitment, transportation, transfer or harbouring or receipt of a child for the purposes of exploitation. Exploitation shall include, at a minimum, the exploitation or the prostitution of others or other forms of sexual exploitation, forced labour or services, slavery or practices similar to slavery, servitude or the removal of organs.

(2000 UN Convention Against Organized Transnational Crime,
quoted in UNICEF Innocenti Research Centre 2003: 6)

Additionally, there have also been efforts to verify how many children are actually trafficked for sexual purposes. But there are difficulties partly because there is a genuine confusion between trafficking in general, trafficking for sexual purposes and networks of illegal migration. As a result, although there are concerns that the numbers of children trafficked for commercial sexual exploitation are growing, it is not clear if this is actually the case (Anderson and Davidson 2002). The ILO estimates that, within Southeast Asia, around 250,000 women and children are trafficked annually but not always to work in the sex industry.

Understanding of the social conditions that lead to trafficking is also considerably improved thanks to research and advocacy. Anderson and Davidson (2002: 54) show that trafficking takes place in contexts where there is little state support to 'unskilled migrant workers and/or other categories of exploitable persons (such as wives, au pairs, adopted children, beggars)' and where 'workers and other exploited people have little or no opportunity to organize effectively to protect themselves from abuse'. Children are not in danger of being trafficked when they live in conditions of security and well-being.

Recent evidence sometimes also points to the involvement of parents and families in direct financial transactions with traffickers or organizers of sex work (UNICEF Innocenti Research Centre 2003). This accounts for why the commercial exploitation of children for sexual purposes is a particularly acute problem in poor communities as well as in transitional and recently marketized countries and in conflict situations, where social disruption and rapid impoverishment both occur. Such conditions not only create opportunities for women and children to work in the sex industry, trafficked or not; they also provide opportunities for law-breaking and sometimes create considerable disposable income for men who may well choose to spend it on buying sexual services.

After the Stockholm conference and the mission statement of elimination of child sex trafficking, ECPAT began to publish an annual database of state responses to the call for action, in an effort to name and shame states and force them to take the issue seriously (ECPAT n.d.). ECPAT also successfully campaigned for ratification of the Optional Protocol to the CRC which deals with the sale of children, child prostitution and child pornography, which was passed in 2000. An Optional Protocol against trafficking was also attached to the UN Convention Against Transnational Organized Crime, also in 2000. Since the campaign began in the 1990s, many states have also introduced legislation that aims to eradicate child sex tourism. Legislation has been introduced in 32 countries, including those of Western Europe, the USA and Canada, which allows for the prosecution of child sex tourists on their return to their country of origin, and which attempts to address demand-led sexual exploitation of children, although this legislation is effectively cosmetic since is extremely difficult to put into effect.

Overall, campaigning by ECPAT has been successful in putting the issue on the international agenda and in drawing attention to the plight of children who find themselves caught up in the global sex industry. Although its origins were in child-saving ideologies and abolitionist debates, ECPAT has moved beyond those ideas to frame their arguments in terms of rights. ECPAT has contributed to research that has attempted to push global images of child sex past sensationalist reporting about children selling sex in exotic locations to one which is mediated by a more nuanced understanding of child sex work as part of a wider problem of gendered and generational poverty and abuse within local and regional contexts, made worse in times of conflict and crisis. There is some recognition that poverty, lack of respect and lack of opportunities explain how children come to enter the sex trade, whether trafficked or not. ECPAT has funded innovative research such as that by O'Connell Davidson and Sanchez Taylor (1996), which clearly shows how abuse of girls can become normalized and, over time, contribute to child prostitution. O'Connell Davidson and Sanchez Taylor (1996:10) note, for example, with respect to girls working as prostitutes in the Dominican Republic, that sexism, not sex tourism, lies at the core of prostitution:

> The incidence of child abuse, incest and rape of girls between the ages of 12 and 15 is very high according to … UNICEF research and it is also the case that girls are often initiated into sexual activities at a very early age by someone in their close circle of family or neighbours … Many girls are sexually exploited by family and friends from the age of 12 onwards and prostitution becomes a logical extension of this when they need to financially support themselves.

But whether 'rights' captures all the complexities at issue in child sex work – and whether ECPAT fully recognizes these complexities – is more open to question. Certainly a focus on trafficking can be misleading, if children's rights are the core issue. Does this focus, for example, draw sufficient attention to the attention of children who do not leave their country of birth to work in the sex industry – those not trafficked – or who opt 'voluntarily' to work in the sex industry? Their plight remains largely unaddressed. A focus on trafficking means identifying, in effect, children who are working in receiving (Northern) countries, yet UNICEF estimates that the bigger problem by far is still in the developing world. In Vietnam, for example, up to 35 per cent of all sex workers are below the age of 17. In Lithuania, up to 50 per cent of all prostitutes are estimated to be under 18 years old (Department of Labor 2003). High-profile campaigns against trafficking also run the risk of ignoring the rights of trafficked children who do not go into sex work, even though, according to the ILO (2005a), more than half of all trafficked people work in other areas of the global political economy. Here it is the desperate situation of children trafficked to work as paid and unpaid domestics and agricultural and factory labourers, of whom some 8.4 million are estimated to be bonded labourers and therefore unfree, that is largely being ignored.

Equally, there are concerns that the focus on trafficking plays into the hands of law and order concerns in the highly developed countries where the treatment of trafficked children falls far below what states should be delivering according to the CRC. In much of Western Europe, special police units are being set up to combat trafficking, trade in trafficked people and break up trafficking rings. Such units have an international crime, not a rights rationale. They do not aim to meet the needs of trafficked children but to catch international criminals. They also operate within immigration guidelines, which means that children are left unsupported. According to UNICEF UK:

> If a child is picked up who is being trafficked, they might end up in a detention centre with asylum seekers or a foster home. These options don't give them a secure place to go. They leave them scarred and vulnerable and at risk of being trafficked again … We need to make sure that children who are rescued are only returned to their country of origin if it is safe to do so and to make sure that they don't fall into trafficking again.
>
> (BBC 2006)

The campaign against children in the sex industry in comparative perspective

The fact that the sexual abuse of children is an issue 'with high value content' (Keck and Sikkink 1998: 200) has allowed ECPAT to put trafficking on the agenda in that Western publics and governments can be sensitized relatively easily to the plight of sexually abused children. The CRC has created an international frame from which ECPAT can and does borrow in order to make demands on governments. But this is something of an exceptional issue area – and even here, rights concerns are eliding all too easily into abolitionist debates and government concerns about illegal migration and transnational crime. Getting other concerns onto the agendas of states and international organizations, even when campaigns invoke rights and the CRC, is harder. Although the CRC has spawned a number of transnational campaigns in which NGOs attempt to use the rights codified in the CRC to make claims on behalf of vulnerable children, most are less successful than the campaign against sex tourism. Of course, success is difficult to measure. But if by this we mean influencing the public debate, it would be hard to deny that ECPAT can command the ear of policy-makers. Partly as a result of the campaign, we can identify some international and domestic initiatives. There is also the beginning of coordinated responses to trafficking and the commercial exploitation of children for sexual purposes, even if these responses still fall short of the ideals of the CRC and the best interests of the child.

The relative success of the campaign to take children out of the sex industry can be contrasted with the other less successful campaigns. It stands in sharp contrast to campaigns, for example, to link the rights agenda with poverty eradication. The international campaign Make Poverty History was mirrored by a similar demand to Make Child Poverty History, coordinated by UNICEF, in 2005. The campaign aimed to encourage Western governments to take the Millennium Goals seriously, and in particular those that referred to children. Calls were issued to implement the World Fit for Children programme agreed in the Special UN Session on children in 2002. This programme was explicitly couched in the language of rights and set out to encourage governments to make policies that would ensure the best possible start in life for children, including access to a quality basic education, free and compulsory primary education and ample opportunity for children and adolescents to develop their individual capacities. It also promised measures to support families, eliminate discrimination and tackle poverty. In this context, UNICEF re-launched the campaign for all donor states to meet the target of 0.7 per cent of GNP to be spent on international aid, for changes to international trade legislation that would allow poorer countries to trade more effectively and autonomously within the global economy, and for debt relief for the poorest countries. UNICEF also launched campaigns on behalf of child AIDS victims. At least 15 million children have been orphaned by AIDS and around 600,000 children were born with the virus in 2004 alone. Yet these campaigns have been much less successful and much less high profile. It is perhaps not hard to understand why. While ECPAT focus on the centrality of legislation as the solution, campaigns against child poverty require the deployment of massive amounts of financial resources over a long period of time and across a range of areas. It is not a question of Western governments simply introducing new laws which, in any case, dovetail with domestic concerns over migration and security. Moreover, aid and poverty do not command the prurient attention of the sensationalist Western media. Additionally, it is hugely difficult to force Western governments to commit significant resources to overseas development over time and to win funds for long-term projects where the benefits are not immediate. At the same time, although democratization in the developing world has created a consensus around the importance of liberal norms politically, this has not been matched by policies to redress inequity; indeed, the success of global democratization relies to an important degree on leaving the structures of inequality untouched, something Prezworski (1986) noted as early as the middle of the 1980s. So it is also difficult to bring pressure to bear on governments in the developing world to address rights claims that require spending; the international norm, in short, focuses on political not social and economic rights.

All this tells us something important about the ways in which liberal rights have been absorbed into global politics. It suggests that the liberal rights agenda, at least as far as children are concerned, can have an impact on some policy domains – but probably not on others. Where rights cost money, whatever the strength of claims in theory, and even when international pressures are brought to bear, governments are much less likely to prove receptive to the need for change. Moreover, because the CRC regime specifically refers to the progressive implementation of rights, this has become in practice an opportunity for governments to ignore poverty and deprivation. The result is that the CRC is probably a more useful tool for the pursuit of political rather than social and economic rights.

Conclusion

We have sought in this chapter to describe the regime of liberal governance for children set in train with the CRC. Despite widespread ratification, formal monitoring is poor and ineffective. The momentum for right-based policy reform is weak, although key actors are willing to endorse the CRC agenda. The social marginalization of poor children continues and, in some ways, may even be worse now than in 1989 (UNICEF 2006). Nevertheless, the CRC has created a powerful human rights discourse, which can – and is – sometimes used as the basis for civil society actors to press for reform, although this is confined principally to political and civic, rather than social and economic, arenas. This highlights the disjuncture between the formal rights children are now said to possess and the reality of many children's lives, which are characterized by situations of vulnerability, violence and neglect.

International campaigning by NGOs is of course only one level of civil society activism. And it may be less efficient in terms of building effective coalitions and implementing reform than national or regional campaigns. Finally we should note that rights-based campaigns, which draw on the liberal rights principles of the CRC, have taken off in the developed and the developing world. Here, because of the very different traditions of civil society organization and political systems, generalizations are particularly difficult. In the following chapter, we explore the utility of rights claims on behalf of children in Latin America, a region particularly sensitive to liberal rights.

7 The governance of children in Latin America

In this chapter, we examine how the global shift towards a discursive recognition of rights for children is played out in Latin America. Latin American NGOs are generally receptive to rights talk and human rights groups play an important role within local civil societies. Consequently, rights-based claims resonate strongly in the region. Nevertheless, demanding rights for children in Latin America presents particular difficulties. These include the fact that, although children are visible on the streets and in the workforce, they have traditionally been invisible in politics and policy-making domains; in addition there is deeply rooted child poverty, normalized in the eyes of both governing and social elites; social stratification based on class, colour and gender, which has marked out rigidly different experiences of childhood; long-standing histories of societal and state violence; and unresolved difficulties with regard to democratic institution-building, including significant failures in the policing and criminal justice systems. In this context, it is not surprising that policy responses after ratification of the Convention on the Rights of the Child (CRC) have been thin. Few institutional mechanisms to address children's rights violations have been created. The CRC has changed advocacy strategies; it has even set in train some important legal rights-based reforms; but it has barely penetrated, in any meaningful way, the policy agenda of regional states.

This chapter is organized in the following way. First, we explore some of the protection and rights issues that arise in the region. Second, we discuss the transformation of national and regional advocacy strategies and the extent to which the CRC presents as a useful tool to civil society groups concerned with the rights of children. In the final section, we explore state responses to the CRC and the extent to which states commit to rights-based policy change.

Children and rights violations in Latin America: the legacies of structural inequality

In aggregate terms, Latin America is the least poor region of the so-called developing world. In comparison with sub-Saharan Africa and Asia, Latin

American children are less likely to be orphaned under the age of 18, suffer serious and life-threatening diseases such as AIDS or fail to complete primary education. Around 15 per cent of children in Latin America are not registered at birth, compared to 55 per cent in sub-Saharan Africa and 63 per cent in South Asia – although we need to remember that these figures are particularly difficult to get right (PI 2005). Infant mortality is, *grosso modo*, much lower than for other developing areas, except in the poorest countries of the region such as Haiti and Bolivia (see Table 7.1). This comparative picture, however, hides stark differences between and within countries, and it distracts many aid donors who concentrate most of their resources elsewhere as a result. In fact, poverty is the first, most widespread and most extreme rights violation children in Latin American experience. Around 43 per cent of all Latin Americans and around 60 per cent of the region's children are poor. This affects the life chances, health and quality of life of all these children, shapes the environment in which they grow up and

Table 7.1 International infant mortality rates (per 1,000 live births)

Countries	1990	1999
Latin America		
Argentina	25.2	18.4
Bolivia	80.0	58.8
Brazil	47.8	32.2
Chile	16.0	9.98
Costa Rica	14.8	12.37
Cuba	10.7	6.87
Uruguay	21.20	14.50
Venezuela	24.60	20.20
Europe		
Austria	7.80	4.40
France	7.30	4.80
Germany	7.00	4.82
Greece	9.70	6.02
Hungary	14.80	8.40
Italy	8.20	5.42
Portugal	10.90	5.60
Switzerland	6.80	4.56
United Kingdom	7.90	5.70
North America		
Canada	6.80	5.30
United States	9.40	6.90
Asia		
China	33.06	30.24
India	80.0	70.90
Indonesia	60.0	41.92
Japan	4.60	3.60

Source: World Bank, World Development Indicators (2001)

limits the choices they make. Moreover, because poverty is difficult to escape from, it is also likely that they pass on the legacy of deprivation to their own children.

Poverty in Latin America is not the result of insufficient national resources or assets; not is it the consequence of a sudden withdrawal of investment or global transformation. Certainly, the implementation of neoliberalism in the 1980s and 1990s led to massive job losses, lower wages and the withdrawal of the state from social provision, resulting in increases in the number of poor people and a greater burden on poor households (Moser 1996; Lloyd-Sherlock 1997; Gindling 2005; Gonzalez de la Roca 2006). But poverty is rooted in Latin America in persistent forms of social inequality and embedded patterns of state bias, which has led to the concentration of social and economic resources in the upper and middle strata. Wealth and capital are more unevenly distributed in Latin America than anywhere else in the world. Although global inequality decreased almost everywhere between 1960 and 1995, it increased in Latin America (Justino and Acharya 2003). In a landmark study of inequality in Latin America, the World Bank noted that:

> The richest one-tenth of the population of Latin America and the Caribbean earn 48 per cent of total income, while the poorest tenth earn only 1.6 per cent. In industrialized countries, by contrast, the top tenth receive 29.1 per cent, while the bottom tenth earn 2.5 per cent. Using the 'Gini Index' of inequality in the distribution of income and consumption, Latin America and the Caribbean, from the 1970s through the 1990s, measured nearly 10 points more unequal than Asia, 17.5 points more unequal than the 30 countries in the Organization for Economic Cooperation and Development, and 20.4 points more unequal than Eastern Europe.
>
> (World Bank 2003: 23)

Economically, this disparity in lifestyles, life chances, income and well-being was sustained by the emergence of a large informal sector (Portes *et al.* 1989). Poverty is reproduced through the unequal distribution of public goods, unjust educational systems, unequal access to health and embedded forms of discrimination, and elite-dominated governments have systematically deferred expenditure on public investments except where elites themselves have stood to gain. Most Latin American countries created impressive networks of public universities for the middle and upper classes – long before an effective system of primary education for all children was in place (World Bank 2003), even though access to decent education is crucial in preventing the inter-generational transmission of poverty (Attanasio and Székely 2001). Side by side sophisticated hospitals, excellent universities, modern shopping malls and architectural masterpieces designed by architects of global stature live communities without even access to basic healthcare, vaccination and clean water. Over time, poverty and structural inequality have become normalized in Latin America through ideologies and practices of discrimination based on class, race and gender.

Politically, this situation rests on restricted and limited forms of citizenship and the persistence of clientelism which democratization in the 1980s and 1990s has so far proved unable to challenge or change (Grugel 2007a). We can see this clearly in Brazil, the largest and most unequal country in Latin America and the tenth economy in the world, where democratization began in 1983. The European Commission noted in 2002 that 'redistribution mechanisms are inefficient or are tilted towards the needs of the middle or upper classes. As President Cardoso once stated, Brazil is not an underdeveloped country, it is an unjust society' (European Commission 2002: 13). In fact, it would require transferring only 5 per cent of the income of the wealthiest 20 per cent of the population to the poorest 20 per cent to reduce the poverty rate to 7 per cent – but even this seems to be impossible for the state to carry through (UNDP 2005). Elsewhere in the region, the picture is almost as bad. Even in Argentina, traditionally one of the countries of the region with the highest social indicators, around 50 per cent of children are now classified as poor, measured by their ability to access basic goods. In Bolivia, where poverty rates have historically been extremely high, of the four million children and young people under the age of 18 (around half of the total population), around 70 per cent live in poverty. Only 50–70 per cent of children receive even their first dose of basic vaccines against polio and other life-threatening illnesses, and over 30 per cent of infant mortality is due to diarrhoeal diseases – a problem that can be almost entirely eradicated simply through access to clean water.

In so far as children are concerned, state biases of this sort translate into almost unimaginable differences in terms of life possibilities, hopes and experiences between the children of the wealthy, and even the relatively well-off, and poor children, especially if they belong to minority groups such as indigenous communities. Given that children are formally guaranteed a range of rights under the CRC, which was ratified quickly across Latin America, the multiple deprivations many experience should be understood as rights violations. All poor children experience forms of state neglect and abuse; girl children and indigenous communities are particularly at risk and unprotected. We discuss some of the rights violations children experience in more detail now.

Working children

Fewer children work in Latin America than in Asia, although here again figures are not fully trustworthy. According to the ILO, around 17.5 million Latin American children aged between five and 14 work, 7 million of whom are in Brazil where over 14 per cent of all children aged between 10 and 14 work. In Paraguay, a third of all children aged between seven and 17 work and 42 per cent of these began working before the age of eight; of these, 37 per cent do not attend school (Department of State 2002). Even in oil-rich Venezuela, at least 13 per cent of children are estimated to be working outside the home. Studies indicate that working children, especially if they do not also attend school, are most likely to find themselves trapped in poverty as adults (Ilahi *et al.* 2000).

Children can be found in a range of occupations from domestic labour to agricultural work or factory production. Poor children, especially girls, have traditionally borne a considerable domestic burden, alongside and sometimes instead of schooling. In Guatemala, for example, almost 40 per cent of girls aged between five and 17 do domestic labour, defined by the ILO as more than two hours a day for children aged between five and nine, more than three hours a day for those between ten and 14 and more than four hours daily for children aged 15 to 17 (ILO 2003b). In addition to unpaid domestic labour, poor children also work outside the home where they contribute in different ways to family income. According to the ILO, around 20 per cent of the income of poor families in El Salvador derives from child labour. The ILO report further that:

> Approximately two-thirds of all working children are concentrated in rural areas where they are mainly involved in agriculture and related activities. In the agricultural sector, child labour is a particular problem in the growing and processing of sugarcane and coffee. Child labour is also a serious concern in non-agricultural sectors, including fishing and shellfish harvesting; scavenging in garbage dumpsites; the making of fireworks; commercial sexual exploitation; and informal activities in urban areas, such as drug trafficking, small-scale street vending and other services.
>
> (http://www.ilo.org/public/english/standards/ipec/timebound/salvador.pdf)

Considerable numbers of children work in commercial agriculture across the region. According to the ILO, 62 per cent of working children in Guatemala are engaged in agriculture, 58 per cent in Nicaragua and 53 per cent in El Salvador (http://www.ilo.org/public/english/standards/ipec/about/globalreport/ 2006/download/2006_fs_latinamerica_en.pdf). Both the ILO and human rights organizations have expressed concern about the scale and nature of child labour in the agricultural sector, and its links with global production chains. In El Salvador, for example, Human Rights Watch (2004a: 4) reported:

> Children as young as eight, cut sugarcane ... Carlos T., an eleven-year-old, began cutting cane when he was nine. 'Last year was the second year I worked,' he said. 'I would leave the house at 5 a.m.' The fields were spread out over a large area. 'When it was far away, we would go by bus; when it was close, we would walk ...' Carlos worked with his

father. As far as the owners of the plantations are concerned, he and many of the other children who cut cane are 'helpers', not employees ... Cutting cane is backbreaking work, and accidents are common. ... Speaking on the condition of anonymity, a former labor inspector told Human Rights Watch that of all forms of agricultural work, sugarcane is the most hazardous. 'Sugarcane has the most risks,' he said. 'It's indisputable – sugarcane is the most dangerous.'

Working in the mining industry is another source of particularly exploitative and hazardous labour regularly carried out by children. In Nicaragua:

about 400 children work extracting gold in the mining district of La India, about 160 kms (100 miles) north of Managua, according to the International Labor Organization (ILO) and the Nicaraguan Commission for the Eradication of the Child Labor. Most of the children belong to families of nearby communities. The children suffer from malnutrition, dehydration, kidney problems and are victims of serious accidents in the mine tunnels.

(Oro SucioNoticias Aliadas 2007)

In Peru, meanwhile, the numbers of children employed in small-scale gold mining has increased steadily over the last 20 years in response to widespread unemployment and economic restructuring in the 1980s and 1990s, which have led poor people to migrate in search of a living. According to an ILO study of one gold mining village in the south of Peru, created in the 1990s:

This new village of Mollehuaca is ... contaminated by mercury and considered to be a high risk area ... There are no permanent health professionals ... Mollehuaca has no public services, whether potable water, sewerage, garbage collection or electricity ... Child labour is part of community life ... [there were] 148 working children, 17 of whom, aged 15–17, live alone or with a non-relative ... The children do the same work as adults. There are also additional tasks, such as taking food to the miners, that are exclusively done by children ... Children working in the tunnels are exposed to very harsh conditions. Such work could entail working underground for 1–2 weeks, eating and sleeping at the mine entrance and working day and night with short rest periods. They use chisels, sledgehammers and picks that require a considerable strength and that are not designed to be used by children ... Considering the dangers that have to be faced in mining, the children working in mining in Mollehuaca do not use any kind of personal protection while working, despite being exposed to hazardous situations such as tunnels collapsing, rock slides, falling, and the worst, exposure to mercury due to direct contact or by inhalation of mercury vapour.

(Martinez-Castilla n.d. and unpaginated)

Children also labour on the street, in factories, (often illegal factories where safety levels are low and production has been out-sourced in order to lower costs) and sex work. Some work for sex tourists, especially in the Caribbean and Central America. Girl children also work as domestic servants, some starting from as young as nine (see, for example, Human Rights Watch, 2004b).

Institutionalized neglect and violence

Poor and marginalized children have traditionally experienced hostility and neglect from the state in Latin America. Some states have even failed in their elementary responsibilities to maintain birth registries in poor areas:

> In Bolivia, fifty per cent of children aged under 1 and 12 per cent of children aged from 0–9 years old lack a birth certificate (CPNV 2001-INE). The causes of this lack of registry are of an economic and cultural character: the cost of obtaining a birth certificate is high, and there is a lack of information on the benefits of registering children. A child whose birth is not registered does not exist in the eyes of the state and therefore does not have access to the basic services and rights guaranteed by law.
>
> (UNICEF 2003)

Even in Argentina, one of the countries in the region with the most developed state apparatus, poor children are still often unregistered despite the creation of a national registry of births early in the twentieth century, as the following example, based on the testimony of a local paediatrician, shows:

> Fabian ... was born in hospital in Buenos Aires. He lived most of his life with his parents, both drug addicts ... Born in 1993, the first four or five years of his life were ones of illness after illness and he was hospitalized in different medical centres in the city. He attended different pre-schools, nurseries and *comedores*. Because he wasn't vaccinated, in 1998 he developed measles which led to severe respiratory problems. He was brought to the children's hospital in La Plata [capital of the Province of Buenos Aires] where he was diagnosed with AIDS ... Following an intervention by the family courts, Fabian took up what would become a permanent residence in hospital because he was now dependent on oxygen ... along with his sister who was also diagnosed with AIDS. His days, his life was lived out in the hospital until, at the age of seven, Fabian died on 10 May 2000. His parents had visited him when they could, sporadically, when their addictions, marginality, illnesses and lack of resources allowed them to ... When we tried to get a death certificate for him – because we had to do it, the hospital – we discovered that Fabian, at seven years old, had no papers. That is, he had to die in order

for us formally to recognize that he had lived. And this despite the fact that Fabian was a child who had passed through the courts on three separate occasions, as well as having been in numerous hospitals. (http://www.lanacion.com.ar/coberturaespecial/porlosdemas/chicoscalle/ seminario/seminario5.doc)

In many countries of the region, children's codes were established in the twentieth century, apparently as a mark of progress and modernity. But such codes tended in practice to criminalize poverty and to justify authoritarian interventions in the lives of poor children and their families. In Argentina, for example, the Children's Code, which dates from 1919, allowed the state to intervene when children were determined to be living 'irregularly' or in a situation of 'moral or social risk'. The state took these children into its indefinite care, while providing no protection or assistance for parents who, however poor or indigent, wished to keep their children. A network of largely unregulated children's homes was established to keep such children out of sight, and out of the way, of 'respectable' society. As late as 2003, it was estimated that around over 15,000 children were living in poorly run and ill-maintained care homes in the province of Buenos Aires alone. The regime in most homes was punitive and children's rights to privacy, emotional and physical respect, and education were consistently violated (Grugel and Peruzzotti 2007).

Poor children are also vulnerable to violence by the agents of the state, especially the police. In Central America:

> Children are frequently victims of social cleansing phenomena. In Honduras and Guatemala, for instance, they are summarily executed by private or public agents or paramilitary groups, who are sometimes even recruited by residents. Governments [sometimes] justify these actions ... Those responsible enjoy total immunity. An alternative report on Guatemala ... to the UN Committee Against Torture in May 2006 stressed the violence of attacks on children, citing the discovery of the bodies of two children living on the street: Heidy Mariol Ruano, 14 years old, stabbed 76 times and Mario Estuardo Esquivel, headless, whose killers have still not been apprehended.
>
> (OMCT 2006)

At the Regional Consultation between Latin American governments and the UN prior to the UN Secretary General's study on violence against children (Pinheiro 2006), the scale of violence in correctional institutions, which can include forced electric shocks, beatings and ritualistic humiliation, was particularly condemned and concern was expressed about the deaths of children in police custody in several countries in the region. In Argentina, according to local NGOs, at least 470 young people were killed by the police in extra-judicial executions between 1983 and 1998 (*Colectivo de ONGs de la Infancia y Adolescencia* 2002: 37). In many cases, the police appear to be able to tamper with evidence and thereby avoid prosecution (Smulovitz and Peruzzotti 2003).

Children and the consequence of civil war

Latin American countries have histories of violent civil conflict and many thousands of children have been traumatized and impoverished by war. Children have been recruited directly into guerrilla and paramilitary organizations, most recently in Colombia where civil conflict is still prevalent. It is estimated that there are around 11,000 child soldiers under the age of 15 fighting in Colombia (Human Rights Watch 2005), despite international pressure and promises by governments, guerrillas and paramilitary organizations to change. Such children are exposed to violence (and encouraged to commit acts of violence themselves), do not have access to education and are often deprived of appropriate family support; girls can find themselves subject to gender-based violence. At the core of the problem is the refusal by adults to see young people as children and a failure on the part of the state to recognize its duty of care to each child as an individual. This is, of course, not a new problem. In Argentina during the military dictatorship of 1976–1983, children became legitimate targets of state terror and the children of 'the enemy' were regarded as part of the booty of war. The coup in 1976 was followed by massive repression of the civilian population, during which many young people were kidnapped, imprisoned, tortured or disappeared. Even children who tried to organize local petitions for cheaper bus fares to school were treated as adult 'subversives'. Nearly 250 teenagers between the ages of 13 and 18 disappeared, most of whom were also brutally tortured (Robben 2005: 229). Children as young as three or four were forced to watch their parents being tortured and abused. A considerable number of babies were kidnapped and sent to live with military officials who then adopted them. Children were treated, in short, as a means to an end – namely, to break and traumatize adults and to refashion society and family into more conservative moulds (Robben 2005).

Violent conflict, if experienced as a child, leaves a traumatic legacy that is difficult to overcome. In Central America, the decades of civil wars are now over. But the emotional, social and economic needs of ex-child combatants and witnesses to violence have not been recognized; and the social and personal costs of displacement at a young age have not been considered. Guns and violence remain prevalent in most Central American societies. In this context, children experience violent death as commonplace. It has become normalized as an inevitable part of the human experience (Scheper-Hughes 1992). One way of surviving socially and physically in a context where adults can rarely be trusted and the state is a source of repression can be to form a social world peopled in a meaningful way only by other young people. Friendship and a sense of social belonging can come from belonging to a gang. Violence between gangs has been made worse by the fact that Central America has become a fixed point in the route to the USA for drug shipments to North America. From the perspective of states, however, the gangs are not alternative worlds for young people trying to live in a hostile environment but simply a law and order problem. In something of a re-run of the debate about the children of the urban poor early in the twentieth century, which led to punitive policies of separation and institutionalization, the gangs are constructed as a threat to 'respectable' society. As such, they have merited a tough law and order response, known as *'mano dura'* or *'super mano dura'*, which means, in effect, criminalizing even gang membership. In the process, as Forter (2006: 174) explains, the rights of young people are being severely eroded:

> Previously, El Salvador and Honduras had implemented significant reforms including specialized procedures and legal norms for the treatment of juveniles in conflict with the law. This exceptional process, however, was revoked under anti-gang legislation resulting in recognition and treatment of juveniles as equivalent to adult criminals. The result, in relation to human rights standards, has been significant conflict with universal rights treaties and more specific international law regarding the treatment of children. The most fundamental principle of human rights law challenged by anti-gang legislation is the right to association. The association with gangs is criminalized under the legal interventions of both El Salvador and Honduras as illicit associations. In this way, it is not necessary to wait for the committing of a criminal act, but belonging to the gang in itself is one, and consequently, by affiliating with the group, detention and condemnation of members is possible.

This is despire evidence, that, as Pinheiro (2006) shows, gang members are victims of poverty and dislocation:

> A survey of 1025 gang men in the greater metropolitan area of San Salvador found that 75.5 per cent of the respondents were unemployed and amongst those employed only half held stable jobs. Only 32 per cent had finished high school.
>
> (Pinheiro 2006: 355)

The CRC: changing advocacy

Advocacy for, and sometimes even by, children pre-dates the CRC in Latin America. Child-focused NGOs are a relatively important sub-set of local NGOs. But the CRC has concentrated the attention of rights and development NGOs on children in a more focused way and, especially in countries where there are strong networks of NGOs, it has contributed to changing how child-centred advocacy works (Grugel and Peruzzotti 2007). The CRC has provided national and international advocacy groups with a justifying frame for making claims, denouncing abuses and demanding rights, and it has led to greater cooperation between local and international organizations in claims-making. UN organization and other international agencies play an important role in research and information provision and sometimes offer support that legitimizes local campaigns. It has forced NGOs to think about constructing networks and alliances and to work together at national and sometimes regional levels. Overall, there is now more advocacy and the tone of claims-making is more confident. In some cases, the CRC has even encouraged a direct engagement with children and young people themselves in deciding agendas.

As a result, different kinds of campaigns have emerged. In contrast to traditional social movement campaigning, however, dependent on large-scale, mass pressure on governments, child-centred advocacy has tended to rely on persuading elites to make changes incrementally. The UN campaign against violence to children, which is about raising awareness and documenting violations as much as making policy changes, is typical in this respect. Another tactic has been the judicialization of claims on behalf of children and young people – a strategy used by human rights groups to good effect in campaigns in the 1970s and 1980s. The struggle for reproductive rights for adolescents is a good example here. Only rarely, however, have campaigns directly included children and young people themselves. On the whole, campaigns have focused on what NGOs see as achievable goals. This has meant, in effect, prioritizing claims that can be addressed by legislative change rather than economic redistribution.

Shaping regional campaigns: global values and the UN campaign against violence

The UN's decision to undertake a global study of violence against children is typical of how children's rights are now being put on the global agenda. Pablo Pinheiro was appointed as Special Rapporteur to lead the study (Pinheiro 2006). The study was supported by UNICEF, in conjunction with international NGOs including Save the Children and TearFund. In so far as Latin America is concerned, it has been actively promoted by the Inter-American Commission of Human Rights. The campaign has engaged governments in thinking about violence and it has captured media attention by depicting the pervasiveness of violence, of all forms, across the region. It has successfully put violence against children on the agenda in a region where, perhaps remarkably, it had been hidden hitherto. In this context, Buvinic *et al.*'s (1999: 48) report is worthy of note:

Estimates place the number of children suffering severe abuse in the region, including abandonment, at 6 million and indicate that 80,000 children die each year as result of parental abuse. One of the few existing population based surveys reveals the magnitude of the problem of domestic violence against children. A full 63 per cent of Chilean children in eighth grade (drawn from a nationally representative sample of 1,533 children) reported that they had suffered physical violence in the home; 34 per cent of them indicated having suffered severe physical abuse, suggesting that serious abuse against children is as great or greater than similar abuse against women.

(Buvinic *et al.* 1999)

It is not surprising, in the light of this, that Pinheiro (2006) judged Latin America one of the most violent regions of the world and explained the prevalence of violence through the existence of deeply rooted regional norms that deny voice and agency to children and emphasize instead hierarchy, discipline and conformity. Physical violence against children is seen as necessary to discipline and educate them.

High levels of violence against children, whether in the workplace, the home or on the streets, have remained hidden until now mainly because violence is experienced differentially by different children. While all children are vulnerable to domestic violence in particular, institutional violence, the violence of abuse and poverty, and violence in the workplace tend to be experienced by poor children. Such children have few resources with which to deal with it and few allies in the adult world who can help them construct ways of defending themselves. Working children and those living on the streets, of which there may be as many as 40 million across the region, are likely to experience institutional violence almost on a daily basis, even though many will not even see as it as abuse – it is simply what is. Violence is also omnipresent in street culture. Many more experience violence as part of the criminal justice and prison systems. But because violence against children has such obvious class connotations, it was often identified as a part of the burden of poverty, rather than violence that the state has an obligation to prevent.

Pinheiro's report changes the construction of abuse and violence in the region and places responsibilities squarely on states to respond. And there is some indication that the high profile of the UN campaign is leading to some gradual rhetorical change within states. Certainly there is a growing sense of awareness that violence on the current scale is not acceptable. In June 2005, Latin American and Caribbean Heads of State signed the Buenos Aires Declaration on Violence against Children, which commits regional governments to creating effective public policies to eliminate violence from children's lives. There is also a growing interest in Latin America in creating child-friendly cities that include spaces where children can feel secure. Nevertheless, it remains to be seen how far these initiatives represent genuine commitments to implementing substantive policy changes.

Judicializing claims: the reproductive rights of girls

Reproductive rights are a good example of how the CRC has allowed rights to enter national and regional policy domains that have typically been dominated by conservative interests. Deep-seated cultural opposition to the sexual agency of women and young people has meant that access to effective, safe family planning remains a major problem in Latin America.

The reproductive rights of women of all ages were recognized by the Cairo Consensus of 1994 and reaffirmed at the UN World Summit in 2005. The CRC explicitly extends these rights to adolescents. Article 24 refers to the importance for governments of developing family-planning services; moreover, the tenor of the CRC is to uphold the primacy of the views and wishes of the child or young person. For the UN, the meaning of reproductive rights for young people is clear: governments must remove the barriers that prevent adolescents making informed decisions about their sexual health. Nevertheless, regional governments have been notoriously slow to take these obligations seriously and many have put considerable obstacles in their path. Although some countries, Brazil most notably, have introduced contraceptive policies that are designed to address the growing problem of HIV/AIDS, policies are not framed in ways that empower and uphold the rights of adolescent girls. Legal access to condoms has little meaning where girls and women are not in a position to take decisions about family planning, and where adolescent marriage and childbirth are common, despite the health, education and quality of life implications they carry with them for young women. Across the region, teenage pregnancies are a leading cause of death in the 15–24 age group (Henriques-Mueller and Yunes 1993). Some countries still authorize legal marriage for girls as young as 14. Around 34 per cent of women have their first child before the age of 20 and between 25 and 50 per cent of teenage pregnancies are unwanted (Henriques-Mueller and Yunes 1993). In short, there are serious concerns as to whether governments are taking appropriate steps to protect the reproductive rights of girls.

Cultural barriers to extending reproductive rights to adolescents are considerable and the Catholic Church has tried to prevent campaigns to extend awareness and access to contraception and abortion. Where states have been more active, is in terms of supporting teenagers once they become mothers (Pereira forthcoming). But this approach is not fully rights-focused, does not challenge the problem of rising rates of HIV infection and, by legitimizing girls dropping out of education, it may even contribute to the persistent gender inequity in pay and employment. Even where laws exist that formally guarantee access to contraception, it is often blocked in practice. In Argentina, for example, which is currently experiencing unprecedented levels of pregnancies among even the 10–14 age group, a sexual and reproductive health law was passed in 2006 but it is still not operative because of conservative opposition. In some countries, there has even been a roll-back as far as access to contraception and abortion are concerned. In reversals of previously more liberal legislation (though still strict by most European standards), abortion has recently been banned in El Salvador, Nicaragua and Chile even when the life of the mother is in danger. In a continent where around four million abortions are performed annually – partly because contraception is often difficult to obtain, especially for young women – this means safe and hygienic abortions are only available to rich women able to go abroad or pay doctors sufficient to persuade them to break the law. The new laws go hand in hand with a decision to actively seek to prosecute women and adolescents who procure abortions illegally. In El Salvador, where 41.6 per cent of women have their first child before the age of 20 (Center for Reproductive Rights 2001) and teenagers rarely have access to contraception, the 1998 law penalizing abortion in all circumstances is a considerable block on the rights of adolescent, to take decisions about their bodies.

This situation is one of concern to international human rights and health organizations and to local rights-based organizations. Moreover, the rising tempo of prosecutions for women who seek abortions creates a climate of real hostility and makes demanding any kind of reproductive rights difficult locally. Once again, there is a clear class bias in the state behaviour – poor women are being victimized and used as 'examples' by the state. One response within the NGO community has been to try and challenge state policies in the courts. An alliance of international human rights and health organizations, including the International Women's Health Coalition, the Centre for Reproductive Rights, and women's organizations in Latin America, with support from the UN Population Fund in particular, is challenging both individual abuses and the new abortion laws through the Inter-American Court of Justice. Although the cases being taken to the Court are individual, there is the hope that victory, which may involve compensation payments for victims, will lead to states re-thinking their policies. One case involved an adolescent in Peru who was refused a termination requested on the grounds of severe fetal abnormality; another was a 13-year-old in Mexico who was refused an abortion after being raped. Moreover, in 2006, following pressure from international rights-based groups, the Inter-American Commission condemned the law banning even therapeutic abortions in Nicaragua on the grounds that it is violation of the rights of women and girls.

Bringing children in: street children in Brazil campaign for rights

Most campaigns for children's rights in Latin America are led and fronted by adults from civil society organizations. But, occasionally, children have managed to exercise agency and demand rights for themselves. One example of this is the campaign by Brazilian street children to win rights for themselves.

'Street' children are undoubtedly now the most visible manifestation of the problems of child poverty and social exclusion in Latin America and the discovery that children were living and working on the street, often putting themselves at risk, provoked a reaction from the global media even before the CRC. Although estimates indicate that around 40 million children live and work on the streets in Latin America, more than anywhere else, 'street' children were 'discovered in' Brazil (Hecht 1998) because of the campaign of eradicating such children in the 1980s:

> Over the past decade, street children, especially in Brazil, have become a focus of attention of the media, featured everywhere from the New York Times to Amnesty International Reports, BBC evening news to the Ladies Home Journal ... Lucrative direct mail campaigns have been launched in the US to raise money for projects with street children, And street children have proved a dubious curiosity for visitors to Brazil [and] a favourite subject of photographers ... Street children have been made something of a Brazilian cultural emblem.
>
> (Hecht 1998: 3)

The global campaign of raising awareness about the existence of such children created an opportunity for the children to organize themselves, at least temporarily. In the context of widespread social movement politics in the 1980s in Brazil and a democratic opening-up of the political structures, some children seized the opportunity to speak for themselves. This kind of agency by children is crucial if the CRC is genuinely to address the needs of children; but, because it rarely happens, it makes the movement in Brazil all the more remarkable. A national Street Children Movement was established in 1985, in a similar way that to the emergence of other kinds of social protest organizations at the time. Following traditional patterns of social movement organization in Brazil, a conference was held in the capital Brasilia to define the problem and try and win the ears of government. More than 500 children attended (Rizzini *et al.* 1992). The inadequate and often violent response of the state to children living or working on the streets was a recurrent theme of the conference and many children used it to offer personal testimonies of the abuse they encountered when they came into contact with the police and the State Foundation for the Welfare of Minors (FUNABEM). So, it was both the international encounter with street children, in conjunction with pressure from inside Brazil and, indeed, from the children themselves, that forced the government to acknowledge the existence of children on the streets. The children at the conference put together a petition that was then signed by over a million others. Coinciding with the beginning of democratization, the petition created a willingness in government to respond. The result was the inclusion of a detailed charter of children's rights in the Constitution of 1988 and a new Children's Code, based on the CRC, in 1990. The Code decreed that all children had the right to 'life, health, food, education, sports, leisure, preparation for a future profession, culture, dignity, respect and liberty' (Article 4). Children were no longer to be treated as legal minors but as full rights-bearing individuals. The children were thus crucial in achieving an important legal victory, even though the Code has not really shaped policies in the ways that they hoped for.

States' responses to the CRC

We can see from the discussion above that the key to effective advocacy is putting issues on the agenda of states – and forcing states to see through an effective policy response. But, unfortunately, the CRC has served states mainly as a vehicle for declaring their good intentions, not as a blueprint for reform. Democratization in Latin America in the 1980s meant that states were keen to ratify international rights treaties as an external signal of their return to the international community. Latin American states were therefore all among the first wave of countries to sign and ratify the CRC. But there have been few signs of a shift from discursive acceptance of children as rights-bearing people to the embrace of a reform agenda, and not many direct improvements to the well-being or security of children (Grugel 2007b). Some countries have introduced legislative change that defines children, formally at least, as rights-bearing subjects; others have resisted even this. Some have made some changes, mainly of a bureaucratic nature, to how welfare and services are delivered. Many have formed closer relationships with children's NGOs, often in the hope that NGOs will deliver services for children on their behalf. But overall, state agencies have been able to avoid fulfilling their obligations to children. Children remain largely invisible in the domain of policy-making. Child protection systems are rarely thought about, yet alone in place. There is, in short, a huge gap between the legal obligations states have assumed and the actual behaviour of state agencies.

There are three reasons for this. First, and most importantly, there is the issue of the state. State biases, which explain children's exclusion in the first place, mean that there is still a generalized tolerance within the state of government failure with regard to children. Children are seen as peripheral to politics, and pre-CRC ideas that locate children exclusively within the private sphere (except for those who are deviant and must be disciplined for the sake of 'respectable' society) persist within the formal and informal structures of contemporary democratic regimes. State elites still do not see children as having welfare claims in their own right. Even within the judiciary and the legal profession, many of whom welcomed the CRC, there is still a reluctance to see children's rights as justiciable, especially with regard to social and economic entitlements (Van Bueren 1999). Issues of state capacity, meanwhile, raise doubts as to whether rights can be effectively delivered, at least within in a reasonable time frame. Resource scarcity,

tax-gathering deficits and budgetary constraints undoubtedly make it difficult for governments to respond quickly and effectively to the needs of
children. Moreover, the CRC envisages only that governments will implement according to the 'maximum extent of their available resources' (Article
4), which gives licence to states to argue that they need only to make partial
and slow progress towards implementation. Finally, because children are
not voters, there is no pressing electoral need for governments to take their
wishes and needs into consideration.

Secondly, there is the unwieldiness of rights as a tool for public policy. As
we discussed in Chapter 1, rights do not easily make the transition to policies (Grugel 2007b). Whose rights? Which rights first? Should legal reform
come first or should states address socio-economic violations? Resolving
these questions is extremely difficult. Moreover, sometimes there are confusions as to what rights actually mean. Fonseca (2002) uses adoption policies
in Brazil as an example of how rights-based policies can actually backfire
for children. In Brazil, 'informal' adoptions, where children live outside
their birth family, have traditionally served as a coping mechanism for poor
households. They were made illegal after the CRC and family courts have
insisted, as far as they are able, that all adoption processes must be legally
ratified by the courts. This has sometimes forced poor families to give up
their children or to conform with non-traditional patterns of child-rearing
that are foreign to them. It has also had the unintended consequence of
stimulating transnational adoptions of children from low-income families,
allowing the state to register children placed temporarily in care as abandoned and then to put them on international adoption registers. Rights
have been used here to justify punishing the poor. Thirdly, there is strong
social opposition to the concept of children's rights, especially from conservative elites across the region.

In short, progress towards alleviating rights and addressing the needs of
vulnerable children has been extremely slow across the region. This is not to
say that nothing has changed at all – but the pace of change is slow and,
when change does take place, it tends to be in the shape of legal, rather than
substantive, reform. We can illustrate this with a case study from Argentina.

Argentina: state neglect, reluctant reform and the limitations of rights claims

Like everywhere else in Latin America, children in Argentina are the principal victims of poverty, state neglect and embedded practices of political,
social and economic exclusion. Nevertheless, the scale of childhood deprivation was largely hidden from view, at home and abroad, because of the
persistent twentieth-century myth of Argentine exceptionalism and relative
prosperity. Poverty was traditionally regarded as a problem only in the
poorest and relatively under-populated regions in the North; but both
urban, and rural poverty are, in fact, widespread throughout the country. It

was only with economic meltdown in 2001, and the onset of the most intense economic crisis ever to hit the country, that the pitiful lives led by most children in Argentina became clear. Between 50 and 70 per cent of children live in poverty – the figure varies depending on the source – and the indications are that childhood deprivation is structural; it certainly seems to be untouched by the trend of economic growth since 2003 (Grugel and Riggirozzi 2007). A UNICEF report in 2002 noted that:

> 53 per cent of children and young people under 18, more than six million live in poor households ... 46.7 per cent of the almost 14 million of poor people in the country are minors who belong to families that do not have sufficient income to obtain basic goods such as housing, warm clothes, health and education.
>
> (UNICEF 2002b: 36)

Living standards for children and young people, moreover, seem even to be declining: there are now 2,300,000 more children living in poverty than in 1992 (UNICEF 2002b). Despite official statistics of around 98 per cent literacy, school attendance is falling year on year and, within Buenos Aires alone, at least 12,000 children aged ten and 11 have no idea at all how to read or write (UNICEF 2002b).

A state culture, marked out by a combination of neglect and discipline, largely explains the prevalence of childhood poverty and marginalization, and it has shaped the lived experiences and expectations of poor children. Three examples serve as illustrations: the state's decision to separate poor children from their families with the onset of mass urbanization and immigration in the twentieth century if they were deemed 'unruly'; widespread but ignored violence against poor children by the police and criminal justice system; and the utter failure on the part of the state to respond to the needs of poor children and young people in the economic collapse of 2001.

Argentina developed an extensive system of care homes after the 1919 state-building *Ley del Patronato de Menores* (the Law of the Minor), which gave the state comprehensive jurisdiction over children and young people at the time. The *Ley del Patronato* was designed to address perceived law and order problems associated with the massive influx of poor Europeans and their families into the country. At the time, around 20 per cent of the population of Buenos Aires was aged between six and 15, and the street was regarded as having become unsafe for the middle and upper classes (Grugel and Peruzzotti 2007). As such, the law was designed specifically to discipline the children of the urban poor and those who were deemed to be abandoned, living 'irregularly' or in a situation of 'moral or social risk'. For children of the middle and upper classes the hand of the state barely registered, while poor children grew up with a fear of state agencies and lived under the threat of being separated from their families. Under the *Ley del Patronato*, the family courts were empowered to take children into the custody of the state and order their indefinite detention, and they began to use this power freely and without fear of contradiction, a policy that meant, in effect, criminalizing poverty (Garcia Mendez 1998). Perhaps not surprisingly, many children went from the care homes to the prison system. 85 per cent of the prison population in Buenos Aires today is under 28, 75 per cent of which passed through the care home system as children and adolescents.

Our second example is violence by state and criminal justice agencies. Poor children and youths have always been vulnerable to abuse by the police when they are on the streets and in public spaces – sometimes, even, in their own homes. Indiscriminate police violence is a constant risk. Heavy-handed tactics and violent policing, and the fact that children and young people are systematically injured and killed by police are issues that have been taken up by local and international human rights NGOs since the 1980s. Despite a transition to democracy which is in many ways regarded as exemplary, at least 470 young people were executed by the police between 1983 and 1998, of which almost half were in the province of Buenos Aires (*Colectivo de Derechos de la Infancia y Adolescencia* 2002: 37). Police violence against poor youths following arrest is also common (Amnesty International 2002; *Colectivo de Derechos de la Infancia y Adolescencia* 2002). Meanwhile, those children and young people under 16 who make it to the criminal courts can find themselves dealt with under legislation which dates from the 1970s – the period of the dictatorship – which allows the courts to order indefinite detention without trial (Beloff 1997).

Although the CRC was incorporated into the Argentine constitution in 1994, there was no follow-up reform programme. As a result, the conclusion of the OHCHR following Argentina's report to the UN in 2002 was remarkably critical. Issues of concern included the failure to guarantee health and education for vulnerable children; high drop-out rates from education for poor children; police brutality against children; domestic violence (the introduction of a new law notwithstanding); high infant, child and maternal mortality rates; increasing rates of malnutrition; growing number of cases of HIV/AIDS among youth and a failure by the state to institute policies to tackle the problem; a lack of state awareness about the needs of disabled children; a steady reduction in education spending on the part of the state; the growing number of economically exploited children under 14 years of age; an increase in child prostitution, especially in big cities; the lack of coordinated policies and programmes to combat the commercial sexual exploitation of children; and the poor conditions of children in detention.

The OHCHR report wound up by expressing a view that progress towards implementation would continue to be problematic unless childhood poverty was comprehensively and energetically tackled by the government. It is interesting, therefore, to note the nature of state responses to the economic collapse after 2001. Despite reports of family breakdown, homelessness, widespread hunger, a collapse in school attendance in many poor and peripheral communities, rising levels of prostitution and a growth in child labour and the number of children engaged in hazardous forms of self-generated employment – and, indeed, despite the 2002 OHCHR report – the transitional government of Eduardo Duhalde concentrated its welfare resources on programmes that focused on providing heads of households with income. *Plan Trabajar* (later *Programa Jefes y Jefas de Hogar*), which was introduced with World Bank support, provided approximately US$50 a month to household heads irrespective of family size. *Jefes y Jefas* has since become a semi-permanent subsidy operating within the context of the clientelistic networks that have typically characterized Argentine social spending (Grugel and Riggirozzi 2007). It serves as a good example of how engrained patterns for welfare spending are re-enacted, even in emergency situations. Some five years after the onset of the economic crisis, no specific state programmes to get children back into education or set up training schemes for youth unemployed have been introduced, although there is considerable statistical evidence that, despite growth after 2003, the employment prospects of poor youth have not improved (Grugel and Riggirozzi 2007).

The crisis, international pressure from the OHCHR and UNICEF, and local pressure from rights organizations eventually led to state revision of the law on children. By 2002, the two main networks of children's NGOs, the *Comité de Seguimiento y Aplicación de la Convención sobre los Derechos del Niño* (CSACIDN) and the *Colectivo de Derechos de Infancia y Adolescencia de Argentina*, had established three main goals, two of which centred on the need to introduce new national legislation: replacing the *Ley del Patronato*; reforming juvenile justice; and the introduction of a universal benefit for children (interview with Silvia Stucklick, president of CSACIDN, November 2005). In practice, however between 2001 and 2005, almost all campaigning was focused on the first aim – namely, the need for a new Children's Code.

The reasons why children's NGOs decided to prioritize legal reform are complex. In the first place, for many NGOs, the *Patronato* was the root cause of poverty and marginalization, so over-turning it made sense. It was certainly clear that the influence of the *Patronato* continued to shape decisions in the family courts, which, it seemed, virtually ignored the CRC in terms of decision-making:

> Argentina is a leading example now in terms of the application of human rights' treaties, but this is not the case with respect to childhood. The Supreme Court has behaved impeccably when it comes to fulfilling the letter of international human rights treaties, and treated them as part of the constitution even before they were. Argentine jurisprudence

has considered them obligatory points of reference ... [yet] when it comes to childhood, we don't see the same sensitivity. This is essentially to do with institutional resistance: [the state continues to see the child in terms] of the *Patronato.* The[re is] resistance is in the family and juvenile courts.

(Interview with human rights lawyer, December 2005)

But it is also the case, nevertheless, that children in Argentina experience multiple forms of exclusion. Moreover, socio-economic and welfare needs were extremely pressing in 2001 and 2002 when the campaign for legal reform was taking shape. In this context, it is interesting that hierarchy of concerns was established, with legal reform at the top.

Although the first two attempts at reform failed, one because of the contentious issue of reproductive rights, a new law was eventually passed in September 2005, the *Ley de Protección Integral de los Derechos del Niño.* The new law makes few specific policy commitments in terms of children's services. Instead, it sets out to achieve a sea change in state–children relations by insisting that the state must treat children as subjects of rights, and it sets up the state as the guarantor of those rights. On paper a very wide-ranging law, in practice the impact of the *Ley Integral* so far has largely been confined to the care home system. Changes here are undoubtedly being introduced, consisting for the most part of passing the responsibility for care onto service-based NGOs, although it is not clear yet that the new services will necessarily be run any better, since there appear to be few child protection policies in place. Other kinds of changes – children's budgets, for example, educational reform or well-funded campaigns around sexual health and reproductive rights, all of which are urgently required – are slower or non-existent. In fact, the meaning of the new law in terms of the detail of policy is very unclear. Although the state has undertaken to rethink its relationship and its responsibilities towards children, there are few signs that government has reflected seriously on what this might mean. Children did not figure, for example, in the debate over how to spend the windfall bonanza that Argentina gathered after the introduction of export taxes after 2003 and the government chose instead to pay the IMF in full, even though the monies could have been used effectively to pay for services for children (see Grugel and Riggirozzi 2007). It seems that the many obstacles to child-centred social and economic reforms – embedded state preferences, budgetary constraints and choices, the tax system and tax collection, vested interests, etc. – remain untouched by the new law. It is hard to escape the view, in short, that, from the perspective of the state, whatever the intentions of government, the introduction of the new law has offered an easy, high-profile, visible and measurable proof of its commitment to the CRC and the principle of legal rights for children, without having to introduce other more substantive, costly or socially divisive reforms.

Conclusion

What are we to make of the introduction of rights-based governance for children in Latin America? Certainly, the CRC has made children more visible in the region. Policy-makers, international organizations, local groups and sometimes even children themselves have a much greater awareness of how states *should* treat children. Equally, however, there are serious limitations in practice as to what rights politics has achieved. Indeed, children seem to grasp perfectly the disparity between rights in theory and rights in practice, if the children interviewed by Snodgrass Godoy (1999) in Guatemala in the mid-1990s are anything to judge by. Talking about how the police and other institutions of the state treat them, one said:

> We have rights ... but if they surround you and you tell them 'we have rights too. We have rights too.' 'Why do you have rights? The only right you have is the right to be killed.' That's what they say to you ... Our right is the right to be killed. The police will kill us for being on the street, for not going home, for not having a family. Rights aren't worth a lot to us.
>
> (Godoy 1999: 423)

But, despite the failures of government to implement changes – and in some cases even to make the plight of children and young people worse – it would be wrong to conclude that nothing has changed. The CRC has changed the tenor of demands on behalf of children, led to serious research that details the lives of children in the region and mobilized communities to press for claims on their behalf. Sometimes it has even mobilized children themselves. Moreover, it has made governments aware that they must, at least, make a rhetorical show of addressing the needs of children. Latin American governments are susceptible to international pressures and they are therefore willing to make legal changes that formally guarantee rights to children. The problem is that the social and economic capital, far more than the constitutional and legal change, shapes policy outcomes. This means that states promise reform but rarely deliver it. Changing this requires more than advocacy: it requires root and branch reform of the state and political practices as a whole.

Conclusion

Over the space of the last seven chapters, we have discussed the scope and effectiveness of rights-based governance, not only in attaching a rights framework to emerging governance regimes and discourses, but also in terms of their utility for claiming rights in practice. In exploring how the architecture and instruments of global governance provide new spaces for political activism, as well as obstacles, our central argument, drawn from our regional case studies, points to the importance of *claiming* rights. But making claims requires first that issues such as poverty, workplace conditions or social exclusion are conceptualized, in a collective way, as rights *violations*. Constitutionalizing rights globally certainly makes it more possible to understand marginalization as a violation of rights. On its own, however, codifying rights is not enough to make effective redress possible. In order to be effective on the ground, rights must go beyond the purely legal domain, inherent in conceptions of liberal global governance as the 'the rule of law' or 'good governance'. They must inform state policies. For this to happen, ordinary people, or civil society groups that represent them, must be able to lay claim effectively to the rights they hold in theory (see Hertel 2006). This argument derives from our case studies, which represent some of the most marginalized groups of people in two different regions of the South: children and foreign workers. It also stems from a perspective that puts ordinary people as the central concern of research on global governance. By taking a 'bottom-up' perspective, the starting point of our discussion has been the possibilities and limitations opened for human rights activism by emerging global rights frames. In this way, our study marks a shift from a vision of liberal global governance as a way to manage ordinary people, to one which posits global governance as a potential opportunity structure for activism as well as a space of regulation.

A discussion of the emergence of rights-based 'soft' global governance has been, in short, the first strand of this book, while the second strand has been to uncover some of the spaces where rights-based activism emerges and from where rights claims are being made from within civil society. In this way, we establish a link between global governance, rights-based regimes (norms, laws, institutions) and people – an important gap left by the existing literatures (from various disciplinary backgrounds) on governance. Emphasizing the role of civil society in claiming rights, or making rights real, ties in with the fact that global human rights are historically still a relatively new concept and remain very much 'work in progress', a product of ongoing socio-political struggles in an era of enhanced economic globalization. Our argument here concurs with research that suggests that state compliance with global human rights regimes reflects, above all, the dynamic of civil society organization and state–society relations (Keck and Sikkink 1998; Neumayer 2005). We suggest, moreover, that rights-based civil society activism can be effective at the local and regional, as well as the transnational, level, and must be explored at all three levels. Nonetheless, we are aware of the very real obstacles and difficulties in the way of claims-making. Let us begin to explore these arguments in more detail from the 'bottom up' – our case studies.

Children and migrants

On a broad level, poor children and migrants are two groups with a lot in common. They are both among the most marginalized and invisible groups in all societies. In both cases, there are considerable obstacles to their self-organization into effective social movements, whether at the local, national, regional or global levels. When they participate in the labour market, they can be found at the very bottom of the hierarchy, performing work nobody else wants to do in sectors such as agriculture, domestic work, in factories that are at the bottom of global-production chains and sex tourism. They are often 'undocumented' – children may lack a birth certificate and migrant workers frequently lack a legal permit – and many lead 'irregular' lives. They are victims of social cleansing (deportation, violence, killing) and, from the perspective of the state, they are often treated as a 'law and order problem' (national security) rather than from the angle of human rights (human security). Their issues and concerns are often hidden from mainstream society and the attention of the wider public. When they become visible to the wider public, interest can be merely voyeuristic or temporary – newspapers have typically focused on gang violence or death squads with regard to children and, with regard to migrants, the focus often is on the migrant as simply a victim, with an emphasis on the violence and suffering experienced by migrants in the search for work. There is still little public awareness of their day-to-day roles in society and the economy. As a result, they suffer high levels of social exclusion and are targets of low, if any, social spending. They remain largely invisible in policy-making also. Children are regarded firmly as part of the private sphere, with the result that adults, carers and 'responsible' family members are generally supposed to speak for them; with regard to migrants, their transnationality (being simultaneous 'constituents' of both origin and destination countries) means that state responsibilities are difficult to attribute and easy to evade. Both our case studies show the limitations of political enfranchisement with regard to people who are not among the voting population, either because of their age or their non-citizenship status in the country in which they work.

In sum, children and migrants are largely invisible in domestic politics; they face particular difficulties in terms of organizing to defend themselves; and they are both regarded as beyond the pale of citizenship. The result is that both groups face immense difficulties in winning, for themselves, a discursive recognition of their rights or policies that aim to challenge their poverty and/or social marginalization. Global activism, changing intellectual conceptions of personhood and the opportunities of the liberal 'moment' after 1989 have certainly meant some global advances in terms of a legal codification of their rights. In the case of both the CRC and the CRM, ratification of global rights-based constitutions has meant some change to their status. But the direct policy responses after ratification of the CRC and CRM have been really quite thin. Governments have undoubtedly been able to avoid the full implications of rights-based governance, in so far as children and migrants are concerned.

Nevertheless, the global codification of rights has meant, at least in some cases, that children and migrant communities are learning to frame aspects of their lives in the context of rights and rights violations. And, more significantly, it has transformed advocacy strategies on behalf of both groups. Both the CRC and CRM have allowed NGOs, at the local, regional and global levels, to concentrate on rights in a more focused manner and the tone of claims-making has become more confident. Constitutionalizing rights globally has also changed the language of claims from below. But rarely have campaigns directly included children or migrants themselves. Especially with regard to children, consultations at the global level are just beginning to take off, although these are, arguably, more a matter of publicity than a genuine vehicle for children's inclusion. We would suggest that it is vital for both groups to engage in self-organizing and, thus, achieve some degree of self-governance for rights to be taken more seriously. This certainly has not yet happened enough.

NGO activism has meant, nevertheless, that there is now much more awareness – among NGOs, within issue-specific networks, within the courts – about how children and migrants should be treated by states. In terms of both regions, our research points to greater knowledge, growing mobilization and some tentative advances in some issue areas, despite serious limitations in practice with regard to the achievements of rights politics.

At the same time we have expressed doubts as to what rights-based governance, in the context of massive inequalities, can achieve in terms of improving the well-being and lived realities of children and migrants at least in the short term. The problems are various. In addition to the difficulties of representation and voice described earlier, social and economic capital shape policy preferences and outcomes far more than constitutions and laws. For Morton (2006), this kind of global social marginalization is intrinsically rooted in capitalist development and the expansion of global markets. If this is the case, the impact of liberal rights can only even be a limited one because human rights claims will not be strong enough to contest material power. This explains why rights claims that address injustices based on economic, not political, disenfranchisement are so difficult to make. Beyond debates about the power of the capital, however, there are other issues. States have embedded preferences and it is always difficult for new claimants to be heard. State capacity, moreover, especially in the South, is limited. This means that the social reforms, which are so necessary for rights claims to be addressed, are hugely difficult to carry out in practice. It does not mean, in our view, that the partial victories that are possible, and which can make a significant difference to the quality of ordinary people's lives, are not worth pursuing.

Rights, activism, states and global governance: bridging the levels of interaction

When we take a rights-based approach, whether to development, governance or the law, we are, in effect, expressing a view that structural injustices constitute a violation of rights for individuals and communities. Rights-based approaches, therefore, raise questions as to the root causes of injustice and who bears the responsibility for redressing rights abuses and the provision of rights in general (Ellis 2006). The philosophical starting point for many rights-based approaches is a faith in the agency (as well as the entitlements) of ordinary people and a belief that they are capable of analysis, reflexivity and action. In practice, social action is generally understood to be collective action rather than individual efforts. Coalitions of ordinary people and civil society movements, whether within global, regional and local governance structures, are thus viewed as Janus-faced in that they simultaneously build collective identities within society that allow for the construction of common grievances and strategies of action, and serve as a conduit into, or a pressure on, elite policy debates, posited both at the national and the transnational level. In other words, social organizations such as trade unions, social movements and NGOs serve as crucial intermediaries between states and international institutions – the world of policy-making, in short – and society.

An important literature has emerged from the 1990s that has attempted to capture and theorize the different ways that these societal coalitions operate, organize and try to shape policy outcomes. The path-breaking work by Keck and Sikkink (1998) in particular on transnational advocacy networks kick-started a flurry of studies on the ways in which civil society organizations emerge and operate and, at least sometimes, are able to shape global politics in a more progressive direction. The result has been that we now understand much better how transnational NGOs and coalitions of civil society actors network at the global level. But there is something of a tendency to disregard the 'local', including the ways in which local NGOs, and trade unions, respond to changing global norms and the impact of those norms on their modes of organization. The emphasis, in sum, is on the 'scale shift', the diffusion of global values and the emergence of transnational collective action (Della Porta and Tarrow 2005). But this can mean that attention tends to slip away from the role of the state, and the continuing significance of local groups in advocacy out-comes can be overlooked (Grugel 2004).

In this book, we have consciously tried to redress this imbalance by refocusing attention on the specificities of place, geography and local and regional modes of organization. But we are not suggesting that local or regional social organizations should be understood in a manner dis-connected from global politics. What we are arguing for is a more detailed exploration of what Della Porta and Kriesi (1999: ix) refer to as the differ-ent ways in which 'social action in a given time and place is increasingly conditioned by social actions in very different places'. This means that there is a need to take into account the politics of the global when we examine local, as well as transnational, social movements. But it also means that we need to take into account the different ways in which states and regions also matter, both in terms of rights agendas and with regard to state responses. In some cases, regional institutional mechanisms, formal and informal, also play a tentative but emergent role, as with the Inter-American Court of Human Rights. We also suggest that there is a need to refocus attention on the authority of states, in the context of globalizing structures of authority and complex and overlapping forms of social protest. After all, simply from a formal-legal perspective of rights-based global regimes, the authority of the UN, the source of so many rights-based regimes, lies in the fact that it is a tiered system based on states. States also matter because they are the prin-cipal site where claims are made and policy changes implemented – whether pressure comes from local or transnational networks. And as our discussion shows, civil society can only achieve 'success' (whether incremental or pie-cemeal) when working *with* governments rather than *against* them.

Additionally, we suggest, and wanted to delineate, the complex and overlapping ways in which local NGOs and civil society organizations contribute, adapt to and use changes in global norms. One response from within civil society is to become what Tarrow (2001) refers to as 'rooted cosmopolitans' – that is, social activists who are rooted in specific national contexts but who regularly link up with activists from other countries in transnational networks. Activists of this sort are generally regarded as having 'multiple belongings' and 'flexible identities' (Della Porta and Tarrow 2005: 237). What is being emphasized here is the increasingly blurred distinction between transnational and local networking, and between transnational and local identities. But there are other ways in which the emergence of global norms can have an impact at local levels. Some activists remain, resolutely, local in their identity and their concerns focus entirely on local injustices and local rights claims. If we think, for example, of the network of local groups which pressured the Argentine state for legal changes that would formally recognize children as rights-bearing citizens after the ratification of the CRC, most activists had little or no direct connection with transnational networks. At most, they networked with local offices of international organizations such as UNICEF. Yet these groups were affected by, and aware of, changes in global politics. We have tried, in effect, to explore new ways in which global regulation and norm-based global governance transform activism at the local level, and we have tried to show how the targeting of vulnerable groups in international treaties can open up some possibilities for activism at the local level and change how small groups, apparently only loosely connected to global advocacy movements, frame grievances and engage in contention. We have shown how, with reference to migrant workers in the Philippines, for example, employment-based local rights claims are gradually emerging and, with reference to children in Latin America, how local struggles take place to introduce legal reform and child protection policies, led by local NGOs.

We hope that we have not painted an overly rosy view of civil society or an exaggerated image of what activism can achieve, whether at the local or the transnational level. There are many difficulties within civil societies that can prevent groups from forming effective alliances. It should also be remembered that civil society itself is a space of power struggles and contestation. Relations between activists are not always cooperative and they do not always pursue common goals. This is true at the local and the transnational levels. Both the transnational and the national non-state domains are spaces of dispute and contestation between different civil society actors, as well as between activists and states/global organizations. Activists, whether local or transnational, do not always agree on aims, strategies or processes. The issues around which rights struggles coalesce is an eminently political question that reflects, *inter alia*, which groups have voice and the relative authority of some groups from within society in comparison with others, relative capacity for organization, the ability to place issues on the political agenda and forge the necessary links with appropriate political leaders, and sometimes whether groups count on support from the state or not. The traditional dominance of urban over rural areas, and the social and political capital of (mainly) middle-class and highly educated activists, can play a dominating, and conflictual, role in shaping rights agendas at both local and transnational levels. All this means that, with regard to children and migrants, priorities in rights terms are certainly not agreed on: should social and economic reforms come first? What is the legitimate space for toleration of cultural differences in terms of policies for children and migrants? And should policies for children be in the context of family policy or children's entitlements be ring-fenced? Some of these disputes reflect technical disagreements about 'best' policy while others are a consequence of the very different ideological strands that influence children's and migrants' rights activists. Some are the result of differences between maximalist approaches and more pragmatic responses. And some reflect conflict between the different priorities of Northern activists and those from the South.

Civil society actors face a range of practical challenges when they try and influence local and global governance processes, including the fear of co-optation, the difficulty of deciding which goals to prioritize, the problem of alliances and the need for funding and campaigning, all of which can act as sources of division. States, meanwhile, sometimes co-opt groups and influence the agenda. The resultant differences between 'insider' and 'outsider' groups can lead to disputes between civil society groups that affect their capacity for effective mobilization. Equally, the relationship between transnational activists and local movements is not always harmonious. The possibility of what Klein (2001) calls 'activist solitudes' is ever present. Local groups may not feel represented by transnational activists who seem apparently more able to access global policy debates or shape global discourses. They may even feel left out, ignored or betrayed by transnational actors whom they see as assuming 'elite' roles in governance networks. Local groups, meanwhile, can all too easily be accused of not seeing the 'big picture'. As Tarrow (2005) points out, transnational activism carries with it an inherent risk of imposing an inappropriate frame for local struggles with the result that the momentum of local contention is lost or obscured. At the same time, unintended negative consequences can sometimes occur from relatively successful campaigns which affect relations between activists. Hertel (2006: 97–98) cites the example of a campaign to eliminate child labour in Bangladesh's garment industry. One result of taking girls off garment assembly was a loss of economic independence and a fall in self-esteem for adolescent girls who had previously been employed in clothing factories, with the consequence that they were unable to delay early marriage. Nevertheless, when transnational advocacy connects with local struggles, it can prove effective and it can resonate locally as well as globally. The campaigns for reproductive rights and against violence to children in Latin America serve as good examples here.

Although the literature on transnational advocacy is concerned with the ways in which international politics opens up opportunities for activism, the connection with emerging frames of global governance has rarely been made in a sufficiently direct way. As Della Porta and Tarrow (2005) point out, part of the problem lies with traditional modes of theorizing the international system. Neither realism nor liberalism allowed for the idea that international institutions could play a defining role in global order or act as a setter of global norms. Globalization studies, meanwhile, tended to emphasize the changing global architecture via an 'analytical economism' (Phillips 2005a) that ignored the agency of ordinary people and local social movements (Grugel 2005). All this meant that students of social movements, whether local or transnational, found it difficult to enter into a fruitful dialogue with scholars of international order. Fortunately, that is now changing. International institutions can become sites for contentious politics (Grugel 2006) and Della Porta and Tarrow (2005: 235–236) speak of, and analyse, some new opportunities for activism generated through a 'multilevel opportunity structure' or the emergent multi-level frames of governance. Bandy and Smith (2005: 232–233) explicitly link the emergence of some transnational networks to the activities of international organizations such as the UN. This link is strongest, it seems, in terms of the legitimacy UN activities have given to networks of human rights activists. We have tried to take this argument further by positing the notion that the impact of global norms of human rights can be seen not only through the development of transnational networks but also through changing strategies of local groups. In this way, global norms are becoming embedded in local contexts. The long term impact of this change is something that undoubtedly would repay further analysis.

Linking rights and development

In addition to a concern with rights and global governance, we have tried to link the emergence of human rights discourses to changing notions of development. In this, we draw on the view that established ideas of what constitutes development, usually understood in some way as a state-led project, are in crisis. Instead, development is increasingly posited as a process of individual and collective well-being or human betterment. This has provided a route for human rights to seep into discussions of development, aid and cooperation, and we outlined in Chapter 1 the ways in which notions of development have gradually come to reflect concerns about individual and collective rights and entitlements. We want to be clear – we are supportive of rights-based development and see the possibilities of linking a development agenda to global governance as a positive step forward and as important in and of itself. This is a significant path, we argue, to putting people and communities first. Equally, being able to lay claim to internationally and nationally codified human rights is very positive for marginalized communities and the civil society organizations and the groups which represent them. The international codification of rights, and the use of global rights constitutions within development strategies, can serve as a vital tool to redress wrongs done to groups such as children and migrants, even if codification does not fully take into account the causes of marginalization in the first place. Indeed, if rights-based governance does not embrace and address development needs, the whole edifice of liberal global governance risks being perceived, especially in the South, as a mere adornment on an international agenda that is primarily concerned with economic liberalism or Western security and power. As such, there are powerful, if pragmatic, reasons why some states have committed themselves to the implementation of some aspects at least of the rights agenda, along-side organizations committed for reasons of principle to rights-based development.

Nevertheless, despite the fact that liberal global governance and, in particular the global codification of rights, can sometimes create openings for pressing rights claims, and despite their increased relevance within global politics, we are fully aware of the limitations of liberal rights as a route to combating embedded inequality and socio-economic injustices. Global-rights conventions, even when they are ratified, are certainly not a magic bullet, transforming structural injustices overnight. Moreover, there are certain ethical dilemmas when we posit global development through the lens of Western liberalism. Liberalism is all too easily associated with intolerance of cultural difference and with modernist assumptions of lineal paths of progress. All this undoubtedly gives rise to some questions about the real value of codifying liberal rights for marginalized groups such as children and migrant workers. Since we have already identified some of the ways in which rights discourses have opened opportunities for activism and this has been an important focus of the some of the earlier chapters, here we will consider some of the potential weaknesses and shortcomings of the project of development through global rights.

Above all, we take seriously three criticisms. First, those of Gledhill (2005) and Archer (2005) that rights discourses are difficult to apply in the short term and in conditions of multiple deprivation. Secondly, that rights-based development risks assuming that poor people can be the agents of their own development – and, by implication, also risks attributing their marginalization to their own failure to act. And thirdly, there is the tendency discussed earlier, namely the failure fully to engage with state power. There is something of a belief that, if only people can be persuaded to lay claim to rights, they will be able to persuade or force states to listen. It is certainly the case, as we have argued, that making rights real depends, in part, on civil society mobilization and political struggles within civil society which are, in turn, shaped by historic and embedded practices that have built up over time in particular places. But shifting attention towards the possibilities of agency from below in this way can imply that the focus of attention moves away from the responsibilities of states to provide for social, as well as economic, development. We would do well here to remember Tarrow's (1998: 141) warning against exaggerating the capacity of civil society groups to effect change on their own and under-estimating the capacity of states to respond to challenges from below:

> Whatever the source of contentious claims, it is political opportunities and constraints that translate them into action ... While the opportunities and constraints in their environments give challengers incentives to mobilize, it is their cultural, organizational and practical resources that are the foundation of social movements. But three things are missing

from this two-stage image of contention and movement formation. First, it deals with social movements as if they emerged, made claims and evolved all on their own. Second, it ignores the fact that the shifting of opportunities and constraints does not cease with the triggering of collective action. Third, it leaves out authorities, who do not sit idly by as challengers contest their rule; they respond weakly or strongly, selectively or generally, intelligently or stupidly to the challenges of contention.

The capacity of state actors to subvert or ignore human rights campaigns is very considerable, although it has rarely been explored in detail. In one of the few works on this topic, Hertel (2006) paints a compelling, if somewhat depressing, picture of state capacity to resist well-funded and well-organized campaigns for labour rights in Bangladesh and Mexico. We have also tried to show in this book some of the ways in which states ignore their legal and moral obligations to children and migrants. But, as White (1994) suggests with regard to child labour, states now tend to make cosmetic changes so as to appear to be in compliance with international norms. Increasingly, states respond to global and local pressures for rights by introducing legal reforms but, at the same time, ignore breaches in the law and fail to provide resources for policy changes. What this means in Latin America for children, for example, is the introduction of some initiatives with regard to child labour or children in care but a failure to tackle poverty or provide resources to improve public education. Power relations in society are not challenged and, without this, it is impossible for rights, especially economic and social rights, to become institutionally embedded or be taken seriously. We can think of this as states accepting the principle of rights in theory but not in practice (Grugel 2007b; Piper and Satterthwaite 2007). If states are able to offer simply a symbolic redress of grievances while avoiding more costly transformations, there is a risk, that rights-based advocacy will be seen as a liberal project that fails to grapple with the real issues of engrained power. In these circumstances, delivering 'rights' can become a ritualistic and limited display of conformity with international norms rather than a serious attempt at grappling with injustice.

Once again, then, we return to the question of the state. The range of problems in the South which prevent states accepting the need to make rights real go beyond the frequently mentioned budgetary constraints: realizing rights in practice is also a question of expertise, know-how and rational target-setting and implementation on the part of government. It requires government capacity and a willingness on the part of state agencies to confront the beneficiaries of the status quo. It also means transforming embedded state cultures and long-standing state practices of cooptation and patronage. Turning rights in theory into rights in practice demands stengthening state capacity for positive social intervention, as well as building domestic constituencies of support for change. It also requires rethinking the role of courts, lawyers and the judiciary, for as van Bueren (1999) points out, the legal profession does not generally see itself as a force for economic and social change, and has little experience and understanding of economic and social issues; yet a human rights approach to poverty and development invites, indeed requires, national courts and regional and international tribunes to actively promote redistribution and economic and social well-being. In our view, this adds up to an urgent need to complement rights-based approaches with a much deeper understanding of how states work – and how specific states, and specific arms of the state, work in specific contexts and policy domains.

Our case studies reveal a complex and nuanced relationship between legal rights-based change, whether at the global, regional or national levels, and the introduction of rights in practice. They certainly do not provide evidence of a simple passage from rights in theory to rights in practice. There is, as a result, a need to guard against the overly optimistic assumptions that concepts of rights-based development can sometimes generate. The view that legal rights (rights in theory) necessarily constitute a first step to successfully claiming rights in practice ignores the complex relationship between law and politics, on the one hand, and policy and power, on the other. At least with regard to Latin America and Southeast Asia, the gap between the legal and constitutional rules of the game and the actual behaviour of state agencies is very considerable. Resources, class bias and political struggle, far more than the law itself, shape policy outcomes. This is the context in which rights claims are made and the reasons why, despite organizational strength, so many campaigns are unsuccessful.

Rights and the politics of knowledge

In earlier chapters, we stressed how little was known about the lives of rights-deprived individuals and communities before the CRM and the CRC. Poor children were mainly invisible to society and to policy-makers, except in cases where they were seen as deviant and in need of discipline. As for migrants, even though states have long allowed, or at least tolerated, the presence of, non-nationals in the economy, they have not been interested in building up knowledge about the lives migrants lead. Policies have been aimed at managing migration and protecting national labour markets and, in the process, the experience of migration has tended to pass unexamined. The codification of rights for children and migrants has undoubtedly changed this reality. We now know much more about the complex lives children and migrants lead. Partly we know more because the CRM and the CRC, by calling migrants and children into personhood, stimulated the seeking of significant academic and policy knowledge by international bodies, governments, universities and NGOs. But we also know more because the CRM and CRC created new knowledge-gathering agencies and encouraged NGOs to professionalize their own research at the same time as it legitimized third-sector knowledge-gathering. If we think, for example, of the role that the UNICEF-funded Innocenti Institute has played in acting as a nexus for research and knowledge diffusion about children, independent of governments, it becomes clear that one of the main outcomes from constitutionalizing rights is that it offers visibility to previously invisible communities and stimulates serious research into the lives of the target groups.

The new knowledge certainly points to the disjuncture between the rights people should have and the ones they really have; but, equally, it also provides solid evidence that can be of considerable use to advocacy groups. Knowledge and effective networking go together and the more that has become known about the lives of children and migrants, the more pressing the case for reform. The utility of the research carried out by UN-funded bodies partly explains the emergence of partnerships and increasing interdependence between UN agencies and relevant NGOs. The work of UNIFEM in Asia in the promotion of female workers' rights that we talk about in Chapter 3, for example, comes directly out of the close working relationship between UNIFEM and women's organizations. In short, we suggest that the significance of knowledge-generation, which has been an unintended outcome from global rights charters, has often been overlooked. We have tried to show here how there is increasing agreement between international bodies, NGOs and local activists, based not on sentiment but on a detailed understanding of lives as they are being led, on the importance of rights-based reform. Once again, states are lagging behind here and are obstructing the implementation of change.

The agenda of rights: which rights come first?

Rights-based global governance begs the question which rights matter most? From a liberal perspective, the answer is clear: political rights take precedence over economic and social rights. Rights-based approaches to development tend to assume that political rights – to participation and inclusion – come first and that they can then become a springboard for claiming other kinds of rights. This is based, first, on a view that anything other than political rights are too contentious a place to start and, second, on a stagist notion of rights acquisition, apparently based on the experiences of Western Europe, where it is usually assumed that ordinary people, following long periods of social mobilization and protest, won political citizenship before social citizenship. In fact, it is not at all clear that citizenship *was* won in quite this stagist way in Western Europe. If we consider rights struggles in the UK, for example, we can see that the fight for political citizenship (the vote) took place alongside, not before, labour struggles for trade union rights and demands for the introduction of clean water and public health. At the same time, legal advances in both political and social citizenship, once they were achieved, were not in practice universal; men achieved political, social and cultural entitlements long before women. Rights struggles and rights acquisition were subject, in other words, to power inequalities within society more generally. The view that political rights can be separated in any meaningful way from social and economic rights, which underpins the legal rights first approach, may not, then, reflect the ways rights are actually won.

In the developing world, there is even less of a case for separating political rights from social and economic entitlements. Citizenship and winning rights in the South are undoubtedly very messy affairs, involving the simultaneous pursuit of political, social, cultural and economic demands; they are not steady, managed transitions, where political rights rigidly come first and other sorts follow on. In so far as Latin America and Asia are concerned, patterns of citizenship are extremely complex. Moreover, despite democratization and global pressures for rights, state elites in the South often remain intensely fearful of ordinary people. In these circumstances, the impact of global rights charters is still unknown.

Our findings suggest that global governance can serve as a useful instrument for the pursuit of social and economic, as well as political, rights in cases where local activists are able to pursue rights claims on behalf of groups. Indeed, they point to the practical difficulties of separating political and socio-economic rights. The CRC has led to campaigns against child labour as much as, if not more than, demands for political rights for children and young people. Moreover, the right not to work in hazardous conditions and the right of children to protection in the workplace (an economic right) is, at one and the same time, a campaign to provide children with a decent education and time to pursue it (a political right). Campaigns for reproductive rights are posited as both entitlements to economic independence for adolescent girls and as a political right to gender equality in relationships and to control over one's own fertility.

Perhaps one of the interesting aspects of contemporary global rights codes is the extent to which there is now more of an acceptance of the complex patterns of rights acquisition than in the past and an implicit departure from a rigid hierarchy of rights, at least so far as UN institutions are concerned. As we note in Chapter 6 with reference to the CRC, although rights-based global governance for children is shot through with Western liberal idealism, there is also a conscious attempt to overcome the notion of stagism and the CRC conceptualizes all rights – political, social, economic and cultural – as equally important. This is partly why we have argued here that rights-based governance has awakened such expectations on the part of civil society organizations: it seems to point to the opening of a new avenue through which rights claims can be effectively made and a new source of pressure on states, in contrast to the view that rights struggles consist inevitably of a lengthy of process of stages (Grugel and Peruzzotti 2007).

Rights and governance in cross-regional, cross-sectoral comparison

We have taken in this book the unusual step of bringing together the study of two different marginalized communities (children and migrants) and two different regions (Latin America and Asia). Our aim has not been to compare either regions or sectors but to offer illustrative examples of the different ways in which contemporary rights-based global governance creates both opportunities and constraints for advocacy and social action. We chose this approach because of an explicit belief that researchers should try to break down barriers between different area specialisms, different disciplines and different issues. But we also came to the project as two individuals with different regional expertise and knowledge and, initially at least, different sectoral interests. We did not expect, necessarily, to find similar outcomes or strategies of advocacy. To some extent our expectations of difference have been borne out. As we expected to find, context and issue area matter. While labour rights predominate in advocacy by and for economic migrants in Asia, issues rooted in poverty, invisibility and adult power surface more frequently with regard to children in Latin America. Patterns of organization by civil society actors also show difference. Regional institutions and national histories make for different outcomes. But certain similarities have come through too. The particular ways in which gender matters for migrants is repeated in the case of children, for example, indicating that there may be some tensions in the universal rights project and the particular needs of women and girls in the face of entrenched gender inequalities, which may well be reproduced within civil society organizations (Cornwall and Molyneux 2006). With regard to children, Elizabeth Croll (2006) also make the important point that the children's rights approach has led to assumptions about 'girl children' but not a focused understanding of what rights girls need. Another similarity, less easy to document but palpable to us, as we have gone about work in our two regions, is the faith so many activists place in the power of rights ideas to effect changes. In conversations with activists, it was almost always possible to detect some element of optimism that, whatever its limitations, rights-based governance presented an opportunity for change.

We are, nevertheless, fully aware that the different regional contexts have shaped advocacy and outcomes in very profound ways. Even though a case can be made for similarities between the two regions – both regions show high levels of human rights abuse; both have experienced uneven economic growth and vulnerability to financial crisis in recent years; some parts of Asia have experienced democratization as part of the 'third wave', along with almost all of Latin America – it is the differences that have overwhelmingly shaped advocacy, especially where local social movements are concerned. This is perhaps less the case for transnational activists in organizations such as ECPAT or NGOs that are closely tied to international organizations. But for small scale local social movements or NGOs grappling with the meaning and possibilities of new forms of global governance in their own communities, local issues, local beliefs and local patterns of organization triumph and shape mentalities and approaches. Another difference, which comes out in the case studies, is the very different regional attitude to international norms-setting. Whereas Latin America has a generally positive record on ratification with international treaties, Asia has the lowest ratification record of UN and ILO conventions (although there is very considerable regional variation here). Clearly this means that states will respond in very different ways to the challenges posed by global governance mechanisms and global oversight agencies. And finally, we should note the very different ways in which the concept of rights is received in the two regions. Latin America has a history of rights-based struggles before the emergence of global governance. As far back as the 1970s, opposition to authoritarianism was framed largely as a human rights struggle. Moreover, by virtue of its Western origins, its close linguistic linkages with Europe and its dependence on the USA, the region has never developed a justifying ideological alternative to Western liberalism. This is a very different history to that of Asia. Despite assumptions about the emergence of a homogenous global civil society, therefore, we can confidentially assert, on the basis of the evidence presented here, that geography, context and issue matter in global advocacy politics.

Bibliography

Adams, R. (2001) 'On the Convergence of Labour Rights and Human Rights' in *RI/ IR* 56(1): 199–203.

Ahmed, I. (1999) 'Getting Rid of Child Labour' in *Economic and Political Weekly* 3–9 July.

Alcid, M. (2006) 'NGO–Labor Union Cooperation in the Promotion of the Rights and Interests of Land-based Overseas Filipino Workers' in *Asian and Pacific Migration Journal* 15(3): 335–358.

Alder, K. (2005) *En Canarias Buscando el Paraiso* [online]. BBC World Service. Available from http://www.news.bbc.co.uk/hi/spanish/international/ newsid_4993000/4993964.stm [accessed 18 November 2005].

Aleinikoff, T.A. and Chetail, V. (eds) (2003) *Migration and International Legal Norms*. The Hague: T.M.C. Asser Press.

Amnesty International (2002) *The Rights of the Child in Argentina: Text of the submission by Amnesty International on its concerns regarding the Argentine Government's application of the United Nations Convention on the Rights of the Child* [online]. Available from http://www.web.amnesty.org/library/Index/ENGAMR130182002?ope n&of = ENG-384 [accessed 26 March 2007].

Anderson, B. and O'Connell Davidson, J. (2002) *Trafficking – A Demand Led Problem?* Stockholm: Save the Children Sweden.

APMJ (Asian and Pacific Migration Journal) (2006) 'Special Issue: Migrant Labor NGOs and Trade Unions: A Partnership in Progress?' in *APMJ* 15(3).

Archard, D. and Macleod, C.M. (eds) (2002) *The Moral and Political Status of Children*. Oxford: Oxford University Press.

Archer, R. (2005) 'Winners and Losers from Rights-Based Approaches to Development: What can be Gained and What might be Lost through Adopting a Rights-Based Approach to Pro-poor Development?' Paper presented at the conference on the Winners and Losers from the Rights Based Approach, University of Manchester, 21–22 February.

Ashangrie, K. (1998) *Statistics on Working Children and Hazardous Child Labour* (2nd edition). Geneva: ILO.

Asis, M.M.B. (2005) 'Recent Trends in International Migration in Asia and the Pacific' in *Asia-Pacific Population Journal* 20(3): 15–38.

Attanasio, O. and Székely, M. (eds) (2001) *Portrait of the Poor: An Asset–Based Approach*. Baltimore, MD: Johns Hopkins University Press.

Augustin, L. (2005) 'Migrants in the Mistress' House: Other Voices in the "Trafficking" Debate' in *Social Politics* 12(1): 96–117.

Ball, R. and Piper, N. (2002) 'Globalisation and Regulation of Citizenship – Filipino Migrant Workers in Japan' in *Political Geography* (special issue) 21(8): 1013–1034.

—— (2006) 'Trading Labour-trading Rights: The Regional Dynamics over Rights Recognition of Migrant Workers in the Asia-Pacific – the Case of the Philippines and Japan' in Hewison, K. and Young, K. (eds) *Transnational Migration and Work in Asia*. London: Routledge, pp. 213–234.

Bandy, J. and Smith, J. (eds) (2005) *Coalitions across Borders: Transnational Protest and the Neoliberal Order*. Lanham, MD: Rowman and Littlefield.

Barnett, M.N. and Finnemore, M. (2004) *Rules for the World: International Organizations in Global Politics*. Ithaca, NY, and London: Cornell University Press.

Battistella, G. and Asis, M.M.B. (eds) (2003) *Unauthorised Migration in Southeast Asia*. Quezon City, Manila: Scalabrini Migration Centre.

BBC (British Broadcasting Corporation) (2006) 'UK Warned over Child Trafficking' [online]. Available from http://www.news.bbc.co.uk/1/hi/uk_politics/5295296.stm [accessed 1 October 2006].

Bell, D. and Piper, N. (2005) 'Justice for Migrant Workers? The Case of Foreign Domestic Workers in East Asia' in Kymlicka, W. and Baogang, Ye. (eds) *Asian Minorities and Western Liberalism*. Oxford: Oxford University Press, pp. 196–222.

Beloff, M. (1997) 'La Aplicacion Directa de la Convencion Internacional de los Derechos del Nino en el Ambito Interno' in CELS *La Aplicacion de los Tratods sobre Drechos Humanos por Los Tribunales Locales*. Buenos Aires: edicion del Puerto, pp. 623–634.

Bhalotra, S. (2007) 'Is Child Work Necessary?' in *Oxford Bulletin of Economics and Statistic* 69(1): 29–56, February.

Bilsborrow, R.E., Hugo, G., Oberai, A.S. and Zlotnik, H. (1997) *International Migration Statistics: Guidelines for Improving Data Collection Systems*. Geneva: ILO.

Blagbrough, J. and Glynn, E. (1999) 'Child Domestic Workers' in *Childhood* 6(1): 51–56. London: Sage Publications.

Boyd, M. and Pikkov, D. (2007) 'Finding a Place in Stratified Structures: Migrant Women in North America' in Piper, N. (ed.) *New Perspectives on Gender and Migration: Livelihoods, Rights, and Entitlements*. London: Routledge, pp. 19–58.

Boyden, J. (1997) 'Childhood and the Policy Makers: A Perspective on the Globalization of Childhood' in James, A. and Prout, A. (eds) *Constructing and Reconstructing Childhood: Contemporary Issues in the Sociological Study of Childhood*. Cambridge: Falmer Press.

Boyden, J., de Berry, J., Feeny, T. and Hart, J. (2002) 'Children Affected by Armed Conflict in South Asia: A Review of Trends and Issues Identified through Secondary Research' in Reyes, G. and Jacobs, G.A. (eds) *Handbook of International Disaster Psychology: Meeting the Psychosocial Needs of People in Humanitarian Emergencies*. Westport, CT: Praeger Publishers.

Briones, L. (2006) 'Beyond Agency and Rights: Capability, Migration and Livelihood in Filipina Experiences of Domestic Work in Paris and Hong Kong'. Unpublished PhD thesis. Centre for Development Studies, Flinders University of South Australia.

Brysk, A. (2002) 'Introduction: Transnational Threats and Opportunities' in Alison Brysk (ed.) *Globalization and Human Rights*. Berkeley, CA: University of California Press, pp. 1–16.

Bull, H. (1977) The *Anarchical Society: A Study of Order in World Politics* (2nd edition). New York: Columbia University Press.

Buvinic, M., Morrison, A. and Shifter, M. (1999) *Violence in Latin America and the Caribbean: A Framework for Action,* Technical Study Sustainable Development Department, Inter-American Development Bank. Washington, DC: Inter-American Development Bank.

Cammack, P. (2002) 'The Mother of All Governments: The World Bank's Matrix for Global Governance' in Wilkinson, R. and Hughes, S. (eds) *Global Governance: Critical Perspectives.* Oxford: Routledge, pp. 36–53.

Caron, C. (2005) 'Global Workers Require Global Justice: The Portability of Justice Challenge for Migrants in the USA' in Discussion Paper, Committee on Migrant Workers, Day of General Discussion on Protecting the rights of all migrant workers as a tool to enhance development [online], 15 December, Geneva. Available from http://www.ohchr.org/english/bodies/cmw/mwdiscussion.htm [downloaded February 2006].

Castles, S. and Loughna, S. (2003) 'Trends in Asylum Migration to Industrialized Countries: 1990-2001'. Discussion Paper No. 2003/31. Helsinki: United Nations University (UNU) and World Institute for Development Economics Research (WIDER).

Castles, S. and Miller, M. (1993) *The Age of Migration* (1st edition). Basingstoke: Macmillan.

Center for Reproductive Rights (2001) *Political Process and Abortion Legislation in El Salvador: A Human Rights Analysis.* New York: Center for Reproductive Rights.

CESE (Comité économique et Social Européen) (2005) 'Opinion of the European Economic and Social Committee on the Green Paper on an EU Approach to Managing Economic Migration' in SOC/199, CESE 694/2005. Brussels: CESE.

CGG (Commission on Global Governance) (1995) *Our Global Neighbourhood: The Report of the Commission on Global Governance.* New York: Oxford University Press.

Chayes, A. and Chayes, A.H. (1998) *The New Sovereignty: Compliance with International Regulatory Agreements.* Cambridge, MA: Harvard University Press.

Chimni, B.S. (2003) 'Post-Conflict Peace-Building and the Return of Refugees: Concepts, Practices, and Institutions' in Newman, E. and van Selm, J. (eds) *Refugees and Forced Displacement: International Security, Human Vulnerability, and the State.* Tokyo: United Nations University Press.

Chin, C.B.N. (2003) 'Visible Bodies, Invisible Work: State Practices toward Migrant Women Domestic Workers in Malaysia' in *Asian and Pacific Migration Journal* 12(1–2): 49–73.

CHIP (Childhood Poverty Research and Policy Centre) (n.d.) *CHIP - Knowledge for Tackling Childhood Poverty* [online]. Available from http://www.childhoodpoverty.org [accessed November 2006].

Cholewinski, R. (1997) *Migrant Workers in International Human Rights Law – Their Protection in Countries of Employment.* Oxford: Clarendon Press.

CHS (Commission on Human Security) (2003) *Human Security Now.* New York: CHS.

Coalition to Stop Child Soldiers (2004) *Child Soldiers: Global Report* [online]. Available from http://www.child-soldiers.org/resources/global-reports [accessed 25 May 2006].

Colectivo de Derechos de la Infancia y la Adolescencia (2002) *Informe de Organizaciones No-Gubernamentales Argentinas sobre la Aplicación de la Convención sobre los Derechos del Niño.* Buenos Aires: mimeo.

Cornelius, W.A. (1994) 'Japan: The Illusion of Immigration Control' in Cornelius, W.A., Martin, P.L. and Hollifield, J.F. (eds) *Controlling Immigration: A Global Perspective*. Stanford: Stanford University Press, pp. 46–71.

Cornwall, A. and Molyneux, M. (2006) 'The Politics of Rights – Dilemmas for Feminist Praxis: An Introduction' in *Third World Quarterly* 27(7): 1175–1191.

Courville, S. and Piper, N. (2004) 'Harnessing Hope through NGO Activism' in *The American Academy of Political and Social Science* 592: 39–61 (special issue edited by Valerie Braithwaite).

Crawley, H. (2006) *Child First, Migrant Second: Ensuring that Every Child Matters* [online]. ILPA (Immigration Law Practitioners' Association) Policy Paper, February. London: ILPA. Available from http://www.ilpa.org.uk/publications/ilpa_child_first.pdf [accessed January 2007].

Crawley, H. and Lester, T. (2005) *No Place for a Child: Children in Immigration Detention in the UK – Impacts, Alternatives and Safeguards* [online]. London: Save the Children UK. Available from http://www.savethechildren.org.uk/temp/scuk/cache/cmsattach/2414_no%20place%20for%20a%20child.pdf [accessed November 2006].

CRIN (Child Rights Information Network) (2006) *CRINMAIL 796* [online]. London: CRIN. Available from http://www.crin.org/email/crinmail_detail.asp?crinmailID = 1385 [accessed 11 July 2006].

Croll, E.J. (2006) 'From the Girl Child to Girls' Rights' in *Third World Quarterly* 27(7): 1285–1297.

D'Angelo, A. and Pasos Marciacq, M. (2002) '*Nicaragua: Protecting Female Labour Migrants From Exploitative Working Conditions and Trafficking*'. GENPROM (Gender Promotion Programme) Working Paper No. 6. Geneva: ILO.

Dannecker, P. (2005) 'Transnational Migration and the Transformation of Gender Relations: The Case of Bangladeshi Labour Migrants' in *Current Sociology* 53(4): 655–674.

Dauvergne, C. (forthcoming) 'Migration Law –Citizenship Law Dichotomy' in Benhabib, S. and Resnick, J. (eds) *Citizenship, Gender and Borders*. New York: NYU Press.

Davies, S. (2004) 'International Refugee Law – Can New Problems be Met with Old Solutions?' *International Journal of Human Rights* 8(3): 19–33, Autumn.

Deacon, B. (2000) 'Globalization and Social Policy: The Threat to Equitable Welfare' in UNRISD Occasional Paper No. 5. Geneva: UNRISD.

de Ferranti, D., Ferreira, F., Perry, G. and Walton, M. (2003) *Inequality in Latin America and the Caribbean: Breaking with History?* Washington, DC: World Bank.

Della Porta, D. and Kriesi, H. (1999) 'Social Movements in a Globalizing World' in Della Porta, D., Kriesi, H. and Rucht, D. (eds) *Social Movements in a Globalizing World*. New York: St. Martin's Press, pp. 25–34.

Della Porta, D. and Tarrow, S.G. (eds) (2005) *Transnational Protest and Global Activism*. Lanham, MD: Rowman and Littlefield.

Della Porta, D., Kriesi, H. and Rucht, D. (eds) (1999) *Social Movements in a Globalizing World*. New York: St. Martin's Press.

Department of Labor (2003) *Department of Labor's 2003 Findings on the Worst Forms of Child Labor*. Washington, DC: Department of Labor.

Department of State (2002) *2001 Reports on Human Rights Practices*. Washington, DC: Bureau of Public Affairs.

DFES (Department for Education and Skills) (2003) *Every Child Matters* [online]. Available from http://www.everychildmatters.gov.uk [accessed 24 June 2006].

Dommen, C. (2005) 'Migrants' Human Rights: Could GATS Help?' [online] in *Migration Information Source*. Available from http://www.migrationinformation.org/Feature/display.cfm?id = 290 [downloaded March 2005].

Donnelly, J. (1989) *Universal Human Rights in Theory and Practice*. Ithaca, NY: Cornell University Press.

Donovan, P. (2006) Gender Equality Now or Never: A New UN Agency for Women [online]. Office of the UN Special Envoy for AIDS in Africa. Available from http://www.healthdev.org/eforums/editor/assets/publications/pdfs/UN_women_ s_agency_ position_paper.pdf [accessed November 2006].

Doomernik, J., Gsir, S. and Kraler, A. (2005) 'Prospects on Migration Management – Opportunities and Pitfalls' in Fassmann, H., Kohlbacher, J., Reeger, U. and Sievers. W. (eds) *International Migration and its Regulation – State of the Art Report Cluster A1*. Vienna: Austrian Academy of Sciences, pp. 32–55.

Duong, L.B. (2002) *Viet Nam Children in Prostitution in Hanoi, Hai Phong, Ho Chi Minh City and Can Tho: A Rapid Assessment*. Geneva: ILO.

ECPAT (End Child Prostitution, Child Pornography and Trafficking of Children for Sexual Purposes) International (n.d.) *2002–2003 ECPAT Report on the Implementation of the Agenda for Action* [online]. Available from http://www.ecpat.net/eng/ecpat_inter/projects/monitoring/monitoring.asp#2 [accessed September 2006].

Ellis, L. (2006) *A Rights-Based Approach to Development: An Exploration of Cultural Relativism and Universality in Human Rights*. Waltham, MA: Brandeis University.

End Child Poverty Once and For All (2006) 'Unequal Choices' [online] in *Child Poverty in the News*, summer. Available from http://www.pegasus.xssl.net/~admin315/assets/files/newsletters/newsletter_2006_summer.pdf [accessed March 2007].

Ennew, J. (1986) *The Sexual Exploitation of Children*. Cambridge: Polity Press.

—— (1994) *Street and Working Children: A Guide to Planning*. London: Save the Children Fund.

—— (2000) Why the Convention Is Not About Street Children' in Fottrell, D. (ed.) *Revisiting Children's Rights: 10 Years of the UN Convention on the Rights of the Child*. Boston, The Hague: Kluwer Books, pp. 169–182.

Esim, S. and Smith, M. (eds) (2004) *Gender and Migration in Arab States – The Case of Domestic Workers*. Geneva: ILO.

European Commission (2002) *Federative Republic of Brazil – European Community: Country Strategy Paper 2001–2006 and National Indicative Programme 2002–2006*. Brazil: European Commission (Latin America Directorate).

Evans, T. (1997) 'Democratization and Human Rights' in McGrew, A. (ed.) *The Transformation of Democracy? Globalization and Territorial Democracy*. Malden, MA: Blackwell, pp. 122–145.

Feeny, T. (2004) 'Caught between a Crocodile and a Snake: Childhood in a Rohingya Refugee Camp, Bangladesh' in Pattnaik, J. (ed.) *South Asia: A Critical Look at Issues, Policies, and Programs (HC) (Research in Global Child Advocacy)*. Charlotte, NL: Information Age Publishing, pp. 1–18.

Feeny, T. and Boyden, J. (2003) *Children and Poverty: A Review of Contemporary Literature and Thought on Children and Poverty*. Virginia: Christian Children's Fund (CCF) Children and Poverty Series Part I.

Fonseca, C. (2002) 'The Politics of Adoption: Child Rights in the Brazilian Setting' in *Law and Policy* 24(3) 199–227.

Ford, M. (2006) 'Migrant Labor NGOs and Trade Unions: A Partnership in Progress?' in *Asian and Pacific Migration Journal* 15(3): 299–312.

—— and Piper, N. (2007) 'The Construction of Informal Regimes as Sites of Female Agency: Foreign Domestic Worker-Related Activism in East and Southeast Asia' in Dobson, J. and Seabrooke, L. (eds) *Everyday International Political Economy.* Cambridge: Cambridge University Press, pp. 63–80.

Forter, A. (2006) *Youth Gangs, Violence and Human Rights in Central America: A Comparative Study on Policy and Law* [online]. Available from http://www.human rights.uchicago.edu/workshoppapers/Forter.pdf [accessed February 2007].

Franklin, R. (ed.) (2002) *New Handbook of Children's Rights.* London: Routledge.

Freeman, M. (2000) 'The Future of Children's Rights' in *Children and Society* 14(3): 277–293.

Gallagher, A. (2001) 'Human Rights and the New UN Protocols on Trafficking and Migrant Smuggling: A Preliminary Analysis' in *Human Rights Quarterly* 23: 975–1004.

Gamble, A. (2000) 'Economic Governance' in J. Pierre (ed.) *Debating Governance,* Oxford: OUP 1999 pp. 110–137.

Gamburd, M. (2001) *The Kitchen Spoon's Handle: Transnationalism and Sri Lanka's Migrant Households.* Ithaca, NY: Cornell University Press.

Garcia Mendez, E. (1998) *Infancia de Derechos y de la Justicia*: Buenos Aires: Ediciones del Puerto.

Gaventa, J., Shankland, A. and Howard, J. (eds) (2002) 'Making Rights Real: Exploring Citizenship, Participation and Accountability' in *IDS Bulletin* 33(2): 31–39. Brighton: Institute of Development Studies.

GCIM (Global Commission on International Migration) (2005) *Migration in an Interconnected World: New Directions for Action.* Geneva: GCIM.

General Assembly (1986) *Declaration on the Right to Development* [online]. Resolution 41/128 of 4 December. New York: UN. Available from http://www.unhchr.ch/ html/menu3/b/74.htm [accessed June 2006].

Gibson, K., Law, L. and McKay, D. (2002) 'Beyond Heroes and Victims: Filipina Contract Migrants, Economic Activism and Class Transformation' in *International Feminist Journal of Politics* 3(3): 365–386.

Gilpin, R. (2002) 'The Challenge of Global Capitalism. The World Economy in the 21st Century' in *Economic Notes* 32(1): 105–106.

Gindling, T.H. (2005) 'Poverty in Latin America' in *Latin American Research Review* 40(1): 207–222.

Glauser, B. (1990) 'Street Children: Deconstructing a Construct' in James, A. and Prout, A. (eds) *Constructing and Reconstructing Childhood: Contemporary Issues in the Sociological Study of Childhood.* London: Falmer Press.

Gledhill, J. (2005) 'The Rights of the Rich versus the Rights of the Poor'. Paper presented at the conference on the Winners and Losers from the Rights Based Approach, University of Manchester, 21–22 February.

Godoy, A.S. (1999) '"Our Right is the Right to be Killed": Making Rights Real on the Streets of Guatemala' in *Childhood* 6(4): 423–442.

Gomez, E.T. (2007) 'Inter-ethnic Relations, Identity and Business: The Chinese in Britain and Malaysia' in Tarling, D. and Gomez, E.T. (eds) *The State, Development and Identity in Multi-ethnic Societies: Ethnicity, Equity and the Nation.* London: Routledge.

Gonzalez de la Roca, M. (2006) 'Vanishing Assets: Cumulative Disadvantages Amongst the Urban Poor' in Fernandez-Kelly, P. and Shefner, J. (eds) *Out of the*

Shadows: Political Action And the Informal Economy in Latin America. Philadelphia, PA: Pennsylvania State University Press, 97–124.

Gordon, D., Nandy, S., Pantazis, C., Pemberton, S. and Townsend, P. (2003) *The Distribution of Child Poverty in the Developing World: Report to UNICEF.* Bristol: Centre for International Poverty Research.

Gosh, B. (2003) 'A Road Strewn with Stones: Migrants' Access to Human Rights'. Paper prepared for the International Meeting on Access to Human Rights, Guadalajara, 17–18 January. Geneva: International Council on Human Rights Policy.

Grant, S. (2005) 'Migrants' Human Rights: From the Margins to the Mainstream' [online] in *Migration Information Source.* Available from http://www.migration information.org/Feature/display.cfm?id = 291 [accessed March 2005].

Grugel, J. (2003a) 'Democratization Studies and Globalization: The Coming of Age of a Paradigm' in *British Journal of Politics and International Relations* 5(2): 258–283.

—— (2003b) 'Democratisation Studies: Globalisation, Governance and Citizenship' in *Government and Opposition* 32(2): 239–265.

—— (2004) 'State Power and Transnational Activism' in Uhlin, A. and Piper, N. (eds) *Contextualising Transnational Activism – Problems of Power and Democracy.* London: Routledge, pp. 3–21.

—— (2005) 'Democratisation and IPE: Taking the Political Seriously' in Phillips, N. (ed.) *International Political Economy.* Basingstoke: Palgrave, pp. 193–220.

—— (2006) 'Regionalist Governance and Transnational Collective Action in Latin America' in *Economy and Society* 35(2): 209–231.

—— (2007a) 'Democratization and Ideational Diffusion: Europe, Mercosur and the Concept of Social Citizenship' in *Journal of Common Market Studies,* 45(1): 43–68.

—— (2007b) 'Rights in Theory and Rights in Practice: Getting Rights Politics Right for Development'. PSA Development/DFID Conference, University of Birmingham, January.

Grugel, J. and Peruzzotti, E. (2007) 'Claiming Rights under Global Governance: Children's Rights in Argentina' in *Global Governance* 13(2): 199–216.

Grugel, J. and Riggirozzi, M.P. (2007) 'The Return of the State in Argentina' in *International Affairs* 83(1): 87–107.

GTZ (Gesellschaft fuer Technische Zusammenarbeit) (2006) *Migration and Development* [online]. Available from http://www2.gtz.de/migration-and-development [accessed September 2006].

Guy, D. (2002) 'The State, the Family and Marginal Children in Latin America' in Hecht, T. (ed.) *Minor Omissions: Children in Latin American History and Society.* Madison, WI: University of Wisconsin Press, pp. 121–142.

Harrison, G. (2004) *The World Bank and Africa: the Construction of Governance States.* London: Routledge.

Hasenau, M. (1991) 'ILO Standards on Migrant Workers: The Fundamentals of the UN Convention and Their Genesis' in *International Migration Review* 25(4): 687–697, special issue on UN International Convention on the Protection of the Rights of All Migrant Workers and Members of their Families.

Hashim, I.M. (2005) *Research Report on Children's Independent Migration from Northeastern to Central Ghana.* Brighton: Development Research Centre on Migration, Globalisation and Poverty.

Hathaway, O. (2002) 'Do Human Rights Treaties Make a Difference?' *Yale Law Journal* 111(1935): 1870–2042.

Hatton, T.J. and Williamson, J.G. (1998) *The Age of Mass Migration: Causes and Economic Impact*. Oxford: Oxford University Press.

Hatton, T.J. and Williamson, J.G. (2003) 'What Fundamentals Drive World Migration?' Discussion Paper No. 2003/23. Helsinki: United Nations University (UNU) and World Institute for Development Economics Research (WIDER).

Hecht, T. (1998) *At Home in the Street: Street Children of Northeast Brazil*. Cambridge: Cambridge University Press.

Henriques-Mueller, M.H. and Yunes, J. (1993) 'Adolescence: Misunderstandings and Hopes' in Gomez, E. (ed.) *Gender, Women, and Health in the Americas*. Washington, DC, Pan American Health Organization (PAHO) (Scientific Publication No. 541), pp. 43–61.

Hernandez, D. (1993) *America's Children: Resources from Family, Government, and the Economy*. New York: Russell Sage Foundation.

Hertel, S. (2006) *Unexpected Power Conflict and Change Among Transnational Activists*. Ithaca, NY: Cornell University Press.

Hetherington, P. (2004) '500,000 Homeless, Claims Charity' *in Guardian*, 14 December.

Hoffmann, M.J. and Ba, A. (eds) (2005) *Contending Perspectives on Global Governance: Coherence and Contestation*. Oxford: Routledge.

Hondagneu-Sotelo, P. (2001) *Doméstica: Immigrant Workers Cleaning and Caring in the Shadows of Affluence*. Berkeley, CA: University of California Press.

Hoogvelt, A. (1997) *Globalisation and the Postcolonial World – The New Political Economy of Development*. Basingstoke: Macmillan.

Horton, R. (2004) 'UNICEF Leadership 2005–2015: A Call for Strategic Change' in *The Lancet* 364(9451): 2069–2152.

Huang, S. and Yeoh, B. (2003) 'The Difference Gender Makes: State Policy and Contract Migrant Workers in Singapore' in *Asian and Pacific Migration Journal* 12(1–2): 75–98.

Hujo, K. and Piper, N. (2006) 'Transnational Economic Migration and Social Development'. Project proposal. Geneva: UNRISD.

Human Rights Watch (2000) *Fingers to the Bone: United States Failure to Protect Child Farmworkers*. New York: Human Rights Watch.

—— (2002a) 'The Other Face of the Canary Islands: Rights Violations Against Migrants and Asylum Seekers' [online]. *Spain* 14(1). Available from http://www.hrw.org/reports/2002/spain [accessed March 2006].

—— (2002b) 'Nowhere to Turn: State Abuses of Unaccompanied Migrant Children by Spain and Morocco' [online]. *Spain and Morocco* 14(4). Available from http://www.hrw.org/reports/2002/spain-morocco/&handle = sosig1023958540-29690 [accessed March 2006].

—— (2003a) *The International Organization for Migration and Human Rights Protection in the Field: Current Concerns*. Submitted to IOM Governing Council Meeting, 86th Session, 18–21 November. Geneva: Human Rights Watch.

—— (2003b) *'You'll Learn Not To Cry': Child Combatants in Colombia* [online]. Available from http://www.hrw.org/reports/2003/colombia0903 [accessed March 2006].

—— (2004a) 'Turning a Blind Eye: Hazardous Child Labour in El Salvador's Sugar Cane Cultivation'. *El Salvador* 16(2B), June. New York: Human Rights Watch.

—— (2004b) 'El Salvador: Abuses against Child Domestic Workers in El Salvador'. *El Salvador* 16(1B), January. New York: Human Rights Watch.

—— (2005) 'Always on Call: Abuse and Exploitation of Child Domestic Workers in Indonesia'. *Indonesia* 17(7C), July. New York: Human Rights Watch.

—— (2006a) *Maid to Order – Ending Abuses Against Migrant Domestic Workers in Singapore.* New York: Human Rights Watch.

—— (2006b) *Children's Rights* [online]. Available from http://www.hrw.org/doc/?t=children [accessed January 2006].

—— (2006c) *Colombia: Armed Groups Send Children to War U.N. Security Council to Discuss Colombia's Child Soldiers* [online]. Available from http://www.hrw.org/english/docs/2005/02/22/colomb10202.htm [accessed February 2007].

Huntington, S. (1991) *The Third Wave: Democratization in the Late Twentieth Century.* Norman, OK: University of Oklahoma Press.

ICFTU-APRO (International Confederation of Free Trade Unions-Asian and Pacific Regional Organisation) (2003) *Migration Issues Concern Trade Unions.* Singapore: ICFTU-APRO.

ICMC and December 18 (2004) *The UN Treaty Monitoring Body and Migrant Workers: A Samizdat,* Geneva: ICMC.

Ilahi, N., Orazem, P.F. and Sedlacek, G. (2000) *The Implications of Child Labor for Adult Wages, Income and Poverty: Retrospective Evidence from Brazil.* March 2001, mimeo.

ILO (International Labour Office) (1996) *Declaration and Agenda for Action from the World Congress against the Commercial Exploitation of Children,* Stockholm, Sweden, 27–31 August. Geneva: ILO.

—— (1999) 'Conclusions and Recommendations' in *Asia-Pacific Regional Symposium for Trade Union Organizations on Migrant Workers* [online], 6–8 December, Petaling Jaya, Malaysia. Available from http://www.ilo.org/public/english/dialogue/actrav/genact/socprot/migrant/migrant1.htm [accessed June 2005].

—— (2000) *Decent Work and Poverty Reduction in the Global Economy* [online]. Available from http://www.ilo.org/public/english/standards/relm/gb/docs/gb277/pdf/esp-3-add1-a.pdf [accessed April 2006].

—— (2002) *Unbearable to the Human Heart: Child Trafficking and How to Eliminate it* [online]. Available from http://www.ilo.org/public/english/standards/ipec/publ/childtrf/unbearable.pdf [accessed 20 June 2007].

—— (2003a) *ILO Declaration on Fundamental Principles and Rights at Work* [online]. Geneva: InFocus Programme on Promoting the Declaration (ILO). Available from http://www.ilo.org/dyn/declaris/DECLARATIONWEB.CONTACTSHOME?var_language = EN [accessed January 2006].

—— (2003b) *Understanding Children's Work in Guatemala.* Geneva: ILO.

—— (2004) *Towards a Fair Deal for Migrant Workers in the Global Economy,* Geneva: ILO.

—— (2005) *International Programme on the Elimination of Child Labour: IPEC – Child Trafficking* [online]. Geneva: ILO. Available from http://www.ilo.org/public/english/standards/ipec/themes/trafficking/index.htm [accessed April 2006].

—— (2005) *A Global Alliance against Forced Labour.* Report of the Director-General – Global Report under the Follow-up to the ILO Declaration on Fundamental Principles and Rights at Work 2005. Geneva: ILO.

—— (2006) *Multilateral Policy Framework for Labour Migration* [online]. Geneva: ILO. Available from www.ilo.org/migrant/download/tmmflm-en.pdf [accessed October 2007].

—— (n.d.) *IPEC Country Profile: El Salvador* [online]. Available from www.ilo.org/public/english/standards/ipec/timebound/salvador.pdf [accessed January 2007].

—— (n.d.) *ILO Fact Sheets on Child Labour in Latin America and the Caribbean* [online]. Available from http://www.ilo.org/public/english/standards/ipec/about/globalreport/2006/download/2006_fs_latinamerica_en.pdf [accessed January 2007].

ILO-IPEC (ILO-International Program on the Elimination of Child Labour) (1999) *Children in Prostitution in Northern Vietnam: Rapid Assessment Findings.* Geneva: ILO.

ILO Socio-Economic Security Programme (2004) *Economic Security for a Better World.* Geneva: ILO.

IOM (International Organisation for Migration) (2003) *World Migration Report.* Geneva: IOM.

IOM and FOM (Federal Office for Migration Switzerland) (2005) *The Berne Initiative - International Agenda for Migration Management.* Geneva: IOM.

Iredale, R., Piper, N. and Ancog, A. (2005) 'Impact of Ratifying the 1990 UN Convention on the Rights of All Migrant Workers and Members of Their Family – Case Studies of the Philippines and Sri Lanka' in unpublished report prepared for UNESCO. Bangkok: UNESCO.

Ireland, K. (2003) *Wish You Weren't Here – The Sexual Exploitation of Children and the Connection with Tourism and International Travel.* London: Save the Children UK.

Jackson, R. and Roseberg, C. (1982) 'Why Africa's Weak States Persist: The Empirical and Juridicial in Statehood' in *World Politics* 35(1): 1–24.

Johansson, R. (2005) 'Role of TU in Respect to Migrant Workers: Summary of Responses'. Unpublished background paper. Geneva: ILO.

Johnston, P. (2001) 'Organize for What? The Resurgence of Labor as Citizenship Movement' in Katz, H. and Turner, L. (eds) *Rekindling the Movement: Labor's Quest for Relevance in the 20th Century* [online]. Ithaca, NY: Cornell University Press. Available from http://www.newcitizen.org/PublicActions.htm [accessed 18 June 2007].

Jones-Correa, M. (1998) 'Different Paths: Gender, Immigration and Political Participation' in *International Migration Review* 30(2): 326–329.

Joppke, C. (1998) 'Why Liberal States Accept Unwanted Migration' in *World Politics* 50(2): 266–293.

Jordan, B. and Duevell, F. (2003) *Migration – The Boundaries of Equality and Justice.* Cambridge: Polity Press

Justino, P. and Acharya, A. (2003) 'Inequality in Latin America: Processes and Inputs'. PRUS Working Paper No. 2. Brighton: Poverty Research Unit, University of Sussex.

Kaldor, M. (2003) *Global Civil Society. An Answer to War.* Cambridge: Polity Press.

Keck, M. and Sikkink, K. (1998) *Activists Beyond Borders: Advocacy Networks in International Politics.* Ithaca, NY: Cornell University Press.

Keohane, R.O. (2002) 'Global Governance and Democratic Accountability' in *Miliband Lectures*, Spring. London: London School of Economics.

Khagram, S., Riker, J.V. and Sikkink, K. (eds) (2002) *Restructuring World Politics: Transnational Social Movements, Networks, and Norms.* Minneapolis, MN: University of Minnesota Press.

Klein, N. (2001) 'Reclaiming the Commons' *New Left Review* May–June. http://www.newleftreview.org/A2323.

Klein Solomon, M. (2007) 'GATS Mode 4 and the Mobility of Labour' in Cholewinski, R., Perruchoud, R. and Macdonald, E. (eds) *International Migration Law – Developing Paradigms and Key Challenges.* The Hague: T.M.C. Asser Press, pp. 107–128.

Kofman, E. (2007) 'Gendered Migrations, Livelihoods and Entitlements in Eur-
   opean Welfare Regimes' in Piper, N. (ed.) *New Perspectives on Gender and Migra-
   tion: Livelihoods, Rights, and Entitlements*. London: Routledge, pp. 59–102.
Lan, P.C. (2003) 'Political and Social Geography of Marginal Insiders: Migrant
   Domestic Workers in Taiwan' in *Asian and Pacific Migration Journal* 12(1–2): 99–125.
Law, L. (2002) 'Sites of Transnational Activism: Filipino Non-government Organi-
   sations in Hong Kong' in Brenda, S.A., Yeoh, P.T. and Huang, S. (eds) *Gender
   Politics in the Asia-Pacific Region*. London: Routledge, pp. 35–69.
Layton-Henry, Z. (ed.) (1990) *The Political Rights of Migrant Workers in Western
   Europe*. London: Sage Publications.
Lebovic, J.H. and Voeten, E. (2006) 'The Politics of Shame: The Condemnation of
   Country Human Rights Practices in the UNCHR' in *International Studies Quar-
   terly* 50(4): 861–888.
Lee, H.K. (1997) 'The Employment of Foreign Workers in Korea: Issues and Policy
   Suggestions' in *International Sociology* 12(3): 353–371.
Levitt, P. and Nyberg-Sørensen, N. (2004) 'The Transnational Turn in Migration
   Studies' in *Global Migration Perspectives* 6. Geneva: GCIM.
Ljungman, C. (2005) 'Human Rights and the International Development Coopera-
   tion Agenda' in Mikkelsen, B. (ed.) *Methods for Development Work and Research:
   A New Guide for Practitioners* (2nd edition). London: Sage Publications.
Lloyd, A. (2002) 'Evolution of the African Charter on the Rights and Welfare of the
   Child and the Africa Committee of Experts: Raising the Gauntlet' in *International
   Journal of Children's Rights* 10(2): 179–198.
Lloyd-Sherlock, P. (1997) 'Policy, Distribution, and Poverty in Argentina Since
   Redemocratization' in *Latin American Perspectives* 24(6): 22–55.
Loveband, A. (2004) 'Nationality Matters: SARS and Foreign Domestic Workers'
   Rights in Taiwan Province of China', in *International Migration* 42(5): 121–139.
Lyons, L. (2005) 'Transient Workers Count Too? The Intersection of Citizenship and
   Gender in Singapore's Civil Society' in *Sojourn* 20(2): 208–248.
Machel, G. (1996) *Impact of Armed Conflict on Children: Report of Graóa Machel,
   Expert of the Secretary-General of the United Nations* [online]. New York: United
   Nations Department for Policy Coordination and Sustainable Development
   (DPCSD). Available from http://www.unicef.org/graca/a51-306_en.pdf [accessed
   March 2006]
Marcus, R. (2003) 'Impact of Poverty on Children and Ways of Tackling it: Save the
   Children's Global Experience' in Civil Society Forum organised by Save the Children
   UK and held on 6 November in Tegucigalpa, Honduras. London: Save the Children.
Marcus, R. and Wilkinson, J. (2002) *Whose Poverty Matters? Social Protection, Vul-
   nerability and PRSPs'* in CHIP Working Paper No. 1. London: CHIP.
Martin, D.A. (2003) 'The Authority and Responsibility of States' in Aleinikoff, T.A.
   and Chetail, V. (eds) *Migration and International Legal Norms*. The Hague:
   T.M.C. Asser Press, pp. 31–46.
Martínez-Castilla, Z. (n.d.) *Child Labour in Traditional Mining: Mollehauca, Peru*.
   Geneva: ILO.
Massey, D.S. and Espinosa, K.E. (1997) 'What's Driving Mexican Migration to the
   United States?' in *American Journal of Sociology* 102(4): 939–999.
McGrew, A. (2002) 'Transnational Democracy: Theories and Prospects' in Stokes,
   G. and Carter, A. (eds) *Democratic Theory Today: Challenges for the 21st Century*.
   Cambridge: Polity Press.

McGrew, A.G. and Held, D. (2002) 'Introduction' in McGrew, A. and Held, D. (eds) *Governing Global Transformations: Power, Authority and Global Governance.* Cambridge: Polity Press.

Migrant Committee (2006) *Protecting the Rights of All Migrant Workers as a Tool to Enhance Development* [online]. Available from http://www.daccessdds.un.org/doc/UNDOC/GEN/N06/423/01/PDF/N0642301.pdf?OpenElement [accessed November 2006].

Molyneux, M. and Lazar, S. (2003) *Doing the Rights Thing: Rights-Based Development and Latin American NGOs.* London: ITDG Publishing.

Morton, K. (2006) 'Civil Society and Marginalization: Grassroots NGOs in Qinghai Province' in H. Xiaoquan Zhang, Bin Wu and R. Sanders (eds) *Marginalization in China: Perspectives on Transitions and Globalisation in China.* London: Ashgate.

Moser, C. (1996) 'Confronting Crisis: A Comparative Study of Household Responses to Poverty and Vulnerability in Four Poor Urban Communities' in *World Bank Environmentally Sustainable Development Studies and Monograph Series No. 8.* Washington, DC: World Bank.

Moser, C. and Norton, A. (2001) *To Claim Our Rights: Livelihood Security, Human Rights and Sustainable Development.* London: Overseas Development Institute.

Muinujin, A., Delamonica, E., Gonzalez, E. and Davidziuk, A. (2005) 'Children Living in Poverty: A Review of Child Poverty Definitions, Measurements and Policies'. Paper presented at UNICEF Conference on Children and Poverty: Global Context, Local Solutions. New York: New School University, April.

Neumayer, E. (2005) 'Do international human rights treaties improve respect for human rights?' in *Journal of Conflict Resolution* 49 (6): 925–953.

Neumayer, E. and De Soysa, I. (2005) 'Trade Openness, Foreign Direct Investment, and Child Labour' in *World Development* 33(1): 43–64, January.

Newland, K. (2005) 'The Governance of International Migration: Mechanisms, Processes and Institutions' [online] in background paper. Geneva: GCIM. Available from http://www.gcim.org/en/ir_experts.html [accessed February 2006].

Newman, J (2005) '*Protection through Participation: Young People Affected by Forced Migration and Political Crisis*'. Working Paper No 20. Queen Elizabeth House, University of Oxford.

Nguyen Thi Van Anh et al. (2000) *Child-Focused Budget Study: Assessing the Rights to Education of Children with Disabilities in Vietnam.* London: CRIN.

NSPCC (National Society for the Prevention of Cruelty to Children) (2005) *Setting the Standard: A Common Approach to Child Protection for International NGOs.* Teddington: Tearfund.

Nyamu-Musembi and Cornwall, A. (2004) 'What is the "rights based approach" all about?' in IDS Working Paper No. 234. Brighton: Institute of Development Studies.

O'Brien, R., Goertz, A.M., Scholte, J.A. and Williams, M. (2000) *Contesting Global Governance: Multilateral Economic Institutions and Global Social Movements.* Cambridge: Cambridge University Press.

Observatorio de la Infancia y la Adolescencia (2005) *Informe de Situacion del Conurbano Bonaerense.* Documento 4 Julio.

O'Connell Davidson, J. and Sanchez Taylor, J. (1996) *Prostitution and Sex Tourism (Dominican Republic).* London: ECPAT.

OHCHR (Office of the UN High Commissioner for Human Rights) (2004) *Special Representative of the Secretary General on Human Rights Defenders – About*

Human Rights Defenders [online]. Available from http://www.ohchr.org/english/issues/defenders/who.htm [accessed February 2007].

Oldfield, A. (1990) *Citizenship and Community, Civic Republicanism and the Modern World.* London: Routledge.

OMCT (World Organization Against Torture) *Universal Children's Day: Stop Violence Against Children 2006* http://www.omct.org/index.php?id=&lang=eng&articleSet=Press&articleId=6646

O'Neill, O. (1989) *Constructions of Reason: Explorations of Kant's Practical Reason.* Cambridge: Cambridge University Press.

Oro SucioNoticias Aliadas (2007) *Nicaraga* [online]. Available from http://www.noticiasaliadas.org/article.asp?IssCode = &artCode = 4119&lanCode = 1 [accessed February 2005].

Overbeek, H. (2002) 'Neoliberalism and the Regulation of Global Labor Mobility' in *Annals of the American Academy of Political and Social Science* 581: 74–90, May.

Papademetriou, D.G. and Martin, P.L. (eds) (1991) *The Unsettled Relationship: Labor Migration and Economic Development.* London: Greenwood Press.

Parreñas, R. (2004) *Gendered Migration, Entitlements and Civil Action in Asia.* Discussion at the Colloquium, Institute for the Study of Social Change, University of California, 2 March. Berkeley, CA: University of California Press.

—— (2005) *Children of Global Migration: Transnational Families and Gendered Woes.* Stanford: Stanford University Press.

Patel, F. (2004) *Chip Policy Briefing 5: Improving Child Welfare in Developing Countries – Lessons in Social Policy from the 'High-achievers'* [online]. Available from http://www.childhoodpoverty.org/index.php/action = documentfeed/doctype = rtf/id = 103 [accessed November 2005].

Payne, A. (2005a) 'The Study of Governance in a Global Political Economy' in Phillips, N. (ed.) *Globalizing International Political Economy.* London: Palgrave, pp. 55–81.

—— (2005b) *The Global Politics of Unequal Development.* London: Palgrave.

—— (2007) *Living in a Less Unequal World: The Making of Renewed Progressive Global Policy.* London: IPPR.

Pécoud, A. and de Gutcheneire, P. (2004) 'Migration, Human Rights and the United Nations: An Investigation into the Low Ratification Record of the UN Migrant Workers Convention' in *Global Migration Perspectives No. 3.* Geneva: GCIM.

—— (2005) 'Migration without Borders: An Investigation into the Free Movement of People' in *Global Migration Perspectives No. 27.* Geneva: GCIM.

Pereira, J. (forthcoming) *Non Governmental Public Action in Adolescent Motherhood: The Cases of Chile,* Argentina and Uruguay. Unpublished PhD thesis, University of Texas.

Phillips, N. (2005a) 'Bridging the Comparative/International Divide in the Study of State' *New Political Economy* 10 (3): pp. 335-343.

—— (2005b) 'Globalising the Study of International Political Economy' in N. Phillips (ed.) *Globalizing International Political Economy.* Basingstoke: Palgrave-Macmillan pp. 1–19.

Pinheiro, P.S. (2006) *UN Secretary-General Study on Violence Against Children: Report to the General Assembly.* Geneva: UN.

PI (Plan International) (2005) *The Right Start in Life.* London: PI.

Piper, N. (1998) *Racism, Nationalism and Citizenship: the Situation of Ethnic Minorities in Germany and Britain.* Aldershot: Ashgate.

—— (2003) 'Bridging Gender, Migration and Governance: Theoretical Possibilities in the Asian Context' in *Asian and Pacific Migration Journal* 12(1–2): 21–48.

—— (2005a) 'Social Development, Transnational Migration and the Political Organising of Foreign Workers' in Discussion Paper, Committee on Migrant Workers, Day of General Discussion on *Protecting the rights of all migrant workers as a tool to enhance development* [online] 15 December, Geneva. Available from http:// www.ohchr.org/english/bodies/cmw/mwdiscussion.htm [accessed February 2006].

—— (2005b) 'A Problem by a Different Name? A Review of Research on Trafficking in Southeast Asia and Oceania' in *International Migration* 43(1/2): 203–233.

—— (2005c) 'Rights of Foreign Domestic Workers – Emergence of Transnational and Transregional Solidarity?' in *Asian and Pacific Migration Journal* 14(1–2): 97–120.

—— (2006a) 'Economic Migration and the Transnationalisation of the Rights of Foreign Workers – A Concept Note' [online] in ARI (Asia Research Institute) Working Paper Series No. 58. Singapore: ARI. Available from http://www.nus.ari. edu.sg/pub/wps.htm [accessed November 2006].

—— (2006b) 'Migrant Worker Activism in Singapore and Malaysia: Freedom of Association and the Role of the State' in *Asian and Pacific Migration Journal*, special issue on 'Migrant Labor NGOs and Trade Unions: A Partnership in Progress?' 15(3): 359–380.

—— (ed.) (2007a) *New Perspectives on Gender and Migration: Rights, Entitlements and Livelihoods*, London: Routledge.

—— (2007b) 'Political Participation and Empowerment of Foreign Workers – Gendered Advocacy and Migrant Labour Organising in Southeast and East Asia' in Piper, N. (ed.) *New Perspectives on Gender and Migration: Livelihoods, Rights, and Entitlements*. London: Routledge, pp. 249–275.

Piper, N. and Ford, M. (eds) (2006) 'Migrant NGOs and Labor Unions: A Partnership in Progress?' in *Asian and Pacific Migration Journal* 14(3), special volume.

Piper, N. and Iredale, R. (2003) 'Identification of the Obstacles to the Signing and Ratification of the UN Convention on the Protection of the Rights of All Migrant Workers 1990: The Asia Pacific Perspective' in APMRN (Asia Pacific Migration Research Network) Working Paper No. 14, University of Wollongong.

Piper, N. and Satterthwaite, M. (2007) 'The Rights of Migrant Women' in Cholewinski, R., Perruchoud, R. and Macdonald, E. (eds) *International Migration Law – Developing Paradigms and Key Challenges*. The Hague: T.M.C. Asser Press, pp. 237–254.

Piper, N. and Uhlin, A. (2002) 'Transnational Advocacy Networks and the Issue of Trafficking and Labour Migration in East and Southeast Asia. A Gendered Analysis of Opportunities and Obstacles' in *Asian and Pacific Migration Journal* 11(2): 171–195.

Piper, N. and Yamanaka, K. (eds) (2003) 'Gender, Migration, and Governance' in *Asian and Pacific Migration Journal* 12(1–2).

Piper, N. and Yamanaka, K. (2007) 'Feminised Migration in East and Southeast Asia and the Securing of Livelihoods' in Piper, N. (ed.) *New Perspectives on Gender and Migration: Livelihoods, Rights, and Entitlements*. London: Routledge, pp. 161–190.

Poniatowski, B. and Jimenez, C. (2005) 'Domestic Workers from Asia and Latin America' in *Report on Workshop on Gender and Migration*, 19–20 October. Tokyo: United Nations University.

Portes, A., Castells, M. and Benton, L.A. (eds) (1989) *Informal Economy: Studies in Advanced and Less Developed Countries*. Baltimore, MD: Johns Hopkins University Press.

Prezworski, A. (1986) 'Some Problems in the Study of the Transition to Democracy. In Transition from Authoritarian Rule: Prospects for Democracy' in O'Donnell, G., Schmitter, P.C. and Whitehead, L. (eds) *Transitions from Authoritarian Rule: Comparative Perspectives*. Baltimore, MD: Johns Hopkins University Press, pp. 47–63.

Pupavec, V. (2002) 'The International Children's Right Regime' in Chandler, D. (ed.) *Rethinking Human Rights: Critical Approaches to International Politics.* Basingstoke: Palgrave, pp. 57–75.

Qvortrup, J. (ed.) (1993) *Childhood as a Social Phenomenon: Lessons from an International Project.* Vienna: European Centre for Social Welfare Policy and Research.

Rahman, M. (2003) *Bangladeshi Workers in Singapore: A Sociological Study of Temporary Labor Migration,* Unpublished PhD thesis. Singapore: National University of Singapore.

—— (2006) 'Migration-Development Nexus Revisited: Family Remittances and Development in Bangladesh'. Paper presented at the International Workshop on International Migration and Social Development, Asia Research Institute, Singapore, 20–21 November.

Rhodes, R.A.W. (1996) 'The New Governance: Governing without Government' in *Political Studies* XLIV: 652–667.

Ricca, C. (2006) *El Salvador: Children in the Farabundo Marti Liberation Front (FMLN) and the Armed Forces of El Salvador (FAES).* London: The Coalition to Stop the Use of Child Soldiers.

Rice, B. (2006) *Against the Odds: An Investigation Comparing the Lives of Children on Either Side of Britain's Housing Divide.* London: Shelter.

Rizzini, I. *et al.* (1992) *Childhood and Urban Poverty in Brazil (UNICEF Innocenti Occasional Papers).* Florence: UNICEF Innocenti Research Centre.

Robben, A.C.G.N. (2005) *Political Violence and Trauma in Argentina.* Pennsylvania: Pennsylvania State University Press.

Rodriguez, R.M. (2002) 'Migrant Heroes: Nationalism, Citizenship and the Politics of Filipino Migrant Labor' in *Citizenship Studies* 6(3): 341–356.

Rozga, D. (2001) *Applying a Human Rights Based Approach to Programming: Experiences of UNICEF.* Paper for the Workshop on Human Rights, Assets and Livelihood Security and Sustainable Development, London, 19–20 June. New York: UNICEF.

Russett, B. and O'Neal, J. (2001) *Triangulating Peace: Democracy, Interdependence, and International Organizations.* New York: W.W. Norton & Company.

Sassen, S. (1988) *The Mobility of Labor and Capital: A Study in International Investment and Labor Flow.* Cambridge: Cambridge University Press.

Satterthwaite, M. (2005) 'Crossing Borders, Claiming Rights: Using Human Rights Law to Empower Women Migrant Workers' [online] in *Yale Human Rights and Development Law Journal* 8: 1–66. Available from http://www.papers.ssrn.com/abstract = 680181 [accessed October 2006].

Scheper-Hughes, N. (1992) *Death Without Weeping: The Violence of Everyday Life in Brazil.* Berkeley, CA: University of California Press.

Scholte, J.A. (2000) *Globalization – A Critical Introduction.* London: Palgrave.

Schuurman, M. and Sutton, D. (2002) *Children are European Citizens Too: Children in the EU Treaty* [online]. EURONET, The European Children's Network of NGOs. Available from http://www.europeanchildrensnetwork.org/docs/ChildrenCitizens2EN.pdf [accessed 20 June 2007].

Simmons, B. (2000) 'International Law and State Behaviour: Commitment and Compliance in International Monetary Affairs' in *American Political Science Review* 94(4): 819–835.

Skeldon, R. (2004) 'More than Remittances: Other Aspects of the Relationship between Migration and Development', UN/POP/MIG/2004, 9 November. New York: Population Division, UN.

Slaughter, A.M. (2004) *A New World Order*. Princeton, NJ: Princeton University Press.

Smith, R. and Paoletti, S. (2005) 'Protecting the Rights of All Migrant Workers as a Tool to Enhance Development' in Discussion Paper, Committee on Migrant Workers, Day of General Discussion on *Protecting the rights of all migrant workers as a tool to enhance development* [online], 15 December, Geneva. Available from http://www.ohchr.org/english/bodies/cmw/mwdiscussion.htm [accessed February 2006].

Smith, W. and Korzeniewicz, R. (2005) 'Regionalism's "Third Wave" in the Americas' in Fawcett, L. and Serrano, M. (eds) *Regionalism and Governance in the Americas*. Basingstoke: Palgrave, pp. 62–84.

Smulovitz, C. and Peruzzotti, E. (2003) 'Societal and Horizontal Controls: Two Cases of a Fruitful Relationship' in Mainwaring, S. and Welna, C. (eds) *Democratic Accountability in Latin America*. Oxford: Oxford University Press, pp. 309–331.

Sørensen, G. (1999) 'Sovereignty: Change and Continuity in a Fundamental Institution' in *Political Studies* 47(3): 590–604.

Stephens, S. (1995) 'Children and the Politics of Culture in Late Capitalism' in Stephens, S. (ed.) *Children and the Politics of Culture*. Princeton, NJ: Princeton University Press, pp. 3–48.

Strange, S. (1988) *States and Markets*. London: Frances Pinter.

Tamas, K. (2003) *Mapping Study on International Migration*. Stockholm: Institute for Futures Studies.

Taran, P.A. and Demaret, L. (2006) 'Action Imperatives for Trade Unions and Civil Society' in *Asian and Pacific Migration Journal*, special issue on 'Migration Labor NGOs and Trade Unions: A Partnership in Progress?' 15(3): 391–404.

Tarrow, S.G. (1998) *Power in Movement: Social Movements and Contentious Politics* (2nd edition). Cambridge: Cambridge University Press.

—— (2001) 'Transnational Politics: Contention and Institutions in International Politics' in *Annual Review of Political Science* 4: 1–20.

—— (2005) 'The Dualities of Transnational Contention: "Two Activist Solitudes" or a New World Altogether?' in *Mobilization* 10(1): 8–27.

The Coalition to Stop Child Soldiers (2004) *Child Soldiers Global Report 2004* [online]. Available from http://www.child-soldiers.org/resources/global-reports [accessed November 2005].

Thouez, C. (2004) 'The Role of Civil Society in the Migration Policy Debate' in *Global Migration Perspectives No. 12*. Geneva: GCIM.

—— (2005) 'Convergence and Divergence in Migration Policy: The Role of Regional Consultative Processes' in *Global Migration Perspectives No. 20*. Geneva: GCIM.

Toor, S. (2001) 'Child Labour in Pakistan: Coming of Age in the New World Order' in *Annals of American Academy of Political and Social Sciences* 575: 194–197.

UN (United Nations) (1989) Convention on the Rights of the Child, General Assembly Resolution 44/25 of 20 November 1989. Geneva: OHCHR.

—— (1995) *Copenhagen Declaration on Social Development and Programme of Action of the World Summit for Social Development* [online]. Available from http://www.daccessdds.un.org/doc/UNDOC/GEN/N95/116/51/PDF/N9511651.pdf?Open Element [accessed April 2005].

—— (1997) *Activities of Intergovernmental and Non-governmental Organizations in the Area of International Migration; Report of the Secretary General*. UN document E/CN9./1997/5. New York: UN Commission on Population and Development.

—— (2000) Convention against Transnational Organized Crime and its Protocols, General Assembly Resolution 55/25 of 15 November 2000. Geneva: UN.

—— (2004) *World Survey on the Role of Women in Development – Women and International Migration.* New York: UN.

—— (2006) *International Migration and Development – Report of the Secretary-General,* A/60/871, 18 May 2006. New York: UN.

Underhill, G.R.D. (2000) 'Introduction: Conceptualizing the Changing Global Order' in Stubbs, R. and Underhill, G.R.D. (eds) *Political Economy and the Changing Global Order.* Oxford: Oxford University Press, pp. 5–22.

UNDP (United Nations Development Programme) (2004) *Human Development Report: Cultural Liberty in Today's Diverse World.* New York: UNDP.

—— (2005) *Human Development Report 2005 – International Cooperation at a Crossroads: Aid, Trade and Security in an Unequal World.* New York: UNDP.

UNFPA (United Nations Population Fund) (2006) *A Passage to Hope – Women and International Migration.* New York: UNFPA.

UNICEF (United Nations Children's Fund) (2000) *Poverty Reduction Begins with Children.* New York: UNICEF.

—— (2001) *Poverty and Children: Lessons of the 90s for the Least Developed Countries* [online]. Available from http://www.unicef.org/publications/pub_-poverty_children_ldcs_en.pdf [accessed 20 June 2007].

—— (2002a) *Chicos y Chicas en Riesgo Educativo El Trabajo Infantil en la Argentina.* Buenos Aires, Argentina: UNICEF.

—— (2002b) *The State of the World's Children 2002.* New York: UNICEF.

—— (2003) *The Situation of Children in Bolivia* [online]. Available from http://www.unicef.org/bolivia/children_1540.htm [accessed March 2006].

—— (2004) *The State of the World's Children 2001* [online]. Available from http://www.unicef.org/sowc01 [accessed February 2005].

—— (2005a) *End Child Exploitation – Child Labour Today.* New York: UNICEF.

—— (2005b) *The 'Rights' Start to Life: A Statistical Analysis of Birth Registration.* New York: UNICEF.

—— (2005c) *The State of the World of the Children 2005 – Childhood under Threat.* New York: UNICEF.

—— (2006) *The State of the World's Children 2006 – Excluded and Invisible* [online]. New York: UNICEF. Available from http://www.unicef.org/infobycountry/sudan_darfuroverview.html [accessed November 2006].

—— (n.d.) Convention on the Rights of the Child [online]. Available from http://www.unicef.org/crc/index.html [accessed October 2006].

UNICEF Innocenti Research Centre (2003) *Trafficking in Human Beings Especially Women and Children.* Florence: UNICEF Innocenti Research Centre.

—— (2007) *Report Card No. 7: Child Poverty in Perspective – An overview of child well-being in rich countries.* Florence: UNICEF Innocenti Research Centre.

UNRISD (United Nations Research Institute for Social Development) (2005) *Gender Equality – Striving for Justice in an Unequal World.* Geneva: UNRISD.

Valentine, G. (2004) *Public Space and the Culture of Childhood.* London: Ashgate.

van Bueren, G. (1999) 'Combating Child Poverty – Human Rights Approaches' in *Human Rights Quarterly* 21(3): 680–706.

Veerman, P.E. (1992) *The Rights of the Child and the Changing Image of Childhood.* Dordrecht/Boston/London: Martinus Nijhoff.

VeneKlasen, L., Miller, V., Clark, C. and Reilly, M. (2004) 'Rights-based Approaches and Beyond: Challenges of Linking Rights and Participation' in IDS Working Paper No. 235. Brighton: Institute of Development Studies.

Verité (2005) 'Protecting Overseas Workers – Research Findings and Strategic Perspectives on Labor Protections for Foreign Contract Workers in Asia and the Middle East' in *Research Paper*, December. Amherst, MA: Verité.

Waterman, P. (2003) 'Adventures of Emancipatory Labour Strategy as the New Global Movement Challenges International Unionism' [online]. Available from http://www.groups.yahoo.com/group/GloSoDia/files/LABOUR%20INTERNATIONALISM/ [accessed June 2006].

—— (2005) 'Trade Unions, NGOs and Global Social Justice: Another Tale to Tell' [online] in *TUs and NGOs Review*. Available from http://www.choike.org/nuevo_eng/informes/1872.html [accessed August 2006].

Watson, A. (2006) 'Saving more than the Children: The Role of Child-focused NGOs in the Creation of Southern Security Norms' in *Third World Quarterly* 27(2): 227–237.

Wee, V. and Sim, A. (2005) 'Hong Kong as a Destination for Migrant Domestic Workers' in Huang, S., Yeoh, B.S.A. and Rahman, N.A. (eds) *Asian Women as Transnational Domestic Workers*. Singapore: Marshall Cavendish, pp. 175–209.

Weiss L. (2000) 'Globalization and the Myth of the Powerless State' in Higgott, R. and Elgar, E. (eds) *The Political Economy of Globalization*, Cheltenham: Macmillan Palgrave.

White, B. (1994) 'Children, Work and 'Child Labour': Changing Responses to the Employment of Children' in *Development and Change* 25(4): 849–78.

White, S. (2002) *Children's Rights, Inequality and Poverty*. London: Department for International Development.

Whitehead, A. and Hashim, I. (2005) '*Children and Migration – Background Paper for DFID Migration* Team' [online], March. London: Department for International Development (DFID). Available from http://www.livelihoods.org/hot_topics/docs/DfIDChildren.doc [accessed September 2005].

Wickramasekara, P. (2006) 'Labour Migration in Asia – Role of Bilateral Agreements and MOUs', Power Presentation, Tokyo, 17 February; available from http://www.jil.go.jp/foreign/event_r/event/documents/2006sopemi/keynotereport1.pdf (downloaded October 2006).

Wilkinson, R. (2005) 'Concepts and Issues in Global Governance' in Wilkinson, R. (ed.) *The Global Governance Reader*. London: Routledge, pp. 5–15.

Wilkinson, R. and Hughes, S. (eds) (2002) *Global Governance: Critical Perspectives*. Oxford: Routledge.

Winton, A. (2004) 'Young People's Views on How to Tackle Gang Violence in 'Post–Conflict' Guatemala' in *Environment and Urbanization* 16(2): 83–99.

Wong, D. (1997) 'Transience and Settlement: Singapore's Foreign Labour Policy' in *Asian and Pacific Migration Journal* 6(2): 135–167.

—— (2005) 'The Rumour of Trafficking: Border Controls, Illegal Immigration and the Sovereignty of the Nation-State' in van Schendel, W. and Abraham, I. (eds) *Illicit Flows and Criminal Things: States, Border and the Other Side of Globalization*. Bloomington, IN: Indiana University Press.

World Bank (2001) *World Development Indicators: 2001*. Oxford: Oxford University Press.

—— (2003) *Inequality in Latin America and the Caribbean: Breaking with History?* Washington, DC:

World Commission on the Social Dimension of Globalization (2004) *A Fair Globalization: Creating Opportunities for All*. Geneva: ILO.

World Organisation against Torture (OMCT) (2006a) OMCT *Statement on Universal Children's Day: Stop Violence against Children*. Geneva: OMCT.

—— (2006b) *Human Rights Violations in Guatemala*. Alternative report presented to the UN Committee against torture (36th Session, May). Geneva: OMCT.

Yamanaka, K. (1999) 'Illegal Immigration in Asia: Regional Patterns and a Case Study of Nepalese Workers in Japan' in Haines, D.W. and Rosenblum, K.E. (eds) *Illegal Immigration in America: Handbook*. Westport, CT: Greenwood Press.

Yamanaka, K. and Piper, N. (2006) 'Feminised Migration in East and Southeast Asia: Policies, Actions and Empowerment' in UNRISD Occasional Paper No. 11.

Yeoh, B.S.A., Huang, S. and Devasahayam, T.W. (2004) 'Diasporic Subjects in the Nation: Foreign Domestic Workers, the Reach of Law and Civil Society in Singapore' in *Asian Studies Review* 28: 7–23.

Zurita, I.F. (2006) *World Economic Forum on Latin America: Managing Global and Regional Risks* [online]. Available from http://www.weforum.org/pdf/summitreports/latinamerica2006/managing_global.htm [accessed December 2006].

Index